Roy King has drawn from years of leadership training and consultation with churches and various organizations to offer a valuable and unique perspective on leadership. While most books treat the subject in a general way, King observes that the life cycle and season of the organization determines the appropriate leadership style. *Life-Giving Leadership* will give insight into the context for various leadership approaches whether an organization is growing, static or declining.

JERRY RANKIN
President Emeritus International Mission Board, SBC

The difference between leaders and followers is perspective. The difference between leaders and effective leaders is better perspective. Roy King takes that last statement seriously. His use of life cycles gives very, very helpful perspectives concerning leaders and leadership. We need more effective leaders. Roy King's book, *Life-Giving Leadership* will definitely support leaders who want to be effective.

DR. J. ROBERT CLINTON
Retired Professor of Leadership, Fuller Theological Seminary

There is no shortage of leadership content in our country, but it's rare that an author address the topic from such a strong biblical perspective. *Life-Giving Leadership* is the most refreshing book I've read in years. It will radically change a leader's perspective on how they execute their leadership role. I can't wait to get it into the hands of the next generation leaders I work with.

MAC LAKE
Visionary Architect, The Multiply Group - multiplygroup.org

My friend Roy King's book is a wise distillation of important themes on biblical leadership. It is a practical, Scripture-saturated, time-tested guide for a new generation of Christ-shaped, kingdom-minded leaders.

PAUL COPAN
Professor and Pledger Family Chair of Philosophy and Ethics, Palm Beach Atlantic University, West Palm Beach, FL; Coauthor of *An Introduction to Biblical Ethics: Walking in the Way of Wisdom.*

Refreshing! Roy speaks, from a deep well of life experience. He reminds us that God is sovereign over all of life and uses negative things like disappointments, betrayals, anger, fear, and worry to produce positive things in us like faith, hope and love. The text is replete with biblical content and a kingdom perspective. In a world of shallow truisms, this book stands apart for its depth, passion and wisdom.

DR. DOUG DORMAN
President, Your Next Step - www.yournextstep.ws
Senior Staff, Global Training Network - www.globaltrainingnetwork.org

I am a huge believer that issues related to organizational lifecycles very much effect the health of local churches. Roy King has given us an excellent tool with this book that drills down deep into what these lifecycles are about for churches. We have to not only know where we are but most importantly; how to get back to a vibrant place of ministry through life-giving leadership.

> DR. HANS FINZEL
> Best-selling author, *The Top Ten Mistakes Leaders Make*

As a member of the rising generation of leaders to whom he's writing, I was encouraged by Roy King's personal reflections on his life experiences. I felt like I was sitting across a table from him listening to him sharing principles shaped by his own relationship with God. In *Life-Giving Leadership* King invites readers to enter into abundant life-giving leadership as modeled by Jesus, to align themselves with him through a reflective biblical perspective of leadership. If you are willing to be encouraged and to grow as a leader, take the time. Read this book and examine yourself through the thought provoking application questions he provides. Those whom you lead will thank you.

> EMILY HALL
> Cross-cultural worker serving in Asia

In a day and time when Christian leaders are straining to meet deadlines, struggling with self-worth and dangerous ideas of success — leading many to walk away from ministry altogether — Dr. Roy King's *Life-Giving Leadership* is a blessing of biblical and practical truth soaked in the grace of God. Dr. King's examination of God's design for relationship and leadership is not just beneficial for Christian leaders to grow spiritually, but for them to gain insight into God's heart for life and in turn reflect his heart to others. I highly recommend this book for any leader who desires to avoid potential burnout and experience God's love to a deeper degree.

> LEE BUTLER
> Pastor, Crescent Hill Baptist Church, Columbia, SC

During our years on staff at Eastwest College we were blessed to have Roy King regularly visit and teach a two-week block course focused on many of the topics addressed in *Life-Giving Leadership*. That particular class always proved very popular with students due to the practical life-challenging material, as well as the transparent, humble manner in which Roy shared his own life. Roy uses the same vulnerable style in *Life-Giving Leadership*. This book is a great practical resource for personal use, mentoring one-on-one and as a tool for regular team gatherings to encourage members and sharpen ministry focus on numerous fronts. I am pleased to recommend this book as a tool for all leaders both young and old.

> PAT MYERS
> Missionary Trainer, WEC, Manila

Life-Giving Leadership is a book I desperately longed for early on in life and ministry. In my twenties and thirties, I would have given anything to sit with a few other young leaders, and a sage leader, guiding us through this book. For example, I believe the chapter on "Two Rhythms of Life Giving Leaders" would have saved me from two ministry burn-outs and Roy King's distilled wisdom in the chapter on a "Four Step Process for Wise Choices" would have pulled me back from numerous dead-end streets. I can't wait to use this material as I mentor individuals and small groups.

ROWLAND FORMAN
Executive Director of Living Stones Leadership Ministries, Auckland, New Zealand; Author of *The Lost Art of Lingering*

Studying under Dr. Roy King in seminary, I was taught many leadership principles that I often use in leading the local church as a pastor. One thing I always default to in leading that Roy taught me is "I can only influence others, and be responsible for myself." This book is just that. Engaging with the heart of God and letting him transform you so that you become a life-giving stream that influences the world you touch. This is a tool I will refer to often moving forward.

CLAY NESMITH
Lead Pastor, Barefoot Church, North Myrtle Beach, SC

I have read more than enough leadership books, but this one was different. It was way more personal, maybe because the author is my dad, but I think also because he speaks really honestly about core lessons in scripture that many other leaders and I gloss over all the time. It reminded me of being around a more seasoned spiritual guide who is gently cautioning me to remember what's important. If you are a leader in the church or are involved in Christian leadership, this book is bound to make you a little uncomfortable. It is not filled with anecdotal stories about churches that are more successful than yours. It is not a list of steps for a new church model that no one in your congregation will go for. You will not find a whole lot of new takes on theology or arguments for or against any hot button issues. On the whole, the most controversial thing about this book is that his isn't a list of steps on how to lead but rather it is an exercise in understanding your own heart and motivations and moving back to an abiding relationship with God. That is precisely why it's uncomfortable. It is really difficult to read this book and not begin to apply its lessons in your life. Reader Beware!

MARK KING
Roy's son, Businessman and Pastor of Soda City Collective, a missional community in Columbia, SC

PRAISE FOR ROY KING'S *HELPING A CHURCH LIVE WELL*

Roy King offers the strategic insights only an organizational architect can deliver. Drawing from a wealth of personal experience, careful study, and seasoned mentoring, this short book provides a 10,000 foot view of the life cycle and seasons every leader needs to understand in order to steward a church effectively through its mission. And while Roy is fully missional in his advice, he includes essentials that other writers often forget: the metastory of God's glory and the motivation of God's compassionate heart for people. *Helping a Church Live Well* will yield more applications per page than most; you will definitely want this in your library!

JEROME DALEY
Leadership Coach and Culture Consultant, Founder of Thrive9

Roy King has written a concise practical guide to understanding organizational life, with special focus on how it applies to local churches. Drawing on his extensive experience as a congregational consultant, Dr. King offers a strategy to help churches engage in an on-going process of walking with God as he builds his Church.

DR. JOHN HARVEY
Dean of the Seminary and School of Ministry, Columbia International University

What I appreciate about Roy King is his heart for Jesus Christ and his Church. His experiences in ministry and his gift of teaching shine through in this application of leadership principles and practices. Helping organizations understand their position in time, the areas that need to change, and how to lead through change brings hope and encouragement to the many challenging times we face. These principles and practices have been a great help to us at China Outreach Ministries.

DR. GLEN OSBORN
President, China Outreach Ministries

I have observed Roy consulting churches and organizations and coaching ministry leaders for several years. I believe God has used him in this service to provide perspective and encouragement. This book is another example of his heart for local churches to prosper as they see where they are and where God wants them to be.

DR. BILL JONES
President, Columbia International University

LIFE-GIVING LEADERSHIP

Life-Giving
LEADERSHIP

ROY KING

LEADER**SPACE**
ALIGNING HEARTS WITH GOD'S PERSPECTIVE

COLUMBIA, SOUTH CAROLINA

Life-Giving Leadership

LeaderSpace
317 S. Shields Road
Columbia, SC 29223
www.leaderspace.org

LeaderSpace provides resources to assist leaders in their personal development and to equip them for developing other leaders. This includes one-on-
one leadership coaching, church consulting, and teaching in organizational
and academic settings.

Cover and interior book design by Kelly Smith, Tallgrass Media.

Cover image by Neil Palmer (CIAT). Creative Commons license (CC BY-SA 2.0).
http://flic.kr/p/9AwBiW

Scripture quotations are from The Holy Bible, English Standard Version®,
copyright © 2001 by Crossway Bibles, a publishing ministry of Good News
Publishers. Used by permission. All rights reserved.

10 9 8 7 6 5 4 3 2 1

ISBN-13: 978-0-692-61711-3

CONTENTS

DEDICATION

THIS BOOK WAS on my "bucket list". I first started thinking about the concept of a bucket list when I saw the movie, starring Morgan Fairchild and Jack Nicholson with that name. Later, after a close brush with death that involved ICU and rehab resulting from an allergic reaction to a blood pressure medicine, I started forming a list in my mind. This book was near the top of my list.

I have file drawers full of information I've been gathering on kingdom leadership since 1977 and I have been teaching a course on the biblical foundations of leadership through the seminary of Columbia International University since 1997. This book represents what I am learning with the students through continually refining that course over the years. Every time I teach the course it seems I am more aware of how much I have received from a generation of leaders and teachers whom my students will never know personally. At best they can meet them in their writings. I sensed a debt to pass on the learning I had received from this preveious generation who have passed on or are now aging and not as visible in public ministry.

How often in class I have quoted one of my guides, such as Ron Dunn, and then said, "But of course he now lives in heaven." I say it so often my students laugh before I get the words out. One student boldly asked me, "Dr. King do you know anything you have learned for yourself?" I thought about it and could honestly say, "Not much." Instead I have received from those who have gone before, let it pass through me and be colored by my experience and gifts, and then offer it to others.

So this book is dedicated to: (in alphabetical order)

1. Dr. Bobbie Clinton — who gave me not only his perspective and values on leadership but also was a sponsor mentor who introduced me to me to others, such as Dr. Terry Walling.

2. Dr. Robert Coleman — who sat across from me when he came as a guest speaker to CIU and I was a seminary student working for the school in financial aid, and asked me, "So, where are your men?" He went on to share his practice of making disciples in seminary and church settings.

3. Dr. James "Buck" Hatch — probably the greatest pure classroom lecturer I have ever experienced and with counseling skills to match. Mr. Hatch planted the seed, "Always start with God." Marriage, family, teaching, leading — whatever — start with, "How does God do it?" Look for clues in the trinity, meditate on every encounter Jesus had on earth with people, carefully look at what God says, and does not say, in the epistles to his children. Always start with God.

4. Dr. Robertson McQuilkin — perhaps the greatest classroom teacher who would send students out with questions that would keep them learning long after they left the classroom. The most frequent comment from Robertson's classes and those reading his books is, "He made me think, and I had to discuss this with my spouse, close friend, etc." Robertson ignited my passion to pray and commune with God. He taught me it was okay to sing straight through a hymnal when I am alone with God, and if I do not know the tune to just make one up. Robertson models being

a Jesus-lover and his leading passion has been to see the church extended among every people group on the planet. God has used his speaking and writing as the earthly means to issue a kingdom call to a large number of men and women.

5. Ron Dunn — I have listened to hundreds of his sermons and some I have listened to dozens of times. He had a unique gift for creatively illustrating and imaginative humor that drills truth deep into the heart. I never met him personally. Some of Ron's messages can be found at rondunn.com.

6. Dr. Bill and Vonette Bright — I became a Christian after hearing him speak at Explo 72 in the Cotton Bowl on "How to be Sure You are a Christian". He convinced me God wanted to use me to change the world. Vonette's prayer workshop became a model for many workshops on prayer and other subjects that I taught over the years. She blended personal stories, Scripture, and guided practice to impart principles I still use and teach today.

7. Dr. Larry Poland — Our paths have crossed a few times over the years. My first encounter was as a college student, sitting with my then fiancée and several hundred other students listening to him deliver a series of messages titled, "Kingdom Mentality." The air was so alive with an electric sense that God was speaking that most of us could not take notes. We were in rapt attention and afterwards carried off in prayer and revival of spirit. Years later I had a personal encounter with Larry. This gentle man won my heart over by graciously encouraging me to teach and give my life to developing leaders.

8. Dr. Terry Hulbert — was the dean of the Graduate School of Bible and Missions at Columbia International University when I came as a student in 1977. One of my favorite gifts from this remarkable teacher was his passion for John 13-17. The Upper Room was the seedbed of teaching that would be developed in the epistles. It was Jesus preparing the disciples to be Jesus followers when Jesus would no longer be on earth to follow in the manner they had

walked for over three years. I will treasure a conversation I had with Dr. Hulbert just a few weeks before he died and a month before I started writing this book. He called me a 'bridge leader'. He encouraged me to spend time with new faculty and to pass on the contribution of the faculty and administration of CIU who were passing off the scene. I pray this book is part of answering that call.

Portions of this book are edited from *Remain in Me: Living Through Change with Wisdom and Grace* by Roy King, International Centre for Excellence in Leadership, Rockville, Virginia, 2014.

FOREWORD

By Reggie McNeal

LIFE IS THE PRIMAL GIFT. None of us asked for it; we just woke up with it and spend all our days figuring out what to do with it. How to live life.

God is in the life business. For him, it's all about life. I would go so far as to say that the kingdom of God can most accurately be characterized as "life as God intends." The kingdom saga is the extent God will go to in order for us to have access to this quality of life. Life is the point of the kingdom, the major focus of God's interaction with planet Earth.

The Bible bears witness to this kingdom-life connection from start to finish. In the first story of the Bible we find a Tree of Life planted in the Garden of Eden. When paradise is disintegrating God sends an angel to stand guard over the Garden's entrance to protect the Tree of Life from being violated. At the end of the Bible in the book of The Revelation John describes a city with a river of life flowing through it, with trees of life flourishing on both of its banks. Jesus said, "I have come to give you life. He then qualifies it as *abundant* life. And he makes possible — through his life, death, and resurrection — for this life to be eternal.

Leadership that reflects the heart of God gives life, pure and simple. Leaders and leadership situations that are life-giving create environments where we are energized in our spirits, so that we believe that life is worth living all over again. It causes us to imagine a better world for ourselves and others. It calls from us our best efforts. It fires up our imagination of a world that could be, one where the kingdom comes on earth as it is in heaven. This is why spiritual leadership should be life-giving. Anything else can hardly claim to be rooted in the heart of God. This is the fundamental truth that Roy King reminds us of in this wonderful volume.

Unfortunately too many of us have been around leaders or leadership cultures that are life-taking. They rob us of life, or cause us to defer life or to substitute something else for genuine vitality. Our souls know the difference between life-giving and life-diminishing. Only the former can claim spiritual authenticity.

Roy King is a life-giving student and teacher of leadership. His insatiable curiosity is accompanied by his wise discernment, a wisdom tempered with humility. His gift of encouragement provides a tonic to all those fortunate enough to share time with him. Roy's engaging and warm personal demeanor grows out a deep reverence for people and for the one who is always party to his conversations and interactions.

I am saying all this about Roy to establish the point that this book flows out of a good life. In these pages Roy shares what he has learned about the workings of God in the lives of leaders who bring about a better life for those they lead. His insights not only will make your leadership better; these truths will make your own life better.

So dig in to *Life-Giving Leadership*. After all, life is what you're looking for!

DEFINITIONS AND ASSUMPTIONS OF LIFE-GIVING LEADERSHIP

Joy is the serious business of Heaven. —*C.S. Lewis*

I AM DECLARING an END to
Life-Taking
Life-Robbing
Life-Stealing
Life-Draining
Life-Wounding Leadership.
I am writing to share good news.

GOD IS INTO LIFE-GIVING LEADERSHIP

God wants you to be receiving *life*. Even more, God wants you to stir up, sow into, and encourage life to come into being and flow out of those you lead. The idea of life as a joyous praise-filled vibrancy, a fruit-bearing effectiveness, and a quality that goes beyond the grave is central to understanding the Bible. The Bible launches its God story with initial life in a garden and ends with eternal life in an amazing city that goes beyond any dream we could have of the perfect future. God is front and center in the story of the people he has blessed with life.

Are you a life-receiving leader?

Would you agree it is difficult to give what you do not possess?

If the essence of leadership is influencing others, how does your time and energy contribute to God's work of making you and them alive?

What do I mean by "life"?

We will reflect on that together as we go on, but here is a description to get us started.

If we interviewed those in your circle of influence, would they describe your impact on them as life-giving? Are they better people; more empowered, energized and effective after they spend time around you? Is helping those you lead enter fully into God's life one of your goals?

I would guess that, regardless of how you answered the previous questions, you could tell me stories of various influencers who have touched your life in ways that were either life-robbing or life-giving. As you picture those individuals, think about the differences between the two. *That difference is what this book is all about.*

Leadership here on planet earth is at its best when it is life-giving, not life-robbing. Now, don't confuse being life-filled with the absence of pain, discomfort, loss, and messy moments. Being alive will very often include sweaty effort, a sore back, and strained brain cells. Just listen to a parent, athlete or business owner whom you consider vibrant and effective; their stories will always include pain and challenges. But also watch their eyes brighten and a smile spread out across their faces as they tell stories of tasting life as they applaud watching the child crossing the stage, the runner crossing the finish line, or the employees rallying as a unified team to resolve a crisis.

We know the difference between being alive or dead. It is obvious in most encounters from house plants to people. But the difference between what *gives and supports* life and what *depletes and endangers* life is harder to discern.

From my experiences of leading and being led, and in many conversations with other leaders, I propose it is possible to discern if leadership is life-giving or life-threatening. People being led by life-giving leaders will demonstrate many of these elements:

➤ They have a sense that being in their role complements and brings richness to other areas of their life.

➤ They have confidence and feel they are being empowered to be at their best.

➤ They have high levels of trust toward those around them.

➤ They have an enduring strength that presses on in times of great difficulty.

➤ They live life joyfully sacrificially giving to others.

➤ They are thankful for what they receive.

➤ They are content and peaceful yet pursuing growth and excellence.

➤ They are consistently taking rest periods and know how to replenish and refresh themselves.

➤ They work with diligence but expect resistance to their efforts.

➤ They have a clear sense of God's objective for their life and prioritize actions according to it.

Sometimes the beating rain and strong wind in a storm can provide essential water in a drought but it may also uproot a tree. It is even more challenging to choose life-giving actions in one's leadership.

1. Do I confront or keep silent about a mistake or a weakness?
2. Do I step in to help or let the weight of responsibility rest clearly on their shoulders?
3. Do I entrust someone with resources or provide a challenge for them to secure the resources?

We would probably say, "It requires wisdom and discernment to make a good decision on the questions listed above." I agree. Can a leader gain wisdom and discernment by being coached by another leader who is consistently observed as being life-giving? YES! Can we come to God the Father, God the Son and God the Spirit as our leadership coaches? This is what I am attempting to explore in this book.

This book is a reflection on over 40 years of leading others. In no way is it a final answer on the way to lead. However, I feel it is time to share some of the questions and initial answers to understanding and multiplying life-giving leadership.

Here is an overview of how I currently understand the flow of God's life-giving leadership, which also provides an outline for this book.

1. We begin by pointing out the FOUNDATION STONES of definitions and assumptions foundational to this perspective on leadership.

2. Every leader must have the essential TOOLS for receiving and giving life-giving leadership. We focus on four: Prayer, The Bible, Witness, and Creative Collaboration with the Spirit.

*The book then shifts from a tools focus to tracking the flow of life. Think of a river as Jesus illustrated in John 7. God gives us living water and then he makes us a stream of life-giving water. We will track the flow of God's grace and truth **to** us, **in** us, and then **through** us to the world.*

3. The HEART of the leader is critical because Jesus is clear that our life flows from an inner spring to the outward flow that touches others.

4. God has set us in a world of limits. Leaders need the proper RHYTHMS in their daily and weekly pace of life. This is essential to keeping our heart connected to God's life.

5. Ultimately leadership involves people. The next area of focus is on RELATING TO people and CHANGING WITH people. God has designed the world so all that is living experiences change.

6. God's life is connected to an overall objective. Life is not just drifting along from one pleasant experience to the next or even just moving one day at a time from birth to death. We live inside the larger story of God offering life to every person on the planet. Life-giving assignments for every Jesus-follower include SPREADING THE GOOD NEWS and MULTIPLYING

LEADERS, leading to the formation of new clusters of Christ-followers. Our goal is every people group on earth having the presence of the salt and light of God's kingdom rule walking among them.

Here's the flow of the book in a visual format:

Tools
    Heart
        Rhythms
            Relating to People
                Changing with People
                    Spreading the Good News
                    Multiplying Leaders

WHO IS THE INTENDED READER FOR THIS BOOK?

As I write, my primary target is the rising generation of leaders. While I believe there may be value to the words for those who have been in leadership for a while, I am seeking to create a tool that could be used to guide conversations between senior leaders and rising leaders.

My desire would be for an older leader to buy two to three copies of the book and invite two or three younger leaders to a time of discussion after reading a section of the book. In the appendix you will find a chart listing all of the exercises placed through the book.

The **"Pause! Try This!"** are opportunities to stop reading and try out the leadership ideas being presented. I have used these with leaders I seek to develop. At the end of each chapter are some **"Thinking it Through"** questions to prompt reflection and interaction with the ideas.

On the chart a leader can discuss with those they are developing which exercises and questions they are going to do and discuss together. Based on the development level of the leader in training some questions or activities are for those who have limited experience and others are for those who have a season of leadership experience behind them. I have also included recommended resources to dig deeper into topics I only have space or knowledge to introduce.

Skim the book together looking at the **"Pause! Try This!"** activities and the **"Thinking it Through"** questions at the end of each chapter. Then check off which ones you want to do. Consider creating a document on your computer or device and begin a leadership journal of the ideas and principles the Spirit teaches you to transform your leadership. You can revisit this journal through your life and keep adding quotes, verses, and key ideas to remind you and pass on to others.

I assume leadership development is happening around the world. I have sought to write for a global church context. It is true that many of my stories come from my leadership and life experience as a North American and will require some grace and adaptation outside of my passport culture. But I have told some of these stories in urban areas around the world and have found that most leaders are adept at using their exposure to global Western culture to filter and make application.

I have intentionally worked at including diverse models of ministry life. I believe biblical principles can be adapted to any setting and have sought to use questions and stories that focus more on leadership relationships than the structures we call churches, ministries, or agencies, which serve as containers for the relationships. You will detect a bias in the writing for informal community over formal structure. I also believe this fluid, consensus driven, flat organizational design is attractive to the millennials and the younger generations coming behind them. I have limited the application and examples of megachurch or program driven organizational models. Please don't assume I am against large or even highly structured and complex systems. I surely believe the Spirit can raise up and bless a great diversity of types of organizations, but I am seeking to wave a flag for diversity in structure and avoid the dangerous assumption that something like the megachurch model is *the* biblical model.

I have been assigned by God to serve Jesus in various ministry structures over the past 40 years as a leader, consultant or coach:

1. Biblical University administration (development, financial aid, alumni) and faculty member
2. Camp, Conference, Retreat organization
3. Youth Pastor
4. Pastor of Mission (congregation of 1,000+ focused on cell groups, evangelism and discipleship)
5. Teaching Pastor (congregation of 450+ engaged in university campus and resort ministry)
6. Two church plant teams (one currently meeting in a home and averaging 17-20 people)
7. Congregations in Rhode Island, South Carolina, North Carolina, Tennessee, Georgia, Alabama, Florida, Washington DC, Washington and Virginia (sizes from 100 to 2,500+ some were mono ethnic, others multi-ethnic, and various age composition)
8. Mission Agencies (consulting and board of trustees)
9. Consulting, teaching and training leaders: United Kingdom, Hungary, Russia, China, Singapore, Korea, Taiwan, Singapore, New Zeland, St. Vincent, and Egypt. (Congregations of various sizes, schools, and mission agencies)

I have attempted to weave in illustrations from most of these experiences.

This book is my attempt to frame a biblical reflection on leadership that leaders can use to shape their own leadership thinking and actions. Once that is clear, and being lived consistently, they can pass it on to others.

Jesus outlined at the end of the Gospels and the beginning of the book of Acts the work of God sustaining itself as those he had trained multiplied their life in Christ to others. Out of the global circle of Christ-followers God raises up leaders to advance, encourage and support the work. May we be a part of what he is doing until he returns.

INTRODUCTION

FOUNDATION STONES

BEFORE WE CAN BEGIN our study it may be helpful for you to get to know some of my way of approaching leadership. Here is a quick outline of what I'll be covering in this introduction.

1. A Glimpse of my personal journey
2. Assumptions that form the backdrop for my approach
3. My approach to the Bible as a leadership textbook
4. A definition of leadership
5. Leadership is not just about the mission — it is holistic in vision
6. Good leaders take on a posture of lifelong learning
7. The Cornerstone — GOD IS A Life-giving LEADER!

MY JOURNEY INTO LIFE-GIVING LEADERSHIP

I was crying. This was not something I did very often in my 30s and certainly not in front of other people. But here I was, unable to hold back tears, and finding myself being comforted by Richard, who served on the staff of a growing church with me. I was held in captivity to a deep sense of disappointment. I was disappointed with myself — I had again fallen short of what I expected a leader in the church to be and do. I felt weak and all of the fight had been wrung out of me. I was ready to quit.

I had not committed a moral failure; there was no blatant sin that could oust me as a ministry leader; but I had lost heart. As Richard listened, he also admitted a sense of being disappointed with the fruit of ministry. We had gone to different universities but had had similar experiences. He had been involved in the Navigators, and I had been very involved in Campus Crusade for Christ, now CRU. We both experienced life transforming encounters with Jesus Christ and had given our hearts freely to love him. Following Jesus included being a witness to his claims and helping others become growing and reproducing followers.

Those college days of ministry had included some relational messes, and we had encountered rejection, indifference and disappointment with those who started the race and then evaporated. But we had also seen a number of changed lives. We saw men and women set free and energized by the Spirit of Christ. We witnessed fellow students marrying, changing majors, and pursuing career paths all marked by their love for Christ and his cause. We were energized by being a part of what God was doing. Every week there was a new story of God's saving grace redeeming a seeking soul.

Richard and I landed on the same church leadership team, first as volunteers, and then as full-time paid staff members. We were serving side by side with our senior pastor and, eventually, two other pastoral staff. What began as a lot of fun with a sense of a God adventure decayed into stressful anxiety and something was lost. It might be easy to throw blame on our senior leader, the elders, or even the expectations of many in the congregation, but, sitting across from each other, we knew that the drift was, in large measure, our own doing.

That day we started on a journey together to regroup and rethink what God expects of leaders in his church. We now live in different cities; we have served in other leadership roles and many years have gone by. But, we still stay in touch and, whenever we talk, there is a deep bond that only can be forged in processing pain together. We seldom revisit the painful 1980s because we both have too much to process with the present and our dreams for the future. However, without a doubt this was a pivotal moment in my own learning, and it has carried forward to this book and is the center of all of the courses I teach in seminary.

My intent is to focus on essentials, and I know this work is not exhaustive. I am sure every leader will scan the table of contents and notice important leadership principles I have failed to include. And they are probably correct in the weight they give to the missing skill or subject. Nevertheless, what I am seeking to lift up are what the Bible considers to be ESSENTIAL for life-giving leaders following the lead of our God.

SOME OF MY ASSUMPTIONS

1. Almost every person has a definition of what leaders are to be, and with it a set of expectations of what leaders are to do.
2. Most have never really examined those views about leadership. Our largely unconscious and unexamined definitions and expectations, absorbed from cultural traditions and life experiences, color every leadership decision we face.
3. Many Christians approach their leadership, to a large degree, more from this cultural and life experience reservoir than from a reflective biblical perspective of leadership.
4. I have chosen to define God's view of leadership as "life-giving leadership" and will make a case for how he models effective and vibrant leadership by how he leads.
5. God leads so that those following him receive effective and vibrant (i.e., fruitful) life. This "fruit" gives glory to him, the caretaker of the vineyard with Christ as our vine and we as his branches.
6. I believe in the principle of "all truth is God's truth", and that in familial, governmental, educational, military, economic, sport, and other arenas where leadership exists, there will be some values and practices that align with biblical leadership. But I also hold that

these same "classrooms" where we learn how to lead are polluted with our sinfulness. Most of this sin shows up in how we use power (primarily authority), and in the motives of the leader's heart which fuel the choices made.

7. We often use effective leadership practices, which work because they align with our Creator's design, but then we twist these practices to ungodly ends because of corrupted power and wrong motives.

8. Like many aspects of God's truth, God's leadership truths appear childlike in simplicity, but when applied are very powerful. Truth coming from the heart and flowing outward to life; abundant life is truly transformational.

9. Notice God's handiwork. Everything he makes alive he makes unique, but to live under his rule we live in *unity*. Unity is not the same as uniformity. Oneness and community are God words for treasuring, appreciating and accepting one another. We are not the same. Each of us is one of a kind. Don Barry, a New Zealand pastor, describes the work of God with a great image:

   God doesn't turn out leaders like chocolate soldiers, but he does allow his people to face common trials and familiar tests. We each have our unique story, but we cover common ground in our journeys.[1]

10. At times, those differences stimulate a response of fear. One definition of sin is anything that threatens the value of our uniqueness and hinders unity. Sin *devalues* and *divides*. Think of how actions such as bullying, racism and prejudice devalue and divide. Think of how words and phrases such as, "I am just a maverick", "I work better alone", "weird" or "personal preference" destructively devalue and divide. Life-giving leadership for the kingdom is very different from other types of leadership. We are *not* producing and then selling a product. We are not just defeating an enemy and securing the land. We are part of a surgical team, gathered around the table, working together as God's changes the heart.

11. This study may challenge much of your inherited view of leadership

and bring you to a crossroads of turning from your current view of leadership and embracing a different path to follow. There is way too much life-robbing leadership, and it will require an intentional change *in* a leader's heart and *by* the leader's attitudes, words, and actions to see more life-giving leaders.

MY CAUTIOUS APPROACH TO USING THE BIBLE TO SPEAK TO LEADERSHIP

One of my mentors in seminary warned of taking historical accounts (Nehemiah rebuilding the wall, Moses leading the people to the promised land, and the birth and expansion of the church in the book of Acts) and deducing principles for all times and places. He pointed out to me that he had never seen the plucking of beards and beatings from Nehemiah, chapter 13, suggested in a current leadership book as a way to correct and train leaders. What we usually end up doing is using the biblical accounts to find a validation for our cultural definitions of leadership and ignore what doesn't affirm our model. To avoid this, I have chosen to focus on broad themes about God's approach to leadership which show up in many parts of the biblical text. Consequently, I have chosen to include many of my references in the end notes, instead of interrupting the flow of the prose with numerous biblical addresses.

I am very wary of trends and fads that sweep through the Christian world packaged in the next new "how-to" book. My shelves contain several of them, but I have found little of lasting value, beyond the exciting story of a journey of some of God's people in a given place and time. Instead, in this book, you will find some rough thoughts describing how to navigate a unique journey with God, which he will faithfully unfold within a community of Christ-followers. I wish to avoid prescribing specific paths, programs, systems or structures. I believe there is a place for many of these elements, and as a community is receiving and giving God's life, the Spirit can easily direct the group on how to wrap the gift of the kingdom presence as the church lives it out. **I choose to focus on the gift, not the wrappings.**

A DEFINITION OF LEADERSHIP

Jesus Offers Life but Never Forces it on anyone.

*You search the Scriptures because you think that in them you have eternal life; and it is they that bear witness about me, yet you refuse to **come to me** that you may have life.*[2]

In creation God speaks and everything comes to life. He breathes and the clay shell of a man comes to life. The Father raises the Son from the grave and, in that act, declares death will not have the last word. His life has won! Jesus teaches Nicodemus that the Spirit blowing like the wind is the one who creates the new birth of a person. A new person, Paul reminds us, is a new creation.[3] We are created with physical life and then the Spirit recreates us with spiritual life. Jesus summed up his ministry of coming to serve and not be served as one giving life—abundant life.[4] There is no question, *life* is the central theme in God's influencing/leadership of humanity. Do note that Jesus is offering life and giving it to those who come, but he does not force feed life to people.[5]

This is consistent with the view we have of God in the Old Testament.

*For my people have committed two evils: they have forsaken me, the fountain of living waters, and hewed out cisterns for themselves, broken cisterns that can hold no water. . . On the last day of the feast, the great day, Jesus stood up and cried out, 'If anyone thirsts, let him **come to me** and drink. Whoever believes in me, as the Scripture has said, 'Out of his heart will flow rivers of living water." Now this he said about the Spirit, whom those who believed in him were to receive, for as yet the Spirit had not been given, because Jesus was not yet glorified.*[6]

Jeremiah provides leadership by giving the people a realistic assessment of their present condition. They have turned from God to other sources of life and the result is like trying to hold water in leaking containers. There is no lack of empty promises and false sources of strength and protection which seduce leaders, but leave both them and the people thirsting for life. Don't look elsewhere for what God is ready to provide.

God places each Christ-follower inside a circle of influence. He then provides resources for us to invest in influencing others toward him and his work. He decides how many are in our circle of influence at any given moment. God desires every person within our circle be granted respect. This blessing of others includes everyone God allows us to influence from the server in a restaurant to the homeless person on the street.

He has created every person with a "thinker", a "feeler", and a "chooser".[7] These three capacities define how we live as a person. In a small percentage of people, one or more of these capacities may be broken, undeveloped, sick or stuck. They may be labeled as "special needs", "not typically developing", or "mentally ill". They, too, bear the image of God and are worthy of being loved as image bearers.

God chooses to never violate the thinker, feeler or chooser in any of his children. He stands at the door to our life and knocks, but he does not tear the door down.[8] He responds to those who come to him in faith—meaning they believe he exists—and he will reward those who seek him.[9] A person opens the door or seeks him, and he responds to the invitation. The same should be true of how we treat those within the circle of our influence.

We can offer what God has given to us, but we do not force ourselves on anyone. Jesus never forced anyone to follow him. He invited and some responded positively. Some turned away and some followed. Jesus loved them all, and he even wept over the rejection he encountered, but he let people determine the level of his influence on them and the depth of their intimacy with him.

Respectful influence is given additional clarity when one looks at the spiritual gifting given to some believers in leadership.

*If service, in our serving; the one who teaches, in his teaching; the one who exhorts, in his exhortation; the one who contributes, in generosity; the **one who leads, with zeal;** the one who does acts of mercy, with cheerfulness.*[10]

*Now you are the body of Christ and individually members of it. And God has appointed in the church first apostles, second prophets, third teachers, then miracles, then gifts of healing, helping, **administrating,** and various kinds of tongues. Are all apostles? Are all prophets? Are all teachers? Do all work miracles? Do all possess gifts of healing? Do all speak with tongues? Do all interpret?*[11]

But the centurion paid more attention to <u>the pilot</u> and to the owner of the ship than to what Paul said.

The Greek word *kubernoeis* in these three passages (see underlined sections) is the idea of the local pilot or navigator going out to a ship full of cargo and leading them into the safe harbor while avoiding the shoals. The pilot lived there and knew the water well. He was able to direct them safely and without loss. He demonstrated life protecting, life cherishing, and life directing influence.

A definition of life-giving leadership would be respectful influence unconditionally imparting blessing and offering direction.

LIFE-GIVING LEADERSHIP IS. . .
RESPECTFUL INFLUENCE
UNCONDITIONALLY IMPARTING BLESSING
AND OFFERING DIRECTION

Leadership is. . . INFLUENCE

The greatest way we influence is to enter into a mysterious partnership with God through prayer. In prayer we are often changed. Those we pray for receive God's influence. God is moving and working in ways the Bible does not fully explain. The center, the foundation, the priority of every leadership strategy to influence should be PRAYER.

Leaders will often need some of their best creative juice to direct those around them to join them in diligent prayer.

God has come to us to influence us. His primary strategy for enticing us to respond has been incredible grace filled, love motivated, GIVING. God joyfully, sacrificially, GIVES for the sake of those he loves. It would make sense then, as we move into our God given circle of influence and because we are made in his image, that a foundational part of our leadership plan would involve GIVING <u>to</u> and <u>for</u> the sake of those we are seeking to influence.[12]

Life-giving leaders follow God. Leaders believe God is *the* leader and their influence is always carried out under him, with him, for him, and ultimately, *by* him. Is there anything that we have to give he did not first give to us?

We are saying, "Follow me as I follow Christ!" offering direction so they may have their own connection to God. The goal for each person we influence is for them to bow their knee to the same King who's kingdom we are in. We are passing out the uniforms, armor and weapons of *his* army. It is *his* harvest. It is *his* family. It is *his* flock. It is *his* body. Leaders in God's economy never mean the statement, "Follow me as I follow Christ," to be understood as "submit to me and I will speak as God to you." We are seeking for our lives to be one large billboard pointing them to King Jesus.

Life-giving leadership strategy must call each person to take responsibility for their own connection to and relationship with God. Every follower should be learning to see, listen, and read God's mission directives, and to follow the map. If a leader is wounded, removed, or rebels and goes AWOL, the army of God marches on. God's leadership looks very different from cultic top down leadership. The Bible clearly balances every Christ-follower having an allegiance to God with a respect for and recognition of God's delegating authority to a group of Christ-followers he calls and gifts to be leaders. But it is never a blind allegiance.

Look at an example of Jesus' leadership.

When he saw the crowds, he had compassion for them, because they were harassed and helpless, like sheep without a shepherd. Then he said to his disciples, 'The harvest is plentiful, but the laborers are few; therefore pray earnestly to the Lord of the harvest to send out laborers into his harvest.' [13]

Jesus had a vibrant, motivated heart and clarity of vision. He operated with deep passion and compassion, and called from conviction for effective, fruitful investment of prayer by his followers. Leaders often have energy rising up from their soul as they become aware of a problem to solve or opportunity for a kingdom advance. Jesus had direction for how the disciples should view others, their time, and their life purpose.

Leaders tend to "see" what others in the room do not quite see yet. It

does not make them better, but they do bring a valuable gift to the group.

In any place that we have served, as soon as we have our first covered dish meal, my wife, Pandora, gets a reputation for her banana pudding. People love it and always want to know if that is what she is bringing to every dinner. Leaders have a banana pudding; it is God letting them see what others in the room may not yet see. It is their contribution to the whole team.

> ➤ They see potential in someone that the person himself does not yet see.
> ➤ They see a problem brewing on the horizon others do not yet see.
> ➤ They see an opportunity for growth and fruitfulness others are not yet aware exists.
> ➤ They catch glimpses, have dreams, and wake up with possible solutions; all gifts from God to bring to the group.

Now, by "see" I do not mean they have all of the ideas or vision for the organization. I think Pastor Don Barry summarizes the biblical view on vision very well.

As I began to contemplate this idea in relation to New Testament leadership, it occurred to me that it wasn't my responsibility to have all the dreams, but rather to minister and lead in such a way that the dreams God had put in the hearts of others would come to fruition. I didn't have to have all the visions and dreams for the community; I had to minister in order to create a community of dreamers. I didn't have to possess any particular kind of personality — larger than life or otherwise. I didn't have to ooze charisma or have divine insight into the future of the church. But I need to have an absolute commitment to serving the dreams that God had put in the hearts of the people I led.

Don describes how, when he shifted to this approach in his leadership, many of the people did not know how to respond.

The thought that God might have placed dreams in their own hearts either hasn't occurred to them at all, or has been buried by a model of church life that has reduced them to passive spectators looking for a genius to follow...As leaders,

I think we are first and foremost 'environmental architects.' We are responsible to create and develop healthy environments in which dreams can be safely pursued ...My greatest challenge as a leader has been to be secure enough to allow them to experiment and succeed, and to purposefully develop a culture in which more and more people would feed the freedom and permission to follow their dreams.[14]

This is what Jesus did with the disciples under Jesus. He shared what he saw and he lived out the heart of God with them. The Spirit then birthed ministry that exploded on the pages of the book of Acts.

The healthy environment Don mentions will need to be holistic in scope because of the complexity of our lives.

Leadership is *holistic* in its perspective

God has made us very complex and interdependent.

Try solving a budget issue when you have a raging stomach problem.

Try disciplining an employee with whom you have no prior relationship.

It is interesting to observe how, within God's design for us, we never really figure out the perfect plan for self-leadership in our life. As we move through stages of life, we stay in a learning curve.

As soon as you learn how to be twenty, you turn thirty.

As soon as you get some stability on parenting children, they become adolescents.

As soon as you forgive your parents for how they failed you and begin to really walk with them as an adult, they enter decline and need you to parent them.

We are always in a learning curve and need to cry out to God in one or more of the aspects of our humanity.

It is helpful to use a grid suggested by Pete Scazzero's *The Five Dimensions of Our Self:*

1. **Physical** — How much you can eat at one time, and the impact of the nutritional value of what you eat, changes as you age and your metabolism shifts. In my sixth decade, I find myself back to scheduling the daily nap I enjoyed as a four-year-old. God made

us to move and yet the intensity, frequency and types of exercise change as we age or recover from certain illnesses. We never finish learning how to manage our physical self.

2. **Mental** — You have to write more things down and review the list of names more often. I have more questions, less answers and yet have more confidence in what I do know than ever before. We never finish learning how to manage our mental self.

3. **Emotional** — Things that caused sleepless nights in my 20s are just expected aspects of life now. Sometimes mountains do turn into mole hills when viewed from a different vantage point. We learn to be thankful for the small things we used to take for granted or feel we were entitled to receive. We never finish learning to manage our emotional self.

4. **Social** — We learn we must balance task completion with being with people. We must balance acceptance with accountability. We need others but do not want to live for being needed. We often have to relearn how to play at each stage of our life and to not miss its value. We never finish learning to manage our social self.

5. **Spiritual** — Often God's mercy and grace helps us find acceptance and peace before God. Yet this same grace inspires us to grow, learn, and stretch to be more. We learn that certain spiritual disciplines fit better at certain stages in the journey. We learn to listen. We never finish learning to manage our spiritual self.[15]

Good leaders are life-long learners!

An important aspect of being ALIVE is never being finished. For those of us motivated by putting a file away or checking off the box on the To-Do list, this may not be encouraging news. God loves to see us grow. Being alive equals growing. And growth equals change; a subject we address in later chapters.

God created us with a *potential* for growth. God created us with gaps, undeveloped capacity, and a flexible adaptable ability to change. Embracing grace and resting in it involves seeing my sin, my weakness, and my flaws and knowing that I am perfectly loved in the life God gives.

The founder of Marble Retreat, a counseling center in Colorado for Christian workers, is known for asking two questions:

1. Is there anything you can do that would make God love you less?
2. Is there anything you can do that would make God love you more?

Are the people we are leading experiencing God's unearned and undeserved love, acceptance, and grace from us, even when we are challenging or assisting them in growth?

Employees are vastly more satisfied and productive, it turns out, when their core needs are met: physical, through opportunities to regularly renew and recharge at work; emotional, by feeling valued and appreciated for their contributions; mental, when they have the opportunity to focus in an absorbed way on their most important tasks and define when and where they get their work done; and spiritual, by doing more of what they do best and enjoy most, and by feeling connected to a higher purpose at work. Social needs include being part of an empowering setting instead of a competitive setting. Competitive goals can have a place when they are organizational wide, but if they turn energy inside and against those on the same team, they become deadly.

Jesus knew the essentials of a healthy environment and included them in some of his final promises to his followers.

*And Jesus came and said to them, '**All authority** in heaven and on earth has been given to me. Go therefore and make disciples of all nations, baptizing them in the name of the Father and of the Son and of the Holy Spirit, teaching them to observe all that I have commanded you. And behold, **I am with you always,** to the end of the age.'* [16]

Jesus never intended to be an absentee leader. His *authority* and *presence* indicate an active, engaged, and very present leader as we join him in his making disciples of all peoples mission. Every Jesus-following leader is to be covered by his life-giving power and personal presence.

GOD IS A LIFE-GIVING LEADER

In this introduction I am seeking to lay down the foundation stones on which to build a solid leadership structure. In a foundation there is a critical cornerstone that is critical to whole building project. This book rests on the truth that God is a life-giving leader.

We will seek to lift up several of God's life-giving attributes as we go through the book. Let's begin with an example foundational to the whole idea of humans being in a relationship with God.

God is relational

George Cladis begins his book on a team based approach to church leadership by searching for a biblical image to anchor his vision of being a godly leader. He writes of his research findings, "In the seventh century, John of Damascus, a Greek theologian, described the relationships of the persons of God (Trinity) as *perichoresis*. Perichoresis means literally "circle dance". . . Based on the biblical descriptions of Father, Son and Spirit, John depicted the three persons in the Trinity in a circle. A perichoretic image of the Trinity is that of three persons of God in constant movement in a circle that implies intimacy, equality, unity yet distinction, and love."[17] He goes on to describe what is experienced in dancing in a circle using the Greek celebration dances as an example. "In a circle we can see each other. No one is left out. We are all interconnected. We hold each other up. I once asked church innovators William Easum (Sacred Cows Make Gourmet Burgers) and Leonard Sweet (coeditor of the journal *Homiletics*) about worship targeted for unchurched people. How do we reach the younger generation today with the gospel of Jesus Christ? They both suggested round tables. "Round tables?" I said, puzzled. "Yes," they replied, "and have the ushers be waiters, serving hot coffee.". . . Round tables create a sense of community and wholeness. Have you ever tried to have a discussion with people sitting next to you on a long couch . . . . Sitting, standing or dancing in the round, we feel together. A sense of community is immediately communicated."[18]

God Addresses Relationship FIRST and then Training

Love, Community, Intimacy, Support, Encouragement, Equality, Mutual Submission, and One in Unity, Purpose and Mission all describe how God reveals himself to us in his leadership. But don't confuse some of our mushy, no right or wrong kind of tolerance as God's love. His love is balanced in grace and truth. He leads through a personal connection, a restoring of a loving relationship initiated by him and sustained by his gracious provision of the resources needed to offer forgiveness, reconciliation and redemption. Once we receive this grace of unconditional love apart from merit, he then begins a process of training and correcting with his truth.

Almost all of the New Testament letters are written to address concerns, problems and dangerous lies in the early church. The first half of each letter is given to reviewing the Christ-centered provision of God's abundant and overwhelming loving grace. *Then*, after securely anchoring the readers in the merciful standing of being God's children, the letter writer begins to discipline, warn and correct. In other words God always justifies and *then* he sanctifies and glorifies.[19]

God is fully present in relationships

One implication of the Triune God in an eternal circle dance with and around his creation is his presence with us. Do you ever pray and have to wonder if God is in the room? Elijah accused the false gods of being in the toilet and inaccessible to the pleas of the priests. That is *never* true of our God. Not only is his presence universal and Omni over all of his creation, he is also personally, relationally connected to every Christ-follower in the Holy Spirit. The assurance of his presence in Matthew 28:20 is one promise that Christ-followers have held on to in times of testing and trial.

Life-giving Leaders develop the skill of being fully present. They are focused on who they are with and attentive to being a part of what is going on. A life-giving leader would not pass through the work floor on the way to their office without noticing and engaging, at least nonverbally, with others in the room.

In Genesis 1:11-12, God speaks and creation breaks out in life and he puts within it the capacity for it to multiply and reproduce—to be fruitful. And God blesses it calling it GOOD! God was present at the moment of creation and has tended and been involved ever since.

Conclusion

God's life-giving leadership stands in sharp contrast to many other styles of leadership. Jesus declared it when he was seeking to recalibrate the definition of leadership used by the disciples.

*And James and John, the sons of Zebedee, came up to him and said to him, 'Teacher, we want you to do for us whatever we ask of you.' And he said to them, 'What do you want me to do for you?' And they said to him, 'Grant us to sit, one at your right hand and one at your left, in your glory.' Jesus said to them, 'You do not know what you are asking. Are you able to drink the cup that I drink, or to be baptized with the baptism with which I am baptized?' And they said to him, 'We are able.' And Jesus said to them, 'The cup that I drink you will drink, and with the baptism with which I am baptized, you will be baptized, but to sit at my right hand or at my left is not mine to grant, but it is for those for whom it has been prepared.' And when the ten heard it, they began to be indignant at James and John. And Jesus called them to him and said to them, 'You know that those who are considered rulers of the Gentiles lord it over them, and their great ones exercise authority over them. But **it shall not be so among you**. But whoever would be great among you must be your servant, and whoever would be first among you must be slave of all. For even the Son of Man came not to be served but to serve, and to give his life as a ransom for many.'* [20]

IT…SHALL…NOT…BE…SO…AMONG…YOU!

It sounds like this was important to Jesus. If you scan the Gospels you will notice this topic comes up several times. Even on the night Jesus would be arrested, he takes a towel and bows down and washes their feet, seeking to drive home how radical the kingdom of God view of leadership is to be. I believe the Christians and Non-Christians of the world are looking for this kind of radical life-giving leadership.

Let's be a part of the kingdom life-giving revolution.

THINKING IT THROUGH

Here are some questions to help you review and discuss what you have just read with a coach or mentor.

1. From your past, identify one leader who was life-giving and one who was life-taking. They may not have worn a formal leadership title but were a person of influence in your life. What do you observe as the differences between the two?

2. Revisit the list of assumptions. Which ones do you strongly agree or disagree with right now? Were any of them a new thought for you to consider?

3. What and who has God placed in your circle of influence or leadership right now?

4. The five dimensions of self-leadership are: physical, mental, emotional, social and spiritual. Which ones do you need someone to assist you in right now? What kind of assistance do you need?

PART ONE

A LIFE-GIVING LEADER'S TOOLBOX

LEADERSHIP IS LIKE most artistic works. Skills can be developed and honed through practice. Improvement requires an openness to one's work being critiqued by others. In humility, one listens to all but, secure in oneself through Christ's power and presence, discerns what to absorb what to let fade away.

Leadership also has an intuitive and creative feel, which is very difficult to teach. You see it, hear it, sense it, or know it—or you don't. The best leaders have their intuitive nature guided by a moral compass. They also recognize the exception that proves the rule and at times will choose swimming upstream against popular opinion. Life-giving leaders expect to experience being misunderstood, expect to be judged wrongly in their motives by an observer, and expect to endure the heat of conflict. There will be personal losses and falling support for one's ideas.

There will also be wins. Good leaders know there will be sweet times of seeing a harvest brought in, a project completed, a person excelling, and goals going down in the record book as completed. There is a deep satisfaction in knowing God has used you to influence others to make a difference, to wade through change, to heal from failure or to accomplish a mission.

In these various exercises of influence leaders need tools. If you observe any master mechanic or artisan, you will see how precious their tools are to them. If you look through their tools, often under their watchful eye, you will see some that look almost new and only come out for a specific task. But other tools look as they are worn to the owner's hand. They rarely get to rest in the toolbox. They are in the leader's hand or laying nearby and are used many times a day.

I want to introduce you to four tools that are essential to the leadership task. As you examine them you may say they are important to many other aspects of life besides leadership. I agree. But I have focused on their contribution to life-giving leadership. There is no claim that these four are exhaustive. Surely they are not. But they are essential. I am convinced that you cannot really follow God into being a life-giving leader without them.

THE FOUR TOOLS FOR LIFE-GIVING LEADERSHIP

1. Praying in Jesus' name: the leader's companion and provision of God's resources
2. The Bible as *the* leader's compass
3. Being a witness to the good news of Jesus' kingdom as the leader's identity
4. The leader's partnership of creative collaboration with the Spirit

CHAPTER ONE

PRAYING IN JESUS' NAME

Praying gives sense, brings wisdom, and broadens and strengthens the mind. The prayer closet is a perfect schoolteacher and schoolhouse for the preacher. Thought is not only brightened and clarified in prayer, but thought is born in prayer.
—E.M. Bounds

IF YOU ARE ASKED, as an outside consultant, to examine any kingdom enterprise, you can determine its effectiveness by listening to how the leaders are praying. Our prayers expose what we *really* believe and are a great predictor of where the time, money and energy of the leadership is going. What we pray about gets our attention! What we pray sets our priorities! What we pray is what we do! A leader who wants a group to behave differently should begin with helping them pray differently. Prayer is not all we do, but if we are not praying, all we do will make little difference.

> We are too busy to pray, and so we are too busy to have power. We have a great deal of activity, but we accomplish little; many services but few conversions; much machinery but few results. —R.A. Torrey

PRAYER CHANGES OUR LEADERSHIP

Here is an example. I saw a pastor's vision become larger and more dynamic as he shared about reading an article by Mike Rogers, from The Navigators, which challenged him to set an alarm on his phone at 9:38, to remind him of Matthew 9:38. When his alarm went off, he paused to pray for the Lord of the harvest to send laborers into the harvest. After a few months of this discipline, the pastor began to see the world news differently. He was reminded to pray for former classmates from seminary who were now missionaries, and he began to see lost people differently. The need for harvest workers changed how he preached and shaped plans for the discipleship of his congregation. The resulting wave of change in attitudes and actions which colored many aspects of his leadership started by praying differently.

Another example comes from a missionary friend in Russia who shared this verse one night after dinner in their flat.

Rejoice in hope, be patient in tribulation, be constant in prayer.[1]

Andy described the dark, long winter days, the cold weather, and the long lines in many places. I remember him saying something close to these words, "Bev and I have served in Vietnam, France and Africa over the past 30 years and we have faced nothing like the challenge here. We have discussed how we can almost feel our hope draining out of us and our impatience escalating in us over big and little things. God is keeping us in a place of constant prayer. I believe it is our greatest encounter with spiritual warfare, but we believe this is because God intends even greater victories."

Call to me and I will answer you, and will tell you great and hidden things that you have not known.[2]

Life-giving leadership involves a God-confidence in spite of our lack of answers to questions in any situation. We are connected via prayer to the one who can direct us through the unknown.

Prayer is a major skill that Jesus uses in leading his disciples and in training them to lead. Christ gave his disciples the right to use his name, authorizing their prayers to the Father. Every Jesus-follower is a priest, coming through the high priest, Jesus, to the Father. The disciples had grown up praying, but Jesus transformed ritualized formulas into quietly bringing their greatest hurts and needs to a caring father.

And rising very early in the morning, while it was still dark, he departed and went out to a desolate place, and there he prayed.[3]

Jesus knew that his mission was not to attract a crowd, but to remain obedient to the Father. It was prayer that set the agenda for Jesus' ministry (Luke 6:12). Prayer preceded the miracles (John 11:42-43); prayer brought him encouragement at critical moments (Luke 9:28-31); prayer enabled him to go to the cross (Luke 22:41-42); and prayer kept him there despite the excruciating pain (Luke 23:46). Follow the Savior's example, and let your time alone with God, in prayer, set the agenda for your life.[4]

Most of us learn to process our lives with a few trusted people as part of our process of weighing, evaluating and making decisions. Speaking and listening in intimate conversation is a natural expression found between life-long loves. My wife, Pandora, shared with me how hard it was when I was unconscious for over 7 days in ICU in 2011. She was present with me, but we shared no verbal or non-verbal communication. She said it was one of the most challenging aspects of that experience.

Recently, my mother became physically and mentally impaired for almost two months. I watched as my dad and those of us present to offer care felt cut off from Mom. We were talking *about* her while she was in the room but not a part of the conversation. It was very challenging to know how to include her in our lives. Love and communication belong together. Love can surely exist in the heart of the beloved without regular exchanges, but the design for love is *connection through open communication.*

Perhaps the greatest love gift our leader Jesus has given us is uninterrupted access into the presence of our holy God.

HOW TO PRAY

Pray Without Ceasing

Remember how the early church was commanded to "rejoice always, pray without ceasing, giving thanks in all circumstances; for this is the will of God in Christ Jesus for you."[5] Because we are indwelt by the Spirit of Christ, we can be in God's presence everywhere we go and anytime we are awake. We are always having an internal conversation with ourselves whenever we are awake, and we can include God in the conversation. David Hansen describes this kind of conversation as, "long wandering prayer".

Long wandering prayer uses the fact that our minds wander as an advantage to prayer rather than as a disadvantage... Our obsessive drive to control our minds in the presence of God, that is, to pray about one thing or stick to one list, may be a form of hiding from God... Ministry is all grace. If my work had flowed from days praying on my knees, perhaps I could connect the dots of discipline, compliance and method to prayer and ministry. Perhaps then I could connect my ministry with my efforts. But going out and fishing while thinking about the problems of the church is not work to be proud of. It's embarrassing... My morning devotions are a matter of discipline. My long prayers are a matter of appetite... I pray all day when I need to exchange my anxious thoughts for the peace that passes understanding, when I want to know the truth that sets free, when I am out on a limb and the branch is cracking, when I feel lonely and I want the presence of the Beloved. The Spirit creates the desire in my soul, and I follow my will. God's open ear is irresistible to me because he has given my new heart, compelling me to pray lengthy, bitter prayers of repentance for the old Adam still at work within me. [6]

At a Pastor's retreat where Dave spoke on long wandering prayer many expressed thanks for the freedom. They had never been told that wandering around aimlessly talking to themselves in the presence of God was one of the pastor's main responsibilities. The apostle Paul tells us to "pray without ceasing" (1 Thessalonians 5:17). What can he mean by that? Can it really mean for us to talk to God in the second person singular all day long? Perhaps he means for us to open all of our thinking to God as a form of prayer.

⏱ PAUSE — TRY IT OUT!

There are biblical examples of inner meditation/conversation and prayer merging together in our hearts. Stop and read the following Psalms and note the shift in person from where the Psalmist is talking to himself, to talking to God, to speaking to others. What does the writer say to or remind himself? What is said to God?

> Psalm 13
> Psalm 42
> Psalm 55

Pray Until Our Heart Changes

Hansen helps us understand how to pray by describing how the writer of the psalms is compressing the journey of the heart that had included dramatic changes in emotions and attitudes over many hours into a short, memorable and repeatable song.

The psalm is a poetic compression of a much longer prayer. The psalm recounts in a minute a spiritual reformation that took hours or even days of personal anguish... That it takes me so long to pray to hope and praise is, well, reality. If it takes me a day to move through sin and despair to hope and praise, that the way it is. But the journey to hope and praise is worth any amount of time and any amount of mental effort. That is why long wandering prayer is not a matter of discipline; it is a matter of desire. It isn't about compliance to law; it is about hunger for grace. Hunger for grace comes from God's grace. Thus long wandering prayer never feels like an accomplishment.

Pray With the Right Motive

Prayer is never earning God's attention. If your prayers become attempts to twist God's arm or deserve his answer you must return to the basic questions, "Who are we addressing? What is the heart of God toward me? What is God like in his basic character?"

If we have problems trusting in God, it's not likely we'll be able to pray this petition from our heart. It's not unlikely, either, that we will have much of a personal relationship with our God.[7]

When I fail to pray, the best I can do is the best I can do. I forfeit my spiritual potential. But when I pray, the best I can do is no longer the best I can do. The best I can do is the best God can do.[8]

Prayer is admitting I need God. I also pray because he is a friend, a companion in my journey. I really do not enjoy traveling without my wife. If I do, as I am enjoying a nice meal, I am thinking how she would enjoy it. If I experience a new place, I think how she would delight in it. During a recent visit to Singapore together, we sought to overcome jet lag the first day by walking in the orchid gardens. I found myself enjoying her enjoyment of the many varieties of flowers, as much as I enjoyed being there myself. In some small way that is what my best times of prayer are, sharing the adventure with Jesus.

> Spread out your petition before God, and then say, 'Thy will, not mine, be done." The sweetest lesson I have learned in God's school is to let the Lord choose for me.
> — D.L. Moody

Pray to Honor Our Relationship

Our prayers operate by some of the same "rules" that apply to any loving honoring relationship:

- ➤ Be specific NOT generic
- ➤ Be submissive NOT demanding
- ➤ Be expectant NOT doubting
- ➤ Be persistent NOT fearful

What means more to you? Someone you work closely with says, "If I have ever hurt you in any way please forgive me." OR "I have been convicted by the Spirit that the way I spoke to you in our last team meeting when you asked the question about why we were changing our outreach strategy was wounding to you and disrespectful of one of God's children. Would you forgive me?"

What means more to you? Someone you deeply love gives you a generic Thank You card printed with the words, "I am thankful for you." OR a handwritten personal note saying, "I am so thankful for the patient and calm way you responded last week."

What means more to you? Someone in the church says, "If you ever need anything just ask!" OR "I am going on a shopping adventure to the market across town. Give me a list of what you need, loan me one of your tote bags, and let me get some things for you."

God is personal and has committed to a relationship. Often the way *we* prefer to be treated is a good clue of how we should relate to our loving and great God.

Pray After Spiritual Victory

And after he had taken leave of them, he went up on the mountain to pray.[9]

Do you know one of the most predictable times for life-robbers to show up in my leadership? It very often happens directly after a spiritual victory. I find the enemy often steps up attacks after he loses face when God wins. Jesus had just fed a huge crowd with five loaves of bread and two fish. I can't believe he didn't even use some coupons for the "cardboard" pizza that is the staple of every youth meeting! Instead of basking in the glory of the crowd, or receiving thanks from the disciples as they carried away the 12 baskets of leftovers, Jesus went up on the mountain alone to be with the Father.

Do not be surprised! There will be crisis storms in our lives following a victory. We need the bread of life that only time alone with the Father can provide to nourish and equip us. There is surely a place to celebrate God's victories in our leadership, but do not let the party rob you from receiving what you need from the Father for what is coming next.

WHAT TO PRAY?

Are my prayers too small for a God who rules over all? God has shaped my prayer life through several Korean friends I have prayed with over the years. One of them introduced me to using the Lord's Prayer as a pattern for anything I want to bring to God.

The six clauses of the prayer help me expand the specific focus of my prayers. I enjoy walking and often use this time for prayer. As I make my way along the trail, I state each phrase of the Lord's Prayer and then let the truth of it be my diving board into the pool of all that is on my heart. Enlarging our prayers is one way we walk with the Spirit and expand our circle of influence and partnership in his work.

Since the Spirit inspired the Scripture, one aspect of praying in the Spirit is praying from what he has written. Praying Scripture also assures my heart that I am praying according to God's will.[10]

⏱ PAUSE — TRY IT OUT!

Use the Lord's Prayer as a template for conversing with God.

Read the next six verses and accompanying paragraphs out loud, stopping after each one to continue the train of thought in your own conversation with the Father.

Our Father in heaven, hallowed be your name...

Lord what an honor to be in your family. What a privilege to bear your name. I am one of your children for whom the Son is building my eternal home. Thank you. I want you to get the honor you deserve from me and everything that I do. There are millions around me right now that do not honor you. Many do not acknowledge that you exist. Help me introduce them to you! You are the King, the Shelter, The Shepherd, The Vine, The Rock, The Bread of Life and so many more. Your names each help me remember truth about you and bend my knee in honor to you.

Your kingdom come, your will be done on earth as it is in heaven...

Your rule over everything is the only solid hope I have to cling to. Not only am I a child of the Father I am a citizen in your kingdom. I will never really be home until I walk into your throne room. I sometime get homesick for other places on this planet where I have lived. They are part of who I am. I want your kingdom to be and more and more what I am like. I joyfully surrender all I have to you. I can think of no safer place to be than under your reign. Help me understand the Bible, for surely you have clearly declared your will in it. May your words be my delight.

Give us today our daily bread...

My life depends on a provision of food and drink. Millions around the world are unsure of where those will come from. Give to me and make me a giver like you. Nothing happens in my ministry without resources. I choose today to look to you, and you alone, today, and each day, to provide what I need. Help me introduce others to you, the one who gives the bread of life. Lord, I lift up each of these people and their needs to you, as I know of them. But I am so glad that you know our needs before we ask. I am not always aware of the hunger of others, please help me see it and bring it to you.

And forgive us our debts, as we forgive our debtors...

The greatest gift you give to me is unlimited forgiveness secured by the blood of the Lord Jesus. Thank you. I want to sit here quietly for a moment and let your Spirit make me aware of any unconfessed sin in my life and also for you to remind me again of what it really means to be forgiven. Now, by your Spirit, make me aware of those I need to forgive. Help me cancel the debt and no longer hold their sin against me as a barrier between us. I would be so lost without your forgiveness, and I am aware that I have no right to withhold this gift you have given me from anyone in my life.

And lead us not into temptation but deliver us from the evil one...

I know that nothing evil comes from you. You do test me to expose what I am blind to in my own heart. You know even more than I do that I need protection. I need protection from my own weak flesh, the world system I am living in, and the evil one. I want to lift up specifically many who need your protection today. I know you will deliver me from evil and bring me safely home. Help me finish well.

For yours is the kingdom and the power and the glory forever...

I close this prayer focusing my faith on you as the all-powerful one. There is no one ruling over you. There is nothing you have created that can surprise or topple you. I affirm that I am yours. Whatever, wherever, whenever, and with whoever, I want to be there with you. I also know there are many today who are afraid and have lost the focus on you in your glory. I have been there many hours myself, as you know. Help me so praise you that others may see you as you really are.

I enjoy doing a workshop using the Lord's Prayer as a framework for everything we want to pray. I explain and model it and then break into groups of twos or threes. I encourage the groups to spend ten minutes on each of the six clauses.

When they return we share how they have been impacted by the time in prayer. It is often rated as the best part of my seminary courses, and many in workshops tell me they plan to put the guide in their Bible and use it often. I have received notes from several missionaries describing how they train new believers to ask, "Lord Jesus teach us how to pray!" and how using the Lord's Prayer helps launch the person's conversations with God.

⏱ PAUSE — TRY IT OUT!

Questions to evaluate your personal and organizational prayer life

In evaluating a prayer relationship to God, as in evaluating the quality of human relationships, the ultimate reality eludes analysis by quantified criteria. But as in the case of a loving relationship, for example, Scripture does give many specific descriptions of behavior that enable a person to evaluate his love life by more than just an intuitive "feel."

Use these questions to evaluate your own conversations with God and to assist you in planning how to teach others to pray.

Personal Prayer Life

1. Is my prayer life a worthy example for other members to follow?
2. Do I have a regular rhythm for daily times of prayer and plan for special extended times of prayer?
3. What are three hindrances that interfere with my prayers?
4. Do I keep a written record of specific prayer requests and note answers?
5. How do I stir up passion and motivation to pray?

Teaching Others to Pray

How do we teach others to pray? Examples: public instruction, private coaching, testimony, sharing the principles and how you practice them, whole family together, training those who are over a household.

1. Where and when do we pray together?

2. Is prayer a *significant* part of other group meetings, especially decision-making meetings?

3. Is there spontaneous grouping of individuals for prayer on a regular basis, the result of special needs, interests and/or relationships?

4. What biblical passages and personal examples do you use to teach each of these types of prayer:

    a. Praise

    b. Thanksgiving

    c. Confession

    d. Intercession

    e. Faith Goals

    f. Physical needs

    g. For rulers and influencers

    h. For world evangelism

    i. For local evangelism

5. What changes will you make based on this evaluation?

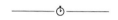

⏱ PAUSE — TRY IT OUT!

Writing out a prayer to God

Take a few moments and write out a prayer. Be *specific* in request, thanks, confession or praise. Be *submissive* in receiving how he answers and avoid a demanding controlling spirit. Be *expectant,* letting trust in his promises color how you come to him. Be *persistent* and enduring, not with empty repetition, but letting your deep burden or passion shine through.

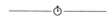

What to Pray? Giving Thanks

Our life-giving leadership is really God leading through us. God is the center, the focus, the power behind our leadership. Our practice of living in gratitude with thanksgiving is a testimony of our belief in God's contribution to our leadership. I have too often slipped into being like a little child running in from playing outside with a bundle of sticks to show to his mother and say, "Look Mom what I made for you!" Do I say, "Look God at this ministry and how we are being the church just for you!" God is really not interested in us doing stuff **for** him, he wants us to do it **with** him and always be whispering, 'Thank You!" for his contribution.

Thanks-saturated prayers like this one make it clear who is the owner and who is the manager.

Lord, I thank you for letting me into your game. I can't believe I get to do this!

> Let us thank God heartily as often as we pray that we have his Spirit in us to teach us to pray. Thanksgiving will draw our hearts out to God and keep us engaged with Him; it will take our attention from ourselves and give the Spirit room in our hearts.
> —Andrew Murray

Gratitude is life-giving

1. It expresses contentment and satisfaction with God's provision.
2. It relieves stress as we acknowledge the fact that ministry is ultimately the result of God showing up.
3. Gratitude is life-giving because it stirs up joy and ignites a celebration in our hearts through the awareness of all we have received from the hand of God:

CONSIDER THIS

Jesus healed ten lepers. One bowed in thanksgiving. Where were the other nine? Does Jesus wonder where I am for all he is doing in my life?[11]

Celebrations of what God is doing grow our faith, expand our vision, and lift our hearts when we feel hopeless and despondent. The Bible is filled with celebrations of the goodness and greatness of God. The Scriptures celebrate victories over enemies, provision of food, healings, deliverance from the Satanic, and beauty in creation. Heaven celebrates the lost being found and the prodigal returning home. Trees moving in the breeze are an expression of praise to God.

God-centered celebration is a critical means to the end of God giving us life. How often do we formally or informally celebrate God showing up? How often do we pause the agenda in a business leadership meeting so we can give thanks for the report that has just been presented? Are we so wired for getting things done that we cannot pause to celebrate and pray?

Praying in Times of Agony and Sacrifice

Every life-giving leader will join in Christ's sufferings as part of the journey into sharing his life.

In the days of his flesh, Jesus offered up prayers and supplications, with loud cries and tears, to him who was able to save him from death, and he was heard because of his reverence.[12]

Jesus was heard, but his request was not answered through his Father sparing him the cross. "Why then, did the Father refuse his request? It was not due to any sin in Jesus' life, nor was it because the Father did not love the Son. The Father said no, despite the unfathomable love he had for his Son because he knew he could not spare his Son and save a world. Likewise, the Lord cannot always spare you and your family and complete his redemptive work in those around you. Are you willing for God to deny your pleadings? Will you intercede with the Father so deeply and intimately that, even in the midst of your tears you are able to say, "Nevertheless, not my will but thine be done." Have you been learning obedience through what you have been suffering (Hebrews 5:8)? If you have, God may choose to make you a source of salvation to others even as he did with his Son.[13]

Pray For Everything

"Do not be anxious about anything, but **in everything** by prayer and supplication with thanksgiving let your requests be made known to God. And the peace of God, which surpasses all understanding, will guard your hearts and your minds in Christ Jesus."[14]

The life God intends for his children includes peace. The opposite of life is anxiety. So God says, "If it is causing you worry, it is big enough to bring it to me." I have often spent more time talking to myself about my worries and ignoring the God living with me. I rehearse various scenarios and plan solutions and still my anxiety is increasing. Where am I looking for peace? If I am looking to myself as the place to find peace, the question I am asking is, "so... how is that working out for you?" And the answer of course is, "Not too well." But there is another path to choose, a life-giving provision.

My children are grown now and making their own money, raising their own families and making their own choices. But, I still love it when they ask to bring an issue to their mother and me to talk over. It tells me they respect our thoughts and value our perspective. They are not asking me to be God in their lives. I turned in my superhero costume long ago. Often the conversation ends with us joining them in prayer for their concern. Many times they leave with a sense of relaxed peaceful confidence that God will bring them through whatever it is before them.

The life God intends for you in your leadership is that kind of relaxed confidence. If you don't have earthly parents you can use as a sounding board for your worries, adopt some. If other people are not available, just go directly to God. It often helps me to take my worries outside into nature. I have walked in the cold to a mountain ridge view or made my way through the summer midnight heat down to the beach, and once there, under the stars, offered up the burdens. There is something about setting my worry in the landscape of God's great creation that renews my faith that the Creator holds everything in the palm of his hand. I can almost hear him whisper, "Hey child, I have got this!"

THINKING IT THROUGH

1. How will you view prayer as a vital aspect of your leadership?
2. How will you pray differently?
3. What will be some of the subjects for your prayers you have ignored or minimized?
4. How can you inspire and train others to pray? (Consider how Jesus did it.)

RESOURCES FOR LIFELONG LEARNING

1. Henry Blackaby & Melvin Blackaby. *Experiencing God Together: God's Plan to Touch Your World.* Nashville: Broadman & Holman, 2002. (Chapter 7 explores Corporate Prayer as a critical ministry of church)
1. Dan R. Crawford. *Giving Ourselves to Prayer: Acts 6:4 Primer for Ministry.* Terre Haute: IN, PrayerShop Publishers, 2009. (Rich resource from the Church Prayer Leaders Network)
2. Jerry Sittser. *When God Doesn't Answer Your Prayer.* Grand Rapids: Zondervan, 2003. (Dr. Sittser has a warm, wise and biblical perspective on prayer)

CHAPTER TWO

THE BIBLE: SOURCE OF GRACE AND TRUTH

Live under the functional authority of the Bible and live at the center of biblical tension. —Robertson McQuilkin

Truth is an acquired taste for most people. —Don Howell

GOD GIVES US many tools. Tools are good things that assist us in being productive. Many of God's tools are very powerful. The Bible is no exception.

For the word of God is living and active, sharper than any two-edged sword, piercing to the division of soul and of spirit, of joints and of marrow, and discerning the thoughts and intentions of the heart.[1]

Anything with great power for good can also become a destructive weapon. Many leaders have been guilty of using the Bible to drain and rob life, rather than to give life. The Bible helps us to be creative, set goals, discern error, and view situations from a variety of perspectives. We can, however, turn this knowledge into a weapon when we use it to devalue, attack, manipulate or control another person.

> God's gifts are powerful and almost any of these gifts in the hands of sinful people can be used to great destructive ends.

God does reveal the essential truth needed to understand how the world operates, why it was created, and what will be its end. This is a very powerful fuel to place in human hands. The Bible's blessings are diverse and powerful. The Puritan Baptist, Octavius Winslow, said 150 years ago:

This precious Word of God has made clear many a perplexity, has illumined many a dark road, has cheered many a lonesome way, has soothed many a deep sorrow, has guided and upheld many a faltering step, and has crowned with victory many a feat of arms in the great battle with Satan, the world, and sin.[2]

But what does it look like when the Bible becomes a weapon? One of the dangers of leaders who handle God's truth is how it can feed a prideful spirit. Confident that we are the source of answers most miss, and convinced we are on God's side of righteousness and truth, we overlook the major theme of the Bible: God revealing himself as compassionate and gracious.

As Aleksandr Solzhenitsyn reminds us, "It is not because the truth is too difficult to see that we make mistakes… we make mistakes because the easiest and most comfortable course for us is to seek insight where it accords with our emotions—especially selfish ones."[3]

Here are some questions designed to set off flashing yellow caution lights in the mind of a leader. A lack of self-awareness, if left unattended, can move a leader from being life-giving to becoming life-taking.

1. Am I aware of my own unanswered questions and the gaps in my own knowledge of God's word and the leadership situation I am facing?
2. Can I clearly and accurately represent the views of those who differ from me? Have I listened well?
3. Can I own a clear and deep conviction without crossing the line into haughty unteachable stubbornness?
4. Whom do I invite to speak into my life and who would cause me to reconsider my strongly held views?

So, with this warning to lead off our thoughts on the Bible, how are we to use God's truth in our leadership?

WHAT ASPECTS OF LIFE DOES GOD OFFER THROUGH THE BIBLE?

1. **The Bible INTRODUCES US** to the living "Word", Jesus, as the source of life.

2. **The Bible DELIGHTS** our heart by connecting us to God's will for us. I like to use the phrases "green light", "red light", and "yellow light" with leadership teams to summarize biblical teaching on an item we are discussing.
   a. Green = When God commands, we quickly obey.
   b. Red = When God prohibits, we quickly abandon and avoid.
   c. Yellow = When God cautions, we slow our actions, look both ways and move ahead carefully.

3. **The Bible DIRECTS** us to make choices leading to a fruitful life.

4. **The Bible DEFINES** my goals and expectations. I give the Bible the right to edit my personal definitions and assumptions.

5. **The Bible EXPOSES** competing allegiances to God and challenges me to remove and destroy any idolatrous practices and beliefs.

6. **The Bible PROBES** beneath my actions to the motives and values driving my choices.

7. **The Bible BALANCES** the quality and quantity of the intakes or consumptions of my life. The truth of God moderates my attitudes, drives and passions.

   > The body makes a great servant but a lousy master for one's life. —Dallas Willard

8. **The Bible LOCATES** the center of God's will as a holding of two truths in tension to one another and an avoidance of moving to a consistent one-sided extreme. God's life-giving leadership is often more in the format of "both/and" instead of "either/or". I would go so far to say that many issues leaders face are tensions to manage rather than problems to solve. I am very grateful to Robertson McQuilkin and Andy Stanley for this humble perspective on truth—Robertson for his view on biblical

theological truth, and Pastor Stanley for his view on the practice of ministry. Here are a few examples:

a. It is possible to hold a high view of marriage and yet offer a compassionate response to those who have seen marriage die and end in divorce.

b. There will always be cultural and generational differences on the best ways to engage in worship, especially with music and the performing arts.

c. Technology is probably not the tool of the anti-Christ or the solution to almost every problem.

d. God is sovereign AND we are judged for our personal choices.

e. We are called to love with grace AND truth.

While it may make life simpler to live from a place of consistency and have one right answer for every concern, godly wisdom calls life-giving leaders to a journey of grace, moderation, and the possibility of several good options. The center of biblical tension needs to understand, honor and embrace all aspects of truth. Life is found at the intersection of two truths held in tension as we dance with his Spirit. Jesus could attend both a wedding feast and a desert fast.

HOW ARE LEADERS TO APPROACH AND UTILIZE THE BIBLE?

God made us to be learners. Have you ever noticed how "dumb" babies are? They have to be taught almost everything. Each child must learn to walk, learn to talk, and learn to work the mouse on the computer. The same is true of our spiritual learning curves.

And Jesus increased in wisdom and in stature and in favor with God and man.[4]

Wait a minute! Jesus "increased". Jesus walked with us in all aspects of our humanity. What incredible mystery in the incarnation and hope for us in our frail humanity. Jesus understands my need to figure things out.

Out of all knowledge how much do we have? We know very few things with certainty but nothing exhaustively. When you allow your mind to roam across topics from the nature of the universe, to electricity, to why ice cream tastes so good, to why grandchildren are the greatest to every grandparent, we begin to appreciate our vast ignorance. God's special revelation, we have named as the Bible, contributes knowledge that we could never discover by ourselves.

> We know very few things with certainty but nothing exhaustively.

So how has God designed us to learn? Here are just a few principles of learning:

1. **We have teachers**. While we can learn a great deal by reflection in most areas of learning, we usually have to utilize a guide (someone who has been where we attempting to go) to reach a fuller understanding.

2. **God has built limits into our ability to acquire knowledge.** That is the difference between general revelation (creation) and special revelation (the Bible). God is the teacher opening up treasures of truth for us to discover. The Bible is accurate, revealed truth graciously given by God through the activity of the Holy Spirit. He serves as our teacher, taking our learning beyond our limits.

3. **We learn through asking questions.** From Genesis three to Revelation, God approaches people by asking them questions. Why? Does God have to learn? No, but he uses questions to trigger learning and new perspectives IN us. Would you like a good devotional study? Go through the Gospels studying every question Jesus asks. Questions are one of God's primary tools to enable us to have what Jesus called having eyes that see or ears that hear. So when my 20 month old granddaughter walks through our house and points to almost every item asking, "What's that?" she is using her limited language to exercise a God designed way of learning.

⏱ PAUSE — TRY IT OUT!

Applying principles of learning

Think about an aspect of ministry you are seeking to LEARN to do or do better. How do the three principles of learning listed above apply?

Questions: one of the best learning tools.

One of my leadership proverbs is, *"Leaders lead by helping the people revisit good questions, rather than a quest for the one perfect answer."*

There are basic questions to assist you in drilling into the biblical perspective on any proposed ministry action. Effective leaders lead through collecting and asking questions that prompt the learning of everyone around them. It has been my privilege to work with ministry leaders in several different cultures. I have discovered that if I work hard to craft good questions, as opposed to bringing answers from my own culture, they are better served.

Questions cross cultural boundaries better than answers.

One form of questioning is to conduct experiments and follow with an evaluation. We learn through experimentation. God gives us the capacity to attempt something new, to fall down (fail), to learn from that failure, and move on to experiment with another attempt. Would children ever learn to walk if they could never fall down? *Doing* followed by *evaluation* (asking more questions) is one of the best ways to learn. We stand in a circle of grace. We have freedom to experiment, to be creative, and to learn from our attempts.

Seeing learning, growth and change as messy — but worth the cost.

Assume for a moment a group of ministry leaders are seeking to determine a strategy for evangelism. There are several strategies being discussed, and some in the group are emotionally invested in certain approaches. The options can quickly deteriorate into:

➤ Everyone going off in their own direction, which often dilutes and diffuses our impact.

➤ Painful destructive and often paralyzing conflict

➤ Damage to personal relationships over disagreement

> ➤ External consensus but internal resentment and resistance.

The process I am going to suggest to bring ministry under the functional authority of the Bible may feel tedious and messy but I assure you it is worth the cost.

Many of us, myself included, have been trained to ask only one question about any activity we are considering. "Will it work?" Pragmatism rules the agenda of many of the leadership meetings I have attended. We can easily justify whatever actions we are convinced will move us toward our goal. This is dangerous on so many levels.

Just because it worked over "there" does not mean it is God's will for us over "here" or at this time in our journey. Some questions to ask:

> ➤ How are we defining "works"?
> ➤ Is our "goal" even in alignment with God's goals?

It is *spiritually motivating and renewing* to revisit God's perspective on our task. Somehow, when we review several biblical passages, we freshly catch God's heart for those outside his family. God's Word helps us ease our tight grip on our personal preferences. Coming to the Bible melts me so I can be poured into a different shape.

As we seek to shape our strategy by biblical teaching, it *clarifies a shared vision and common set of values* in the leaders being trained. This common perspective sets the front-line leadership free to seek creative solutions that fit their context. As we know, specific methods come and go in popularity. The tendency is to determine strategy by copying or cloning from other ministries, which seldom produces effective results. Biblical teaching gives us a narrow direction and destination balanced with wide boundaries on specifics.

Being able to distill the biblical perspective on any aspect of our ministry will help those who are *struggling with change* to see how the new approach is undergirded with biblical principles. Biblical reflection on how we conduct ministry deepens ownership and redefines the newly proposed approach as only one particular expression of living out biblical truth.

A FOUR STEP PROCESS

Let's organize our questions into a four-step process to help us make wise choices and illustrate it with an example. Our example concerns our practice and conviction in the use of alcohol.

Step 1 — DEFINING THE BASIC IDEA

What is the basic idea behind this method or activity? Create a simple sentence that states the action in terms of being practiced or avoided.

> ➤ Is there agreement on defining the basic idea by everyone involved?

Examples of basic ideas:
1. A Christian may choose to drink alcoholic beverages.
2. The Bible prohibits a Christian from choosing to drink alcoholic beverages.

After studying the passages relevant to the basic idea (Step 2 Gathering & Step 3 Reflecting) you may need to refine the definition of the basic idea or problem. If there is more than one possible definition, everyone involved in the decision needs to agree to a specific definition to bring under biblical authority.

> ➤ Is there more than one basic idea related to this practice that needs to be brought under biblical authority?

Example of refining a basic idea:
1. Some may define consuming alcohol in pubic as different from consuming alcohol privately in one's home.
2. Others would further limit "public" to family celebrations such as a wedding versus going to a bar.

In this example, we will need to create more than one basic idea so that we can speak specifically to how biblical truth relates to each of the definitions of the practice.

Step 2 — GATHERING Biblical Teaching

Look up all passages related to the basic idea. Go on an exploration through the Bible to uncover all biblical material that is related.

> ➤ What are key words or phrases to use in searching for relevant passages?
>
> ➤ Use a concordance to find passages containing key words from the basic idea.
>
> ➤ Use a topical Bible to search by the basic idea.
>
> ➤ As you locate passages, use cross-reference system to locate additional relevant passages

Example: Look up "wine", and "drunkenness". In a topical Bible, look up "alcohol", "drinking", and "abstinence". These will get you started:

Verses concerning the use of alcohol:

1. Leviticus 10:9
2. Proverbs 20:1
3. Proverbs 23:19-21, 29-31(drunkard presented in the same category with glutton and slumbering leading to poverty)
4. Isaiah 5:11, 22, 23
5. Hosea 4:11
6. Matthew 11:19
7. Luke 21:34
8. 1 Corinthians 5:11
9. Galatians 5:21
10. Ephesians 5:18
11. 1 Thessalonians 5:7
12. 1 Timothy 3:8
13. Titus 2:2-6

Study each passage. Be sure and take the passage in its context as the author originally intended its meaning. Here are a series of questions you can use to prompt reflective learning every time you read.

Using the SPECKA approach to arrive at a personal application for each passage. Is there...

> A **Sin** to confess?
> A **Promise** to claim?
> An **Example** to follow?
> A **Command** to obey?
> **Knowledge** to understand?
> An **Application** to my life?

Now consider *each* passage in light of the basic ideas from step one. How does the passage assist in setting the level of authority of the idea or practice?

Options
> The basic idea is commanded (must do)
> The basic idea is prohibited (must not do)
> The basic idea is permissible (some level of practice is allowed but not required)
> The basic idea is compatible (no examples of practice and not specifically taught but the basic idea does not violate clear biblical teaching)

Does this passage introduce a balancing truth that limits or modifies the basic idea?

Does this passage address the motives or character-related issues impacting the practice of the basic idea?

Example of motives or character related to the practice: Does Paul's teaching on laying down one's freedom for the higher goal of loving or not creating a barrier to the gospel (Romans 13-14; 1 Corinthians 8-9;10:23-33) apply to one's choice of consuming alcohol?

Step 3 — REFLECTING on Biblical Perspective

Create a summary of what is learned from *all* of the passages.

Summarizing helps you form a synthesis of the related passages. Create a summary of what the Bible teaches from all of the passages you gathered in Step 2, and if necessary, summarize each of the basic ideas as you further refined the concern in light of the passages and the questions being asked.

The summary should answer these questions in terms of each basic idea of a belief or activity:

1. *Is it required or prohibited?* Is this activity or belief commanded or forbidden in Scripture?

2. If not commanded or forbidden, *is it obviously required or prohibited by clear biblical principle?*

3. If not required or prohibited, *is it permitted but not required by scriptural teaching?*

4. There are no examples or specific teaching and the basic idea does not violate any clear teaching. If so, *the basic idea is compatible and can be practiced or not practiced with freedom.*

5. *Have I brought this activity into alignment with ALL biblical data that is related either directly or indirectly?* Often this part of the summary reminds us of cautions or extremes to avoid if we choose to practice the basic idea. This addresses what the proper heart attitude should be behind the practice or not practicing of the basic idea.

6. *Is it allowed with moderation or balance?* Does the emphasis represented by this activity maintain balance with all other related biblical truth in such a way as to maintain the biblical emphasis? For example, deeds of compassion are commanded and modeled by example in the New Testament, but they should not replace or take priority over sharing the gospel.

7. *Is it to be practiced or not practiced with freedom?* If this activity is extra-biblical, am I careful to make this fact clear and divest it of ultimate authority, both in my own thinking and for making demands of others?

Example of "extra-biblical": I teach at a Bible College and Seminary. There is very little direct biblical support for a training institution as we structure them today. I would consider this activity "extra-biblical." The justification for a school rests on it assisting the church in accomplishing the commands and principles outlined for it. In my summary, I must admit that a school *may* be an acceptable practice but is not required by the Bible. Other models of training leaders may well prove to be more cost effective and could lessen the impact of the creation of a professional clergy—which has historically sidelined the "laity" from certain ministries of the church. In favor of schooling, the in-depth study of the Bible, theology and church history may contribute to less overall corruption of the gospel, including the inhibiting of error and cults. Recent reports from some of the house churches in China would add evidence to this concern.

Since the Bible is my authority in determining the level of influence that this practice exerts over the church, it is important to determine how this basic idea fits with the foundational beliefs of our faith.

Is it Primary? This means that how this basic idea is conducted is critical to preserving biblical Christianity. This practice is a boundary issue, which cannot be compromised.

Is it Secondary? These practices fall within a circle that when we get to heaven we will discover many Christians throughout history had a variety of practice and therefore I refuse to make it a boundary issue. I can choose to live in submission to my contemporary authorities and lay down my freedom to engage or forbid this basic idea to be in alignment with the required policy of those with whom I serve.

Example of reflecting on primary and secondary:

If the basic idea is: *A Christian may choose to drink alcoholic beverages.*

The summary may conclude that *it is not required* of Christians to consume, and is *also not prohibited,* but is *permitted in moderation by example and by forbidding the extreme of drunkenness.*

Consuming alcohol is not essential to life (such as bread and water) so a person may *refrain from consuming for the sake of love or witness or just personal preference.* Since it is not required that a Christian consume, and we know some Christians may have a personal history where consuming would tempt them to abuse or extreme, it is permissible to have a non-alcoholic option for the Lord's Table.

There is clear teaching against drunkenness that must be obeyed and confronted as sin if disobeyed.

If my mission agency leaves the choice up to the team on the field, I can limit my choice to what is acceptable to those God places in authority over me.

Since this is a secondary issue, I am free to fellowship with believers holding a variety of positions on consuming alcohol without being divisive. (Romans 14:4)

Step 4 - IMPLEMENTING & TAKING ACTION

According to Matthew 7:24-27, Matthew 28:19, and John 14:15, the goal of the Christian life is not simply regular study leading to understanding but obedience. Obedience is an expression of love for God. Disciples are taught to obey. Bringing practices under biblical authority must lead to action but should not violate the command to love in grace and truth.

1. **How do our choices in responding to the basic idea develop or manifest humility?** Clarifying biblical authority for a practice lets me put weight on what God commands or prohibits and yet limits claiming God is on my side on issues that come out as permissible or are extra-biblical. I can know some things with certainty, without having to claim to know all things exhaustively.

2. **What are possible threats to the unity of believers impacted by this basic idea?** Learn to appreciate the diversity of God's family and how God not only accommodates but enjoys the difference and diversity. I value my brother and sister, seeking to love them. My study of bringing a practice under biblical authority must always be lived out with grace. The biblical rationale of a practice should never be used as a club to beat our fellow Christians or seen as a competition to win. Violating the law of love is always a wrong use of biblical authority.

3. **To what degree am I responsible for implementing or enforcing the choice on this basic idea?**
   Implementing the changes needed to bring a practice under biblical authority requires clarifying my level of authority over others. Just

because I form a strong conviction on a basic idea does not grant me authority by God to be demanding or divisive. I must carefully examine my heart and God's assignments for me.

⏱ PAUSE — TRY IT OUT!

Think of a leadership decision made by those over you which you do not agree with or support. Now apply these questions to thinking through how you should respond.

Some questions for personal reflection:

> Is this issue a core truth necessary to preserving the gospel or is it a secondary issue that sincere Christians may disagree on?

> Do those who supervise or hold authority over me allow me to support the choice being made, even if my personal conviction is different and I am willing to hold it privately and not be divisive?

> Can I support the choice without harboring bitterness or going on a mission to force adoption of my view?

> Am I willing to resign and go to a ministry more compatible to my view?

Read Romans 13:8-15:7

Summarize the biblical teaching on relationships with differing views. Did your answer include these options?

> Loyal support of my leadership

> Serve as a change agent in a constructive manner if given permission to lead in that manner

> Leave without being intentionally destructive to those around me.

Example: If I am committed to a position of personal abstinence but my organization has given missionaries freedom to choose, I must watch my heart and attitude toward those who choose to consume. I also do not have freedom to go on a campaign for my position that divides the field workers and turns them against one another. Assume that the position of missionaries serving with other agencies is different from my organization. Again I must carefully examine any judgments I am forming.

LET THE WORD LIVE IN US

Your words were found, and I ate them, and your words became to me a joy and the delight of my heart, for I am called by your name, O LORD, God of hosts.[5]

Feed on God's Word in both an *intentional rhythm* and seeking *teachable moments*. Mine every experience for growth. Be as concerned about what God is saying to you as what you are saying to him.

I have spent considerable time studying the word "joy" and all related words, like rejoicing, through the Bible. I think joy is to be a standard we live out every day. As I choose God's Word as my dessert, it raises my joy gauge. Yes, the Bible commands me to be joyful. It is not something that happens naturally for me. But I can also seek out sources of joy and God's word is central.

Look at Jesus:

➤ Childhood—discusses Scripture in the Temple
➤ Ministry launch in wilderness/temptations—responds with Scripture
➤ End of ministry on road to Emmaus—reveals himself in Old Testament passages
➤ Throughout his ministry—opens the Scriptures with disciples and often with other Christ-followers present

They said to each other, 'Did not our hearts burn within us while he talked to us on the road, while he opened to us the Scriptures?'[6]

What I love about the story of the Emmaus road is that the disciples had questions and confusion filling their thoughts. They had just seen their leader arrested, tried and executed. They had no idea how to take what they had experienced in recent years and put it together with the tragic events. And what does the resurrected Christ offer them? He takes them on an Old

Testament bible study. He frames what he had experienced by the prophetic truths written centuries ago. He really believed there was truth that had been revealed through the Spirit-inspired Scriptures that made sense of the tragic leadership crisis going on around his followers.

God's Powerful Word Makes Us Fruitful

Blessed is the man who walks not in the counsel of the wicked, nor stands in the way of sinners, nor sits in the seat of scoffers; but his delight is in the law of the LORD, and on his law he meditates day and night. He is like a tree planted by streams of water that yields its fruit in its season, and its leaf does not wither. In all that he does, he prospers.[7]

Life-giving leaders are planted deeply in and drawing fruit bearing life from the Word of God. We choose what we will sink our roots into. As we delight in God's Word we go beyond simple understanding into choosing it to clarify our vision and to write in the correct price tags on all aspects of this life. The heart trained by the truth to discern will gain in wisdom and gentleness. It will be wise in perspective, separating the junk from the treasures of this life. It will move gently into relationships with nothing to prove or defend. Wise, gentle people are trees bearing fruit that will attract others to the source; our life-giving God.

⏱ PAUSE — TRY IT OUT!

The truth of God living in you

Try this exercise for four weeks, one day each week. Read Psalm 119 in its entirety in one sitting. It will take 45 minutes to an hour. Consider trying different translations. Read it out loud. Do not write anything down or mark in the text while reading. When you finish, close the Bible and pray some of the thoughts of the Psalm back to God as they come to mind.

On the fourth week, substitute "Jesus' for "law" as you read, as he perfectly lived out God's law for us. Close the Bible, and let your love for Jesus as your guide and teacher come out of your heart to God in your own words.

Resources to Assist in Study

On the next few pages are some helpful resources developed by Robertson McQuilkin and a one-page summary of the four steps in this chapter for bringing a ministry activity under the functional authority of the Bible.

APPROACH TO DETERMINING AUTHORITY OF A PASSAGE

Note: these flow charts and the guide to determining authority of a passage are found in Robertson McQuilkin's books listed in the Resources section at the end of this chapter.

All Scripture is inspired and therefore trustworthy and of profit for the believer. But not all Scripture is authoritative for present day obedience. Christ himself and the Apostles in their writing set aside much of the Old Testament as not having continuing authority. The ceremonial law, for example, was fulfilled in Christ and should no longer be obeyed.

Furthermore, much Bible teaching is directed to a specific, not a general audience, to a specific condition, not of universal application. The command to take no change of clothes and money, given to the disciples, was later set aside, for example. How, then does the interpreter decide what teaching is authoritative for contemporary obedience?

Here are some questions to guide in the decision:

1. Does Scripture itself, either in the context of a teaching or in subsequent teaching, set aside or disallow a given teaching? For all the illustrations above, the answer to this question is "Yes, the Bible itself sets them aside."

2. Is the command or teaching addressed to an individual or specific group? If so, it is not binding on the contemporary Christian. God's command to Moses to take off his shoes was not intended as a universal requirement, for example.

3. Does a teaching appear to be in conflict with other Bible teaching, especially later, more persuasive and clearer teaching, and (esp. in

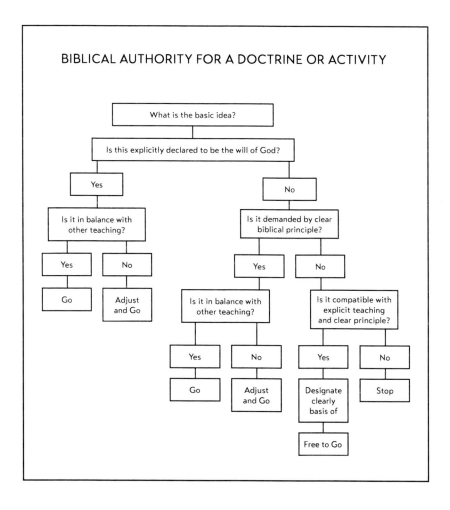

BIBLICAL AUTHORITY FOR A DOCTRINE OR ACTIVITY

What is the basic idea?

Is this explicitly declared to be the will of God?

Yes — Is it in balance with other teaching?
- Yes → Go
- No → Adjust and Go

No — Is it demanded by clear biblical principle?
- Yes — Is it in balance with other teaching?
  - Yes → Go
  - No → Adjust and Go
- No — Is it compatible with explicit teaching and clear principle?
  - Yes → Designate clearly basis of → Free to Go
  - No → Stop

the New Testament)? Preference should be given the later, more persuasive, clearer teaching.

4. Is the teaching based on an historical event or example? This does not have authority in and of itself. To be made authoritative it must be based on direct commands or stated principles. Only then does history set a precedent for demanding obedience. Much of Acts, for example, falls in this category. Just because the disciples or even Apostles did something doesn't make it mandatory for others unless Scripture, either in context or elsewhere, says so.

A SUMMARY OF QUESTIONS TO BRING PRACTICES UNDER BIBLICAL AUTHORITY

Step 1 — DEFINING

1. What is the basic idea? Identify the practice, activity or belief to examine in light of the Bible.
2. Is there agreement on one or more basic ideas to bring under biblical authority by everyone involved?

Step 2 — GATHERING

Look up all passages related to each basic idea. Go on an exploration through the Bible to uncover all biblical material that is related.

1. What are key words or phrases to use to search for relevant passages?
2. Use the SPECKA approach for each passage.
3. How does the passage assist in setting the level of authority of the idea or practice? Some options:
   a. Required
   b. Forbidden
   c. Permissible — freedom to practice or not practice
   d. Extra-Biblical
4. Does this passage present balancing truth, limits or modifications to the basic idea?
5. Does this passage address the motives or character-related issues surrounding this basic idea?

Step 3 — REFLECTING

Create a summary of what is learned from all of the passages.

1. Is it required or prohibited?
   a. Is this activity or belief commanded or forbidden in Scripture?
   b. If not commanded or forbidden, is it obviously required or forbidden by clear biblical principle?
2. If not required by Scripture, is it permitted by scriptural teaching, compatible with Scripture?

3. Have I brought this activity into alignment with all biblical data that might be related either directly or indirectly? Often this part of the summary reminds us of cautions or extremes to avoid if we choose to practice the basic idea.

4. Is it allowed with balance? Does the emphasis represented by this activity maintain balance with all other related biblical truth in such a way as to maintain the biblical emphasis?

5. Is it to be practiced or not practiced with freedom? If this activity is extra-biblical, am I careful to make this fact clear and divest it of ultimate authority, both in my own thinking and for making demands of others?

Since the Bible is my authority in determining the level of influence this practice exerts over the church, it is important to determine how this basic idea fits with the basic foundational beliefs of our faith.

1. **Is it primary?** This means that *how* this basic idea is conducted is critical to preserving biblical Christianity. This practice is a boundary issue which cannot be compromised.

2. **Is it Secondary?** These practices have had different historical expressions by Christians, therefore I refuse to make it a boundary issue. I can choose to live in submission to my authorities and lay down my freedom to engage in or not practice this basic idea to be in alignment with the required policy of those with whom I serve.

Step 4 — IMPLEMENTING & GROWING

1. How do our choices in responding to the basic idea develop or manifest humility?

2. What are possible threats to the unity of believers impacted by this basic idea?

3. To what degree am I responsible for implementing or enforcing the choice on this basic idea?

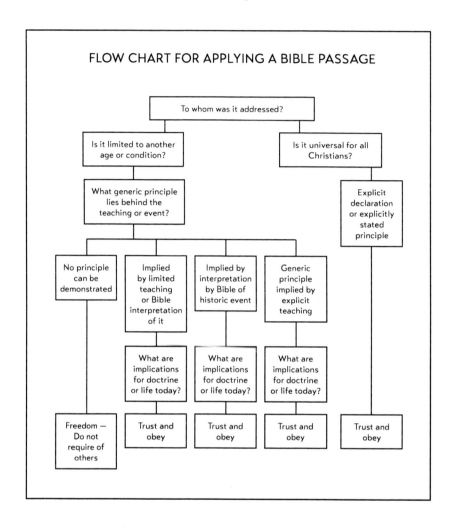

FLOW CHART FOR APPLYING A BIBLE PASSAGE

To whom was it addressed?

Is it limited to another age or condition?

Is it universal for all Christians?

What generic principle lies behind the teaching or event?

Explicit declaration or explicitly stated principle

No principle can be demonstrated

Implied by limited teaching or Bible interpretation of it

Implied by interpretation by Bible of historic event

Generic principle implied by explicit teaching

What are implications for doctrine or life today?

What are implications for doctrine or life today?

What are implications for doctrine or life today?

Freedom — Do not require of others

Trust and obey

Trust and obey

Trust and obey

Trust and obey

RESOURCES FOR LIFELONG LEARNING

1. McQuilkin, Robertson. *The Five Smooth Stones: Essential Principles for Biblical Ministry.* Nashville: Broadman & Holman, 2007. ISBN: 978-0-8054-4518-3. (See Unit One and the appendix on Cross-Cultural Communication)
2. McQuilkin, Robertson. *Understanding & Applying The Bible (revised edition).* Chicago: Moody Press, 2009. ISBN: 978-0-8024-9092-6.

3. Vanhoozer, Kevin. *Is There Meaning in This Text: The Bible, The Reader, and the Morality of Literary Knowledge*. Grand Rapids: Zondervan, 1998. ISBN: 0-310-21156-5. (In a very accessible but deeply thoughtful style Dr. Vanhoozer helps us see how evangelical hermeneutics answers challenges of post-modern and allegorical views of language and meaning.)

CHAPTER THREE

WITNESS TO THE GOOD NEWS OF JESUS' KINGDOM

As I have read the Gospels over the years, the belief has grown in me that Christ did not come to found an organized religion but came instead to found an unorganized one. He seems to have come to carry religion out of the temples into the fields and sheep pastures, onto the roadsides and the banks of the rivers, into the houses of sinners and publicans, into the town and the wilderness, toward the membership of all that is here. Well, you can read and see what you think. —Jayber Crow

WE ARE A WITNESS...

I WAS WATCHING the news recently as they interviewed witnesses to a train accident. The witnesses spoke of what they saw, heard and felt as they went through the terrible experience. The interviewer never used the verb "witnessing". Yet I often hear Christians use the word witnessing as in, "Our team went witnessing in the neighborhood." Does our use of the word reveal we have shrunk the meaning of the idea of being a witness to a specific activity that we do for a defined amount of time in a certain set of circumstances? Does that subtly separate our experience of the life-giving King Jesus from the rest of daily life? *A witness is what you are all of the time, not something you do occasionally.* In a similar way, are we not we commanded to be the people of God going and making disciples, not to only engage in a set time of "discipling"?

*But you will receive power when the Holy Spirit has come upon you, and **you will be my witnesses** in Jerusalem and in all Judea and Samaria, and to the end of the earth.*[1]

Jesus told the disciples, just before he went to the cross that people would know they were his disciples by the love they had for one another.[2]

He spoke of neighbor-love and used the Samaritan helping the child of Abraham as a definition of a neighbor.[3] Jesus also spoke of enemy-love and then demonstrated what it looked like on the cross, "Father forgive them…"

Very early in the ministry of pulling together the twelve, Jesus told some of them they would become fishers of men instead of just fishermen. Their conduct and the content of their personal story of the King and life in his kingdom would be used to catch people and draw them into the kingdom. Others would reject them and see them as enemies who were showing up with a message that challenged the kings of the world or their private little kingdoms. Jesus is always a threat to other gods and rulers who call for allegiance and cry out, "serve me!" but then turn the followers into slaves and drain them of life. An individual's sinful heart is the biggest competitor to the kingdom of God and it cries, "No one will rule over me. I will not bend my knee!"

The life and testimony of the first generation witnesses surely repelled some, but it also enticed others to abandon all other kings and swear allegiance and declare identity through baptism with the kingdom of Jesus. I believe it is a weakness in how we establish new believers when leaders delay guiding them to live as witnesses until they have been a believer for a year to two, as though being a witness is an "advanced" course not required of every child of God. Actually, the call to be a witness is core to the new identity of being a Jesus-follower and supported by the Spirit who comes to live inside at new birth to empower witnesses to live for King Jesus' glory everywhere they go.

In 1 Thessalonians Paul recounts how the church is being formed out of a response to the truth of God's word and a demonstration of the power of God.

*For we know, brothers loved by God, that he has chosen you, because our gospel came to you **not only in word, but also in power and in the Holy Spirit and with full conviction.** You know what kind of men we proved to be among you for your sake. And you became imitators of us and of the Lord, for **you received the word** in much affliction, with the joy of the Holy Spirit, so that you became an example to all the believers in Macedonia and in Achaia. For not only has the* *word of the Lord sounded forth from you in Macedonia and Achaia, but your faith in God has gone forth everywhere, so that we need not say anything. For they themselves report concerning us the kind of reception we had among you, and how you* **turned to God from idols to serve the living and true God, and to wait for his Son from heaven,** *whom he raised from the dead, Jesus who delivers us from the wrath to come.*[4]

Paul mentions how their decision to follow Jesus cost them "much affliction". They were witnesses who paid a price shortly after joining the kingdom. He goes on to describe them as those serving and waiting for King Jesus' return. It sounds like the church of Thessalonica had hearts anchored to serving in and living for a coming kingdom.

Let's look at one more example from the church in Rome.

"For the kingdom of God is not a matter of eating and drinking but of righteousness and peace and joy in the Holy Spirit."[5]

Paul is coaching the Roman church through a heated divisive debate between "weaker" and "stronger" brothers in terms of personal freedom to be engaging in certain lifestyle practices. He calls them to relate under the life-giving characteristics of the kingdom they now occupy in the Spirit. "Righteous, and peace and joy" sound like attributes of a desirable neighborhood — even more so when you review the rugged and threatening world of first century Rome.

We are witnesses to good news and it is not *just* Jesus dying on a cross for our sins but Jesus introducing us to a whole new way of living out every aspect of our lives.

We are witnesses to… finding life by losing it… winning by surrendering… and coming truly alive by dying.

A WITNESS TO THE GOOD NEWS OF JESUS' KINGDOM

What is a kingdom? "Basically the idea of a kingdom involves a group of men and women, generally a large multitude, who are under one sovereign power, at the head of which is the king…It has to do principally with power, and the exercise of that power; and if the kingdom is what it ought to be, it involves loyalty and glad obedience of those who are embraced within that sovereignty.[6]

"The kingdom of God is an order of things in connection with which God reigns in hearts softened by his grace, and his will is done. In this form it comes into the world with Jesus Christ and in his person."[7]

But what is the nature of the kingdom? What images does God use that help us see something other than our thousand year old definition of a king residing in a castle lording it over the peons? God is presented in the Bible as the only true and ruling Sovereign. We believe in a real devil, but he is not a co-anything with God. He is under God's rule like everything else in heaven and earth. We were designed to live in a good kingdom under a good king. Replace your mental picture of "king" and "kingdom" as big, cold castles with the biblical images of "garden" from Genesis or "city of God" from Revelation or even Jesus' word "home" or "dwelling place" in John. God made us for himself. When we are living under his *rule* and in a *relationship* of love, trust and obedience, we are truly alive.

Every Christ-follower, from the original 12 to the millions alive today, lives in a story of a King and his kingdom. The Bible is the story of the King of Creation, in love, designing a people who can love him and each other. To do so, he gave them the capacity to freely choose—because love is only love when it is freely chosen and never coerced. His people turned from him and rebelled and were taken captive by the enemy, who they thought promised them freedom and life. Instead he stole from them and killed them.[8] He was the life taker.

The King set out to be the life restorer. He had a deep love for his creation: his people. He pursued them and then came and lived among them. The story of the King redeeming a people to live under his rule and in loving relationship with him begins in the Old Testament and then comes fully into this reality in the New Testament.

The two Testaments are organically linked to each other. The relationship between them is neither one of upward development nor of contrast; it is one of beginning and completion, of hope and fulfillment. And the bond that binds them together is the dynamic concept of the rule of God. There is indeed a "new thing" in the New Testament but it lies precisely here... the tense is a resound-

ing present indicative — the Kingdom is here! And that is a very "new thing" indeed: it is gospel — the good news that God has acted!" [9]

The Suffering King Jesus gave people tastes of his kingdom versus the kingdom of darkness that they were living in. The hungry were fed, sick were healed, dead were raised, those held in bondage by evil spirits were freed. The Kingdom of Life and Light had broken into the darkness. The King, with his own life, paid the ransom to buy his people back. This King then demonstrated he had power over all rule and authority by conquering the greatest enemy: death. "Not is there any doubt what the gospel is: it is the gospel of the Kingdom of God... Demonic powers of darkness and their earthly minions have held this world in deathly thrall. But good news! The Kingdom of God is at hand! The power of the new age has broken in, has grappled with the evil power and defeated it on a Cross, and now moves on to its final triumph! Let men now be summoned to live that new age! Let them renounce their old allegiances and find life as citizens of the Kingdom of the Son of God! [10]

It lies at the very heart of the gospel message to affirm that the Kingdom of God has in a real sense become present fact here and now... In the person and work of Jesus the Kingdom of God has intruded into the world." [11]

The King has returned to the heavenly realm but his followers await his return. They often ask, 'May your kingdom come, your will be done here right now as it rules heaven.' To pray, 'thy kingdom come,' is to pray precisely that the rule of God triumph everywhere. It is a prayer that simply cannot be prayed while we declare that there are areas of life where the will of Christ will not rule, but our ancient prejudice. The Church is to exhibit the righteousness of Christ, nor merely in private morality but in all matters of human relations. [12]

While we wait for his return, he has not left us alone. His Spirit lives in each of his beloved people. Together they are Jesus' body. They are the presence of the King and continually witness to and bless others with the same kingdom life he offered when he was in the flesh. The King's people declare good news and carry out good works. (Ephesians 2:8-10) The church is a gathering of kingdom citizens. It is a treasure because it represents Him. Today the church offers the same message Jesus and his followers did over 2,000 years ago. "Turn and embrace King Jesus, his Kingdom is near!" [13]

The Kingdom of God, then is a power already released in the world. True, its beginnings are tiny, and it might seem incredible that the humble ministry of this obscure Galilean could be dawning of the new age of God. Yet it is! What has begun here will surely go on to its conclusion; nothing can stop it." [14]

This unquenchable wave of kingdom conquering rule is also marked by kingdom followers who are to be different from citizens of other kingdoms. Jesus kingdom is a nation of servants. "But if the Kingdom of God has in a real sense entered the world, then men are called to the service of that Kingdom. For the Kingdom is no empty domain, so many square miles of territory with geographical frontiers—it is people." [15]

Nor is the call of that Kingdom a call to honor or to victory, as the world understands those terms, but to utter self-denial. . . . He who heeds the call of the Kingdom has no destiny save to take up his cross and follow the Servant (Matthew 10:38; Luke 14:27; Mark 8:34). But to those who are called there is given nothing less than the Servant mission: to proclaim the gospel of the Kingdom to all the nations of the earth. [16]

In any event it is repeatedly insisted in the Gospels that the members of Christ's Kingdom are those that obey him. Christ's own are those who have fed the hungry, clothed the naked, shown mercy to the prisoner and outcast—who have, in short, done the works of Christ (Matthew 25:31-46). Those who have not, whatever their profession and creed, simply are none of his. [17]

Exactly here is the relationship of social gospel to gospel of individual salvation, and it is important that we get it. The two are not to be set apart as has so often been done, for they are two aspects of the same thing. Indeed, they are as intimate to each other as the opposite sides of the same coin. [18]

The Church does not announce the Kingdom of God merely as a possibility, or as a thing to be wished for; she announces it as a fact made present in Jesus Christ, even now at work in the world building its structure in the hearts of men. And it is a victorious Kingdom! All history tends toward it; all the future belongs to it; it is a Kingdom that comes! It is as the emissary of that Kingdom that the Church makes bold to speak. [19]

I invite all life-giving leaders to live with a kingdom of God mentality coloring their leadership.

WHAT IS A KINGDOM MENTALITY?

As you read the Bible and watch for the attitudes, words and deeds of kingdom citizens, here is a summary of the confident, hopeful, loving—*alive and offering life*—way they live.

What is a Jesus-follower?

My friend Larry Poland is the first teacher to expose me to a kingdom mentality. He once replied to a person beside him on an airplane who asked what he did, "I am a plainclothes agent in the Jesus revolution, the only revolution that will ultimately be successful." I would have enjoyed being in a seat nearby and seeing where that conversation went. Kingdom witnesses live with an "unshakable commitment to the sovereignty of Jesus Christ and to the growing establishment of his invisible and perfect world order." [20]

How do I become a citizen of God's life-giving kingdom?

- ➤ Repent—turn to God from all other idols.[21] Making an unshaken commitment to change. Perhaps one image of our distorted pride ruling over our kingdom is the little boy standing and looking at his castle of sand in a ten foot square wooden sand box in the back yard and with a shout and raised fists declaring, "I am king of the world!"— Well in reality, not exactly...
- ➤ Become childlike in attitude—with nothing to earn, walking into unconditional love and acceptance from the King.[22]
- ➤ Accept the invitation. "Whatever you say I am ready to change."[23]
- ➤ Bow to the sovereignty of God. He is my savior and king.[24]
- ➤ Abandon rebellion and live in complete submission to the person and authority of Christ.[25]

I expect that there will be various heart responses to the good news of the offer to switch kingdoms.[26] But God never forces his will on us. He is looking for people who will love Him. It is the nature of Spirit to only be where he is wanted.[27]

What does a Kingdom Citizen believe?

Larry Poland uses an illustration of staying at a hotel during his travels and carrying a key ring with two keys on it during his stay. Several times during his visit he walked by a beautiful garden, but every time he approached the gate, it was locked. At check-out he mentioned his delight in enjoying the garden from a distance and his disappointment at finding it locked. The clerk held up his key chain, "sir, this key was to your room and this other key was to the garden." Are we in danger of thinking of the kingdom as only related to the second coming of our King?

⏱ PAUSE — TRY IT OUT!

Read the following selections from Matthew 13 and reflect on these two questions:

1. Do we live in the reality of kingdom citizenship?
2. How does being in his kingdom affect how we live each day?

*Then the disciples came and said to him, 'Why do you speak to them in parables?' and he answered them, 'to you it has been given to know **the secrets of the kingdom** of heaven, but to them it has not been given. For to the one who has, more will be given, and he will have an abundance, but from the one who has not, even what he has will be taken away. . . When anyone hears **the word of the kingdom**_and does not understand it, the evil one comes and snatches away what has been sown in his heart. This is what was sown along the path.'*

*He put another parable before them, saying, 'The **kingdom of heaven** may be compared to a man who sowed good seed in his field, but while his men were sleeping, his enemy came and sowed weeds among the wheat and went away. So when the plants came up and bore grain, then the weeds appeared also.' Then he left the crowds and went into the house. And his disciples came to him, saying, 'Explain to us the parable of the weeds of the field.' He answered, 'The one who sows the good seed is the Son of Man. The field is the world, and the good seed is **the sons of the kingdom**. The weeds are the sons of the evil one, and the enemy who sowed them is the devil. The harvest is the end of the age, and the reapers* *are angels. Just as the weeds are gathered and burned with fire, so will it be at the end of the age. The Son of Man will send his angels, and they will gather out of **his kingdom** all causes of sin and all law-breakers, (Is Jesus saying that the present world we live in is his kingdom? Is God tolerating the pollution of his kingdom for a season? Does he mean I should not look around me and dream of some future kingdom that has no physical expression currently? Instead, I should be living in the kingdom of God as present at this moment.) And throw them into the fiery furnace. In that place there will be weeping and gnashing of teeth. Then the righteous will shine like the sun in **the kingdom of their Father**. He who has ears, let him hear.'*

*The **kingdom of heaven** is like treasure hidden in a field, which a man found and covered up. Then in his joy he goes and sells all that he has and buys that field. Again, the **kingdom of heaven** is like a merchant in search of fine pearls, who, on finding one pearl of great value, went and sold all that he had and bought it. Again, **the kingdom of heaven** is like a net that was thrown into the sea and gathered fish of every kind. When it was full, men drew it ashore and sat down and sorted the good into containers but threw away the bad. So it will be at the end of the age. The angels will come out and separate the evil from the righteous and throw them into the fiery furnace. In that place there will be weeping and gnashing of teeth. Have you understood all these things? They said to him, 'Yes.' And he said to them, 'every scribe who has been **trained for the kingdom of heaven** is like a master of a house, who brings out of his treasure what is new and what is old.'* [28]

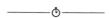

From this passage in Matthew and other kingdom teaching in the Bible we can summarize a kingdom mentality as those children of God with a:

1. **Conquering worldview.** The kingdom is constantly expanding. Jesus predicted it was having a small launch but could not be stopped and would grow. (Acts 2; Acts 4:24-26; Acts 14; Acts 19; Acts 20:25-27; Acts 28:23)

2. **Commitment to a cause with global dimensions.** Matthew 28:19-The disciple making MISSION of the church only makes

sense in light of 28:18. We are carrying the news—the proclamation of "the" ruler, "the" authority, "the" kingdom to potential subjects.

3. **Conviction of invincibility.** The kingdom is not just past or future—but is present. "God's eternal plan is to destroy his enemies, liberate mankind from their grip, and establish his rule upon earth through his Son, Jesus Christ." (Matthew 28:18; 1 Corinthians 15:24-26; Matthew 12:27-28; Romans 14:17-18; Revelation 11:15). The future kingdom in its full experience is surely coming. (Luke 24:45-47; Matthew 24:14; Philippians 2:9-11)

4. **Divine sanction for what they are doing.** Our King created us for victory that will change the ruling order forever. (Matthew 13:47-51; Luke 10:18; John 16:33 1; Corinthians 15:22-25; Revelation 11:15-17; Isaiah 65:17; Isaiah 65:24; Isaiah 33:6). This includes being unwilling to accept status quo as unalterable. We are motivated by a vision of what the world could be like and a determination to make the dream a reality.

5. **Detachment from the evils of the world system** and experiencing the reality of the presence of Christ — kingdom citizens are *in* the world but *not of* the world. (2 Corinthians 6:17; 2 Timothy 4:10; Matthew 13:22; James 4:7). Kingdom children are to live free from all spirits of rebellion and joyfully submissive to the authority of Christ in every aspect of life.

6. **Liberation from the constraints of earthly relationships** only to bathe those relationships in kingdom love. God wants us to enjoy living in the reality of the kingdom every day (Colossians 1:9-17; Colossians 3:1-17; Ephesians 1:16-23).

7. **Release from any expectation of earthly inheritance** and living in hope for the heavenly one. A kingdom citizen freely is giving away all he possesses in the glorious release provided by underwriting from the kingdom treasury. Kingdom economics are the opposite of the world's standard. The kingdoms wealthy are free to give and rejoice in seeing resources make real differences in people's lives.

(Luke 6:38; Matthew 19:23-26; Matthew 13:44-46)

8. **Freedom from all self-righteous and phony rule-keeping** so we are attractively sharing the good news with everyone who will listen.

9. **Lack of loyalty to a denominational or academic "party line"** to share freely the kingdom secrets with all who seek wisdom. *We do not speak with political correctness but kingdom acceptance.* Remember our King was accused of keeping poor company.

The kingdom family operates by its unique values and motivations laid out by our King.

*And do not seek what you are to eat and what you are to drink, nor be worried. For **all the nations of the world** seek after these things, and your Father knows that you need them. Instead, **seek his kingdom**, and these things will be added to you. "Fear not, little flock, for **it is your Father's good pleasure to give you the kingdom**. Sell your possessions, and give to the needy. Provide yourselves with moneybags that do not grow old, **with a treasure in the heavens** that does not fail, where no thief approaches and no moth destroys. For where your treasure is, **there will your heart be also**.*[29]

THE KINGDOM IS THE ONLY TRUTH THAT CAN SATISFY SOUL HUNGER

Dallas Willard defines kingdom as "a range of effective will" and then describes three kingdoms:

➤ God's kingdom,
➤ Satan's kingdom
➤ My kingdom

The gospel teaches that the greatest threat to me experiencing the LIFE (abundant, peaceful, joyful, love filled, fear free life) provided in Christ is what I do with my kingdom. I must lose my life to gain it. I must surrender to win. I must give up to be given to. I must die to live. All of these statements describe a recognition of how my kingdom either is being lived under Satan's kingdom of this world, or I am surrendered to and living under God's rule.

God's revelation through Moses was given to over a million former slaves (born into slavery for over 400 years) having been set free by God. There at Mt. Sinai, God reviews their calling to be his people as Moses is the scribe for Genesis, Exodus, and Leviticus (given over a period of months at their camp site). Here God defines and separates out his people. He lays out their identity. And the first snapshot he holds up from this historical photo album is the creation of the human race. Three truths dominate these first two chapters of Genesis.

1. God, (THE God) is THE creator, the source of all life.
2. Adam and Eve were uniquely made in his image and part of this design includes capacity for RULE (they have a kingdom)
3. Adam and Eve are designed for RELATIONSHIP (intimacy with THE God and one another).

If we zip forward through time to the first fifty years after Christ's death, burial, resurrection and ascension to his throne, we find Paul (2 Corinthians 5, Romans 8) describing how we and all of creation (under our reign) GROANS for its restoration. The restoring of proper RULE and RELATIONSHIP,

> The gospel teaches that the greatest threat to me experiencing the LIFE (abundant, peaceful, joyful, love filled, fear free life) provided in Christ is what I do with my kingdom.

free from the destruction and death is God's aim. The fall of Adam and Eve and their descendants has polluted everything under their delegated influence and has spread globally to all humanity.

Our salvation in Christ does not stop with justification (being saved). Our salvation does not stop with coming into a loving personal relationship that transforms us from the inside out (sanctification). Our salvation includes our glorification and his rule with his people. To preach another gospel results in a loss of worship toward the powerful King whose name, mission and glory we proclaim.

Apart from the kingdom, we have no good news big enough to answer the questions of the aching lost heart. Apart from the King, we have no adventure big enough to contain the human heart. All good theology rests on the rule of God. Apart from the King and his kingdom, there are no satisfying answers to our theological questions.

For God's will to be done, and his kingdom to come on earth as it is in heaven what would need to occur? "What would stand and what would fall?" reflects Frederick Buechner. "Who would be welcomed in and who be thrown the Hell out? . . . Boldness indeed. To speak those words is to invite the tiger out of the cage, to unleash a power that makes atomic power look like a warm breeze." When we pray, we are to pray for God's kingdom, God's *will*, to not only come into our lives and take root, but through us to spread throughout the earth. God's kingdom was announced by Jesus, and makes its way into the world from that beachhead as individuals give their hearts and lives to Christ." [30]

THINKING IT THROUGH

1. Do you agree that the words "witnessing" and "discipling" indicate a shrinking from a lifestyle to certain church based activities?
2. How is being a witness to the kingdom of Jesus different from a focus that stops with personal forgiveness provided by Jesus?
3. How does a kingdom mentality change how you lead?

RECOMMENDED RESOURCES

For anyone interested in current writing on the kingdom read Reggie McNeal. Start with *The Present Future* and then move to *Missional Renaissance, Missional Communities,* and his newest title, as of 2015, *Kingdom Come.*

CHAPTER FOUR

CREATIVE COLLABORATION
WITH THE SPIRIT

We are brought to God and to faith and to salvation that we might worship and adore Him. We do not come to God that we might be automatic Christians, cookie-cutter Christians, Christians stamped out with a die. God has provided his salvation that we might be, individually and personally, vibrant children of God, loving God with all our hearts and worshiping him in the beauty of holiness.[1] —*A. W. Tozer*

Once in seven years I burn all my sermons for it is a shame if I cannot write better sermons now than I did seven years ago.— *John Wesley*

When you meditate, imagine that Jesus Christ in person is about to talk to you about the most important thing in the world. Give him your complete attention. — *Francois Fenelon, Archbishop of Cambrai (1651-1715)*

THE SPIRIT AS OUR CREATIVE
COLLABORATOR IN LEADING

IF YOU MASTER any aspect of theological truth, let it be your understanding and experience of the Holy Spirit. I cannot imagine a life-giving leader who is not a Spirit-filled leader. And yet I find myself in many leadership workshops, and reading many leadership books, where the Holy Spirit is ignored or given only a cursory nod. The emphasis of far too much work on leadership centers on the contribution of the leader alone. Any biblical approach to leadership is going to include the goal of the glory of God and bring in the mission of God that every Jesus-follower has been given.

The Spirit of Christ indwelling us is not a "silent partner" as sometimes occurs in a business. He is the majority investor in the enterprise of God's kingdom through God's people—the church. His name should not be left off of the billing. He does not just apply the saving grace of Jesus and then turn us lose and hope something of value occurs. He is the constant collaborator.

As you scan the New Testament, it is obvious that the Spirit is an active, visible, powerful agent in the work of God. He is sovereign over the grace gifts that are given to every Jesus-follower so they have a way to be in the game.[2] He is active in the warfare and resistance we encounter to spreading the good news.[3] He is the constant source of encouragement, comfort and assurance as we move through this fallen world longing for the return and finale.[4]

We have introduced three other tools essential to the life-giving leaders toolbox: Prayer, The Bible, and the Witness. Notice that all three of these tools have value to us and are energized by the Spirit's activity.

1. We are to pray in the Spirit.[5]
2. The Spirit teaches by illuminating the Bible to us.[6]
3. And in Jesus' closing word to the eleven disciples in Acts 1, he assures them that when the Spirit comes they will have the power to be bold witnesses.[7]

One of the images of the Spirit used by Jesus, and experienced in Acts, is wind. I have worked in a mechanic shop where most of the tools were powered by a high-pressure air hose. The mechanic placed the tool and was involved with the work, but the strength to accomplish the task came from another source. Do not settle for just working for God in your own strength. Go stand in a tire store and watch the mechanic tighten five lug nuts on each of four wheels in just a few moments and without breaking a sweat. Then go off and pray for God the Spirit to be the power in your leadership. Seek his collaboration.

After reading the Gospels and Acts, we should expect the Spirit to work with unpredictable and unique creative expressions. We should also expect that his leading and work will be full of surprises and challenges. Jesus modeled the wild adventure of Spirit led leadership.

And Jesus, full of the Holy Spirit, returned from the Jordan and was led by the Spirit in the wilderness for forty days, being tempted by the devil. And he ate nothing during those days. And when they were ended, he was hungry. [8]

Jesus operated his entire ministry in the filling of the Spirit and being led by the Spirit. Tests and temptations are part of leadership and the Spirit can design those and call us to live in intense seasons of risky exposure. But greater is he that in you than the one who is in the world.

The seventy-two returned with joy, saying, 'Lord, even the demons are subject to us in your name!' And he said to them, 'I saw Satan fall like lightning from heaven. Behold, I have given you authority to tread on serpents and scorpions, and over all the power of the enemy, and nothing shall hurt you. Nevertheless, do not rejoice in this, that the spirits are subject to you, but rejoice that your names are written in heaven.' In that same hour **he rejoiced in the Holy Spirit** *and said, 'I thank you, Father, Lord of heaven and earth, that you have hidden these things from the wise and understanding and revealed them to little children; yes, Father, for such was your gracious will. All things have been handed over to me by my Father, and no one knows who the Son is except the Father, or who the Father is except the Son and anyone to whom the Son chooses to reveal him.' Then turning to the disciples he said privately, 'Blessed are the eyes that see what you see! For I tell you that many prophets and kings desired to see what you see, and did not see it, and to hear what you hear, and did not hear it.'* [9]

Jesus found JOY in the way the Spirit was bringing wins in the effort he was leading. The Father is glorified and the followers are blessed because they were on a work of God. A work carried out by the Spirit.

Philip said to him, 'Lord, show us the Father, and it is enough for us.' Jesus said to him, 'Have I been with you so long, and you still do not know me, Philip? Whoever has seen me has seen the Father. How can you say, 'Show us the Father'? Do you not believe that I am in the Father and the Father is in me? The words that I say to you I do not speak on my own authority, but the Father who dwells in me does his works. Believe me that I am in the Father and the Father is in me, or else believe on account of the works themselves. Truly, truly, I say to you, whoever believes in me will also do the works that I do; and greater works than these will he do, because I am going to the Father. Whatever you ask in my name, this I will do, that the Father may be glorified in the Son. If you ask me anything in my name, I will do it.' [10]

The Spirit was the author of the Father's work through Jesus. Jesus assured them the same works, even greater works, the Father would orchestrate through his followers, operating in his name, by the Spirit. Notice the intimacy of all three persons in the godhead in the work. It is the Father's will, the Son's availability and the Spirit's capacity.

Think back through the Gospels at the diversity and creativity that colored the WORKS and WORDS of Jesus that he credited as being received from the Father and delivered by the Spirit. Are we seeking to copy or clone God's work from one setting into another? Instead can we be anticipating and seeking a fresh, creative expression of God's life for our leadership context, birthed by his Spirit in and through us?

I want you to see the very personal provision of the Spirit. *He is with us.* We never walk alone. He is the source of God's blessings, grace, and truth—making the Father's love and care very relevant and moment to moment. He is the one bringing answers to our prayers. The Spirit is the companion who always listens to our questions and turns on the light to help our struggling eyes see God's heart and perspective.

GOD IS CREATIVE

God is THE creator. He is unique is his capacity to create from nothing. The *logos*, the Son as the living Word, speaks and God's intent comes into being. As I sit writing, I can look up from the screen and see birds, trees, and sometimes the squirrels who torment or entertain my Brittany dog. It is life-giving just to be in God's handiwork and breathe and look around. We are part of his creation. And he made us creative.

We create from the stuff God leaves around for us. Sometimes the creative process is a solitary work and often we are invited to play with others. God gave us our exploring, creating, and the ruling over creation capacity. YES, it gets polluted with sin, like all other abilities and gifts he has provided his children. But it such a core part of his design that the goodness and joy of creating always breaks out. Rejoice!

For many of us, we reach a point in life where we only acknowledged the creativity of the gifted artistic types and assume we are not creative. By failing to affirm our God given and Spirit partnered creative capacity, it yields little of value and fails to ripen into a fruitful contribution. I believe leadership situations are our sandbox and God puts other people, problems, inadequate resources, and many other blessings and challenges, just so leaders can "play" at creating solutions. God creates our opportunities to know the joy of creating with Him. I did the same thing as a parent of young children. We put the pieces in place for an engaging learning encounter.

1. Can you help me put your new toy together?
2. You are more comfortable with new technology than I am, how about helping me out?
3. Your Mom says her low tire light is on, let's take this gauge and check them.

Remember. The fruit of living in my own strength is complaining. The fruit of living by faith in his strength is gratitude. One important way to detect that a person is ready for greater leadership responsibilities is by observing a consistent humble spirit of thanksgiving.

It is the artist who realizes that there is a supreme force above him and works gladly away as a small apprentice under God's heaven.

—Aleksandr Solzhenitsyn

The Spirit's contribution to God's people

One of my life passages is John 13-17, often called the Upper Room Discourse. Dr. Hulbert, my Gospels professor in seminary, taught that in this passage Jesus outlines how the disciples will live the Christian life when Jesus was no longer present with them in the flesh. When the disciples first accepted Jesus' invitation to join him, whenever Jesus was out of their sight the twelve had gone looking for him. Initially, to be a Jesus-follower meant to be able to see and walk along with him. In the Upper Room, Jesus speaks several times of a coming time of separation and in their unnerved state the disciples are full of questions and pledge their loyalty to stay with him. All of their vows will shatter into utter failure in just a few hours, except for John.

Jesus uses their concerns to surface sinful flaws in their hearts. Jesus knows they will require his assistance to stand up to the opposition and resistance that will soon be storming their hiding places. He will reinforce their weak vows by his own Spirit whom he will send in his place. There are several essential resources given by Christ to his followers wrapped in relationship with the Spirit.

These blessings in and by the Spirit will empower us to live a Christ following lifestyle until Christ returns:

1. His constant, personal and powerful indwelling presence (John 14:16-18, 20, 23; 15:5, 8, 9, 11, 16; 16:22-24; 17:15)
2. Being marked by the Spirit; identified as God's children (John 15:3,19-21,26-27; 16:1-3; 17:14)
3. Granted the authority to freely make requests of the Father in his name (John 14:12-14; 15:7, 16, 21; 16:23-24,26; 17:26)
4. Going to the ends of the earth (Acts 1:8) and yet quickly recognizing and bonding with other Christ-followers in a unexplainable unity that is similar to the oneness of Father, Son and Spirit (John 13:34-35; 15:12-13, 17; 17:11-12; 18, 21-23)
5. Sparks of creative illumination in their minds as humble followers seek his wisdom, involvement in and discernment to solve problems and face challenges (John 14:26; 16:7-15, 33)
6. A whole array of grace fueled gifts entrusted to every believer giving them a contribution to God's cause and the welfare of their spiritual family (John 16:14-15; Romans 12:3-8 ; 1 Corinthians 12-14; Ephesians 4:11-12)
7. A taste of their inheritance that they anticipate enjoying with him at his return (John 13:36; 14:1-3; 17:24; Ephesians 1:3-14)

Christ's blood will cleanse their hearts, preparing them to be a holy dwelling place. Then he will send his Spirit giving them God's life. It will be flowing like sap from a vine moves through the branches. They will not attempt to work for him in only the strength of their best effort. They discovered first-hand how that turned out at his arrest. His powerful presence will be the support and an unconquerable force enabling them to stay faithful in life threatening moments.

It is important to notice in John 13-17 how Jesus predicts that his followers will be misunderstood and attacked, and those attacking will think they are doing God a favor. An example is Saul, who later converts and has his name changed to Paul.

The Upper Room is a key passage for preparing the church to live as a misunderstood minority.

In John 13-17, Jesus drops the seeds of truth that will grow into full fruitful plants in the epistles. He offers more truth than they could absorb in the shadow of his betrayal, arrest and death (John 16:12-15).

A basic outline of John 13-17:
1. John 13:1-20 — Humility, not a pride fueled heart, is the foundation of the new community. Competition, gaining the upper hand, concern with who is served and who is serving will create resistance to unwrapping and enjoying the Spirit's contribution.
2. John 13:21-14:14 — As Jesus surveys their weak hearts and confusing questions, he calls them to love one another and graciously offers them a home with the Father.
3. John 14:15-31 — God's gifts come wrapped in relationship; his Spirit's presence and the right to come and ask the Father in his name. Notice the link between loving and taking his commands seriously.
4. John 15: 1-17—Jesus uses the vine illustration to visualize and review the crucial teaching he has just taught in chapter 14. Notice again the priority from Jesus' perspective of believers living together in intimate love and sharing life with him.

5. John 15:18 – 16: 33 — We will be treated by others the same way as they had treated Christ. But he shows how powerfully the gifts wrapped in his Spirit will not just allow his followers to survive but to bear fruit with great joy, peace.

6. John 17 — Jesus prays for those in God's family, honestly admitting to serious danger, but stressing the power of being and loving one another as God himself is one.

⏱ PAUSE — TRY IT OUT!

Resources for Jesus-followers

Reflect on this question as you read through John 13-17.

How will the contributions of the Spirit provided by Christ sustain his followers when they come under attack, rejection and persecution?

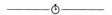

Creative Solutions: A Gift from the Spirit

When I put on my consulting and coaching hat with pastors, missionaries, and church leaders, one constant is a slate of challenges and problems that demand creative solutions. In the first part of this lesson, we stressed the wide breadth of the dynamic power of the Spirit. Now we want to focus on the Spirit as the stimulator of "creative juice" and the one who raises up and provides passionate gifted contributions of service wrapped in unique individuals. He gives leaders perspective, insight and wisdom into challenges, and then he provides the resources for addressing those problems by distributing gifts to uniquely created Christ-followers.

One writer on creativity encourages people to wear four different hats that tap different aspects of creative problem solving. These hats may be worn by one person moving through a creative process or it may be that team members excel in one of these roles.

1. **The Explorer** — moves out, leaves the known paths to uncover new possibilities (sounds like Paul).

2. **The Artist** — Asks, "What if?" and walks around challenges to view them from a variety of perspectives (sounds like Nehemiah).

3. **The Judge** — Discerns the best of options, willing to count the cost and commit so we learn as we move along. Prevents the paralysis of analysis and acknowledges we have to decide before we have certainty in much of what we face (sounds like Solomon).

4. **The Warrior** — Endures, willing to sweat and struggle to see the new solution given a good test. He is the test driver who jumps out of the plane to see if the new cord is really strong enough under stress[11] (sounds like David).

The Spirit stirs up these creative mind-stretching activities in Christ-followers as they seek God's perspective on wise changes.

⏱ PAUSE — TRY IT OUT!

Inventory of creative styles
Reflect on these two questions:

1. As you look at your leadership team, is there one of the four "hats" from the previous section that best describes the type of creativity the Spirit offers through your ideas?

2. Can you identify the creative contributions of other team members?

Is there a way of thinking that can help us stimulate creative solutions that reflect God's heart for beauty and truth? One answer is to jump-start your creative approaches to challenges by reflecting on creation. As we look at God's creation, we see how beauty and design appear as wasteful, and even extravagant. But, a sunset or a ripe tomato is joyful and good just in itself.

The Western culture assigns value based on efficiency, functionality, and productivity. God balances these values with an appreciation of unique variety and expressions. Wouldn't most people prefer a dozen roses grown by God than a dozen plastic ones duplicated and assembled in a factory? Don't be surprised if ministry strategies germinated by the creative Spirit of God look more like a bouquet of wild flowers than manufactured identical plastic ones.

Examples:

1. A congregation in Singapore started by merging three congregations, two using English and one using Chinese. Their history gives clues to what their next chapter or ministry looks like.

2. A missionary with a gift of evangelism and a heart for street people gets permission to open a basement bar on Sunday morning for a bible discussion. The range and depth of problems people carry in with them call for breaking the spiritual chains of various bondages.

3. In the middle of a major city in an English speaking part of the world, a Farsi speaking congregation of over 200 Iranian immigrants has been raised up. What will their ministry be as their 2nd generation children are growing up in the English context?

There is no book on church ministry that can provide answers for these very different gatherings of disciples and seekers. But the Spirit has all that is needed to reflect God's love of diversity, beauty, goodness, and truth.

The ministry of the Spirit includes "illumination" of the Bible. The writers of the Bible were "carried along by the Holy Spirit"[12] in a one of a kind inspiration of the Scriptures. The same Spirit gives the words needed to God's people as he shines light on Jesus, the Word of God, with the living Word of God.[13] He transmitted the truth of God as he inspired the biblical writers, and the Spirit of Christ will make it "burn" in the individual hearts of his followers.[14]

Now we have received not the spirit of the world, but the Spirit who is from God, that we might understand the things freely given us by God.[15]

Because the author of the Bible is with God's people, we can expect him to give us insight into making it relevant and applicable across cultural contexts.

⏱ PAUSE — TRY IT OUT!

Exposing blind spots

The Spirit may expose blind spots in our learning and raise challenges relevant to those amongst which we live. For example, many missionaries from North America come from a middle class culture. One of the cultural blind spots they may inherit is having less of a focus on caring for widows, orphans and victims of armed conflicts.

What challenges do you face in making the Bible applicable to people around you? Are you seeing some parts of the Bible, almost as though God added them while you slept, because they were not often taught in your church background?

⏱ PAUSE — TRY IT OUT!

Anticipating the Spirit's creativity

Reflect on this question:

How would assuming the Spirit of God was with you to birth creative solutions in you change how you investigated and selected approaches to ministry challenges?

Meditate on the relationship between the Holy Spirit hovering in creation of the whole earth to his hovering with you in your expressions of creativity.

Perhaps we tend to box in creativity within a smaller frame than God intended. Creative inspiration of the Spirit is not limited to helping us with challenges or problems. James Long offers another important consideration on creativity. Recalling a conversation he had with Andy Crouch, he writes, "Our conversation turned toward three things that have great value, regardless of how 'useful' they may or may not be: art, worship and people. 'What makes art unique is that it's not useful,' Andy said with no trace of irony. 'I mean, that's almost the definition of art — things human beings do that have no demonstrable utility. And consider worship: God is unlike every other small-g god. He doesn't require our worship for his satisfaction or pleasure or feeling of significance. Similarly, people are not "useful."' Crouch says this to emphasize that people are ends in themselves, not means to an end. You don't use people to achieve some objective. . .I reverence you because you are 'worth you' when you are baby and you can't feed yourself and when you are old and can't feed yourself." [16]

Our creative partnership with the Spirit is not just in digging for answers. He brings color, pleasure, joy, and vibrancy, as well as wisdom, when we need it. [17] The activity of God in and through us goes beyond just function to memorable, heart moving pleasure.

⏱ PAUSE – TRY IT OUT!

Recalling the Spirit's beautiful creations

Reflect: Stop and give thanks for beautiful treasures the Spirit provides for you to enjoy and open your heart to your Creator.

Start with music that moves you and go to vistas you have "photographed" in your memory, foods you delight in, and the feel and smells carried in the wind...

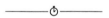

A Part of the Spirit's Provision is to Wrap His Gifts in Christ Followers

To each is given the manifestation of the Spirit for the common good.' [18]

Since God is sovereign, I believe it is okay for me to believe that anything he allows to touch my life should be viewed as a gift from him. Every person, even an enemy, arrives on my doorstep with lessons for me to learn about my God and my loving him and others.

The overflowing grace of God comes to us by the Spirit. And often the Spirit delivers the grace of God wrapped in a person! The Greek word translated "gift", as in spiritual gifts, is from the word for grace.

The Spirit helps us discover, develop, and deploy the gifts he brings to the church. As a consultant, I often encourage the leaders to know the life stories of the unique people God has brought together. God's unique outreach and discipleship plan for a particular church is often revealed in the people he brings together as he builds it.

Examples:

Families with children playing soccer are God's solution for a web of gospel spreading relationships.

Recovering addicts, unskilled laborers receiving training, school teachers, and people working late night shifts in restaurants are treasures the Spirit brings together to spread salt and light in specific dark arenas of the community.

Pastor Don Barry uses the term "redemptive fingerprint" to describe the way God has granted and redeemed our life experiences mixed with talents and spiritual gifts. "A redemptive fingerprint is that unique aspect of kingdom life you are designed to exemplify. It's that unique thing that you can do best. It occurs when there is a convergence of spiritual gifts, passion and opportunity."[19]

⏱ PAUSE — TRY IT OUT!

Partnership of God's Spirit and the Church

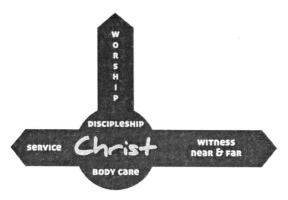

1. The five purposes of the church are shown in the illustration above. **List the specific grace gifts needed to express these purposes.**

If the church was operating at full effectiveness, describe what would be taking place.

2. What do these passages tell us about the **Spirit as the provider** for the church?
   » Ephesians 3:2
   » Ephesians 4:71
   » 1 Corinthians 12:7, 11

3. List the gift abilities needed in a prayer list and begin to pray with each other.

4. In your church, plan music, serve communion, and reserve at least one hour for prayer at a designated gathering. Ask the Spirit to give you God's perspective. How is he growing the capacity of this church through the gifts, failures, skills, struggles, and circles of influence of each person he has brought into this expression of his family?

5. Save some time at the end for sharing ideas on the discovery and deployment of the needed abilities. How will you know when God is answering your prayers?

6. Help every believer pray and then celebrate how God works through them.

7. Close times of prayer by standing in a circle and pray conversational prayers of thanksgiving, rejoicing by faith that God will provide all that is needed for the congregation to effectively live out his purposes.

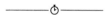

Are Christ-followers a religious minority where you live? How can the love you have for one another be an attractive light of new life in Christ?

Remember, to be a disciple of someone means you follow them. You treasure their teaching, practice it, and joyfully identify with the leader and the cause. So, how could Christ, as he knew his time to return to the father was coming, prepare his followers to carry on without him being present among them? He had the authority to request that the Spirit of God come to be with them in his place. The Spirit brings with him a variety of grace blessings. It is his provision that is essential and central to his followers fulfilling the mission given by Christ.

1. How would the training of leaders change if we focused on the provisions Christ gave in his Spirit?

2. Review the blessings of the Spirit that empower us to live a Christ following lifestyle until Christ returns which were mentioned in this study:

   » His constant, personal and powerful indwelling presence (John 14:16-18, 20, 23; 15:5, 8, 9, 11, 16; 16:22-24; 17:15)

   » Being marked by the Spirit; identified as God's children (John 15:3,19-21,26-27; 16:1-3; 17:14)

   » Granted the authority to freely make requests of the Father in his name (John 14:12-14; 15:7, 16, 21; 16:23-24,26; 17:26)

   » Going to the ends of the earth (Acts 1:8) and quickly recognizing and bonding with other Christ-followers in a unexplainable unity that is similar to the oneness of Father, Son and Spirit (John 13:34-35; 15:12-13, 17; 17:11-12, 18, 21-23)

   » Sparks of creative illumination in their minds as humble followers seek his wisdom, involvement in, and discernment to solve problems and face challenges (John 14:26; 16:7-15, 33)

   » A whole array of grace fueled gifts entrusted to every believer giving them a contribution to God's cause and the welfare of their spiritual family (John 16:14-15; Romans 12:3-8 , 1 Corinthians 12-14; Ephesians 4:11-12)

   » A taste of the inheritance that they will anticipate enjoying with him at his return (John 13:36; 14:1-3; 17:24; Ephesians 1:3-14) **Write out a prayer of gratitude for some of these gifts.**

The Spirit Works In Our Hearts

*Behold, the days are coming, declares the LORD, when I will make a **new covenant** with the house of Israel and the house of Judah, not like the covenant that I made with their fathers on the day when I took them by the hand to* *bring them out of the land of Egypt, my covenant that they broke, **though I was their husband,** declares the LORD. For this is the covenant that I will make with the house of Israel after those days, declares the LORD: **I will put my law within them, and I will write it on their hearts. And I will be their God,** and **they shall be my people.** And no longer shall each one teach his neighbor and each his brother, saying, "Know the LORD," for they shall all know me, from the least of them to the greatest, declares the LORD. For I will forgive their iniquity, and I will remember their sin no more." **Jeremiah 31:31-34 (ESV)***

Here are some of the truths we lead from based on this passage:
> God as husband.
> Spirit writing on heart (see Hebrews 8, 10).
> We bear a new name.
> Have become participants in a NEW covenant created by God.
> We have been honored with the privilege of having God dwell in us; work in us.
> God is delighted to have a people who all the time declare — he is our God. We are his people.

The Spirit Provides Practical Leadership Insight

I have been in an e-mail conversation with Steve Richardson, Director of Pioneers USA, in light of this question. **"How does trusting the Holy Spirit in a person work itself out in my leadership?" Most of the following points are Steve's reflections with my thoughts and biblical passages added.**

Because my leadership is not just me, but the Spirit is working...

1. It gives me hope that people can change, even if they seem entrenched in their ways at present. I am less likely to "write them off" when they mess up, because I know that the Holy Spirit has a long term plan for "finishing his work" in their lives.
2. It keeps me humble, because I view myself as being on the same playing field as other indwelt servants, whatever our titles or roles.
3. When I must have a difficult conversation with someone (like help-

ing them recognize that their present role is not a good fit) the Holy Spirit gives me both courage to move forward and the compassion to speak diplomatically and graciously. Knowing that God has a good plan for them and for their lives always reassures me. I talk with them about how we can seek God's gracious direction for them.

4. It makes me want to hear what people are thinking about me and my life and leadership, even if they bring "hard" news. There is a good chance that the Holy Spirit is speaking through them. I can almost always find a "kernel" of truth in their words, at least.

5. I am more inclined to let the person (like a missionary appointee) participate in significant life and ministry decisions, since we do not feel that we have a "corner on the market" when it comes to Holy Spirit wisdom. We recognize everyone as being on a journey, with the Holy Spirit as their ultimate guide and protector. When I speak or teach, it is good to know that not only is the Holy Spirit working in my heart and giving words to my tongue, but he is also tuning the hearts of the listeners. I encourage not just one idea or answer but in most cases to have at least three good options before seeking to make a decision.

6. It is good to have an "ally" moving through the audience as I speak. I think this awareness of the Spirit's movement in and through people helps task oriented leaders to be more relationally aware. The Spirit of Christ draws his children together in koinonia with the people we serve; he motivates us to break down barriers.

7. The Spirit is a moral "sentinel" making me aware of how I think about and relate to those of different genders. As a male, I need reminding that the Spirit fully indwells and gifts all individuals, male and female. I want to relate to a sister in Christ with full recognition that she is a temple of the Holy Spirit. As Dallas Willard says, "The body makes a great servant but a terrible master."[20] One of the fruit of the Spirit is self-control. God's design is for the spirit to rule the body.

8. I enjoy an expectancy tied to connecting the creative collaboration

with the Spirit illumination. I lead out of a creative anticipation of what the Spirit will illumine/inspire and let us be a part of his kingdom work.

» Psalm 39:1-4

» Luke 12:11-12

» Luke 24:31, 32, 45

WHAT SQUASHES CREATIVE LIFE-GIVING LEADERSHIP?

Be curious always! For knowledge will not acquire you:
you must acquire it. —Sudie Back

Avoid the crowd. Do your own thinking independently.
Be the chess player, not the chess piece. —Ralph Charell

Problem 1: Creative leaders lose perspective on themselves

What happens when a leader loses the willingness to explore and create?

But we have this treasure in jars of clay, to show that the surpassing power belongs to God and not to us.[21]

I am assuming that many of you reading this book are wired like me and tend to be more aware of our weaknesses than our strengths. You can contact me and let me know if I am wrong. This verse is a good reminder when you are thinking about what a fragile, weak "jar of clay" you are. Remember God can show his above-and-beyond power better in a weak vessel. You may not see yourself as a creative genius. Perhaps you feel the gifts you have been given do not add all that much to what God is doing. Live each morning then expecting that the way God will show through you will just assure he gets the glory.

When I was a freshman in college I worked at a small auto garage gas station for a while. You don't see many of those in the States anymore where most gasoline is sold as part of a convenience store. One night a young mechanic, known for his skills with car engines, pulled into our place. He was driving a Vega. Google it and you will read how it was one of the worst cars ever built. It was Chevrolet's first attempt at a small car in the early 70s and it was ridiculed by everyone who knew anything about cars.

We were all shocked to see our mechanic friend driving this ugly yellow

Vega. He walked over and issued a challenge to drag race down the street with anyone there. We all laughed. A friend of mine, the owner of a very fast Camaro, accepted the challenge. No one was betting on the Vega. They lined up down the road at a quiet section of road and the flag was dropped. The Camaro saw nothing but tail lights as the Vega led the whole race. When our friend pulled back in and climbed out, he was almost strutting. We all walked over to see what he done to the car to turn it from a wimp to a street killer (sorry if you don't get early 70s engine talk here!). He had removed the wimpy aluminum block 4-cylinder engine from under the hood and then somehow, where the back seat used to be, he had mounted a 427 cubic inch V-8 engine. It was crazy. That huge engine was sitting right in the middle of that dinky car.

Moral of the story: The Vega was the "clay jar," a sure sleeper and no great impression, an embarrassment for any real man to be seen in. But the power of the new engine brought great fame and glory to the young mechanic. Everywhere he went driving the Vega, people wanted him to work on their car. *How many people will be drawn toward our God as he displays his creative and powerful Spirit in our Vega-like flesh?*

Creative expression to express beauty, truth and life *or* creative solutions to problems and challenges require provisions. We cannot, like God, create out of nothing. He provides color, sounds, rare jewels, smells, and the ability to gauge our touch—all examples of his providing the raw material for his children to be like him and create. Providing the *resources* for creating is just one aspect of God's initiative in making us creative agents, but it is often an important aspect in tackling leadership challenges.

Problem 2: We can be consumed by a scarcity mentality

The resources God provides are adequate for engagement in his assignment for us. Watch Jesus and the disciples. So many times their starting point in a situation is, "There is not enough. We can't do this. There is no way out." And over and over Jesus says, "'Trust me. Ask the Father. He is enough— more than enough." Christ was training his leadership team to approach problems with an abundance mentality! Now don't get me wrong, I am not going down the path of prosperity theology. But sometimes I think we commit an equally greater sin of unbelief and moaning that leads to paralysis.[22]

At the heart of Satan's temptation to Eve was the idea of God withholding what was good. Why do I so quickly assume that God is holding out on me, and it is up to me to lay claim and possess what I need? In John 14, Phillip asks Jesus to let them see the Father. Why? Did he think there was a lack, something missing, in what God provided in the giving of his Son? How often is there buried in my complaining spirit an unstated belief that declares, "God, you are not enough. I do not have what I need to follow you." That is the scarcity mentality. An abundance mentality is knowing that the God who gave us his Son will not withhold anything from us.

He who did not spare his own Son but gave him up for us all, how will he not also with him graciously give us all things? [23]

An Example of Scarcity Mentality

We are in a leadership meeting. We are laying out an exciting ministry opportunity. And we are all aware that we do not have most of the resources to take this on. So, how does the conversation go? "Well, you know we just don't have enough money and we really can't do much so don't expect much to come of it." Stephen Covey and others call this the "scarcity mentality."

I think an abundance mentality helps leaders to not push back from opportunities but instead to:

> ➤ Be committed to organizing and leading a prayer initiative that addresses the needed resources (people, money, etc.).
>
> ➤ Start by asking what resources God has provided. If God gives us an opportunity, it may be that he has also given us something to start with— maybe it is better to start smaller than the full blown opportunity— but get started and grow into it.
>
> ➤ Start by asking what resources can be redeployed. God often prunes before increasing capacity. Often we must go through the painful process of stopping some things before we can start something else.
>
> ➤ Start by looking for resources that may be different from what

we expect. Often our first reaction is to think of the money that is needed. We default to what would seem to be the quickest or easiest provision. But sometimes the provision is not clean and efficient—it is messy and takes us into more relational, life-on-life investments.

> Approach life from a perspective of expecting God's involvement and intervention in the situation, and know that he is not surprised by what is happening. (Matthew 6)

> Value people who ask the hard questions, count the cost, and point out risk. God has provided them to balance the ready to jump folks like me! But do be careful to make sure that a spirit of fear does not crowd out the right moment to take a step of faith together.

One of the most empowering acts of a leader is to invite others into the game. Come join the fun! I can't keep all of these problems and challenges to myself. I need you to bring a fresh pair of eyes and a whole different set of life experiences to the mix. The Spirit will blend it all together.

Problem 3: We are afraid of letting others influence the work

Creative collaboration gives others the opportunity to be a part of the work. It might seem simpler if Jesus, by himself, had preached all the sermons, healed all of the sick, defeated all spiritual attacks, and fed all of the hungry. After all he is the Son of God. But instead, Jesus invited his followers into the work with him. What is even more interesting is how frequently they messed up. They would fail almost every test and seldom gave the right answers. Let's examine a few days in their three years together.

⏱ PAUSE – TRY IT OUT!

Ministry of the twelve — pass or fail?
Read the passages noted in the summary chart below, from Luke 9 and 10.
Reflect on these questions:

1. What was Jesus' response to the poor performance of the twelve?

2. What would this look like for a life-giving leader today?

KEY VERSES	DISCIPLES ACTION	JESUS RESPONSE
Luke 9:6	Ministry of preaching and healing	Takes them on a retreat afterwards
9:13	"We can't feed them"; focus on lack of resources	Feeds them; 12 distribute what Jesus provided
9:20	Accurate confession of Jesus' identity	Keep it quiet for now!
9:28	Eight Days Later	3 man prayer retreat
9:33	Peter, does not know what he is saying	Retreat over after Father speaks
9:40-41	They can't	Jesus confronts lack of faith and banishes the evil spirit
9:46	Prideful arguing; breaking unity, competitive, petty	Jesus teaches with a young child
9:49	"THEY were not of US so we tried to stop them"	WRONG! See who is on the team
9:54	Do you want us to call down fire on them? Lack of compassion on the lost; trying to be like Elijah who they had seen on the mountain though they were powerless in 9:13 and 40?	Jesus REBUKES
10:1		Jesus appoints 72 others to send out! Enlarges the team!

I am not sure of how Jesus was grading, but in my class, they would have failed! Also, based on how the twelve performed, the last thing I would do is to invite others to join the team. Jesus now had 84 students. How many rebukes, conversations, and messes would he have to clean up now! But, Jesus drew a circle of grace around these followers and did not pull back from letting them join in with him.

JESUS INVITED IMPERFECT PEOPLE TO COME OFF

THE BENCH AND PLAY IN THE KINGDOM GAME!

Jesus modeled a grace filled, shepherd's heart that had been described hundreds of years before.

I myself will be the shepherd of my sheep, and I myself will make them lie down, declares the Lord God. I will seek the lost, and I will bring back the strayed, and I will bind up the injured, and I will strengthen the weak, and the fat and the strong I will destroy. I will feed them in justice.[24]

Life-giving leaders will, at times, have a shepherd ministry. The creativity and empowerment of the community of Jesus-followers will require leaders creating safe places for people to learn to enter the kingdom battleground. Life-giving leaders draw a circle of grace and are not afraid of failure. They have tasted Jesus shepherding them through moments of failure and bringing about redemptive growth. They are ready for the Spirit to empower them to shepherd others as well.

WHERE DOES CREATIVITY OFTEN OCCUR?

There are two environments that seem to stimulate creative thought and actions: ***Playful exploring*** and ***the focused intense drive for a goal***.

During playful exploring there is no agenda, other than to see what is around the corner or in the next book on the shelf. Open space is critical to stimulate some types of creativity.

A stressful, pressured focus provides a different type of opportunity. The "just-in-time" situations we mentioned earlier are one example. I recognize focused activity when the environment seems to be a closed space. There is a sense of isolation, the pressure of deadline, a weight is resting on one's shoulders. It is time to step up, step out, and do something.

First, PLAY! God made us to be learners, explorers and discoverers. Creativity is the sweet essence of play. Play is a sandbox becoming a fort or battle field, a swing set becoming a sailing ship bouncing over waves, and clouds becoming dinosaurs plodding across the sky. Play is at its best when the engagement in play becomes the end in itself, and the energy invested is not a means to some other goal. Isn't it great when work is experienced by the worker as play? I delight in playing with my granddaughters.

Here are some recent creative lessons from my granddaughters:

➤ The four year old was walking in my front yard picking weeds with yellow blooms because Papa was behind on mowing. She turns to me and says, "Papa, can we get a napkin with water so I can take these home? *I want to use them in my wedding.*" She then returned to breaking off a hand full of weeds. I was looking forward to hearing how my daughter and son-in-law had set up an arranged marriage, but they assured me that no plans were made yet! They reminded me she attended a wedding with them a few weeks before and the wheels in her little head were still turning from that recent experience. *Are we free to see ourselves in another version of the experiences we observe?*

➤ My 19 month old Eloise loves to stand on the steps of the pool with a floating star toy in each hand and throw them as far as she can out into the pool. She then points for her Mom, or whoever is close to her, to help her swim to retrieve them and returns to the steps laughing so hard she gets a mouth full of water (reminds me I better check the chlorine levels!). As soon as she is back on the step, she is ready to throw them again. *Could our life adventure be better if we shared it with someone and they clapped with us as we completed each section of the journey?*

➤ I never have to BEG these young ones to play. I hand them the new Crayola water wand and special coloring book and they freely go at it. They assume everything they create is good and those who love them will appreciate or value it. Just look at the door of the fridge. *Who tells us we are NOT a great artist, writer or musician? How many, "You are not..." messages do I generate inside of myself and, as a result, stop trying to create?*

➤ As young as they are, both grandchildren know where the toys and craft items are stored at Grandma's house. They know which door leads to the front porch swing, and they always run and bring a book because it is a good thing to take to the swing. And Miss Eloise is a daredevil, so after we read a puppy book; and all good books have dogs according to her, she wants me to keep the swing moving while she stands up, holding the chains on the end, and jumps up down dancing to music only she hears. She assumes I will be her safety net! *Is God sitting in the swing with me, and would he be more than willing to keep me safe, if I would just stand up and dance?*

➤ A week after picking up plastic Easter eggs, we had some strong wind that covered my front yard with small sticks from the oak trees. Before I could mow — remember the story on the wedding weeds — I needed to pick up the sticks. So my four year old helped me have a "stick hunt" and she then piled them at the street for the collection men to pick up. She was mildly disappointed when I told her the "fort" she was building would be gone by the next time she returned. Weeks later when we were out shopping, the wind came up as we walked to the car. She reminded me we needed to do another "stick hunt". She turned *my work* into play just by making it *her play. Can we do that for those we work alongside?*

➤ After a day of play at Grandma's house, they sleep well. They burn up lots of energy, they get tired and sleepy but are not depressed or burned out. The dog, Grandma and Papa also sleep well, and as my wife and I prepare for bed, we laugh and relive the joy of being with them. We feel drained in a very good way. *How often, in our days, can we enter into that kind of joy?*

➤ Both of my granddaughters are better on the tablet or phone than I am. My wife, a preschool teacher, says it is because they have no fear. They do not have the awareness yet of breaking something and then spending hours to get it back to a usable position. They are free to explore and trust it will lead them to something fun or interesting. *Can I set myself and those who work with me free to explore and see what new thing we may discover?*

Our life-giving God wants to unleash our joyful creative dancing through playing with his Spirit. You are free to let worries and needs roll off your shoulders and onto the shoulders of the very present Spirit of Jesus and delightfully anticipate how he will prompt your creative instincts.

Second, FOCUS ON URGENT CRISIS! The challenge, when faced with need to be creative *right now*, is to set some boundaries and to say, "The next hour is for focused activity." Remove distractions from the environment and go to work. We may also need to set aside an hour to browse, explore, make some new friends over coffee—let our world and our thoughts expand and visit new territory. But without boundaries what happens?

One of the challenges life-giving leaders face is to correctly discern the moment. Here is a question that can create real tension for a leader. "Is this a moment for unstructured play or a call to intense work?" To be honest, I like to play. But my wife will also tell you I have a hard time playing if a pile of work with a deadline is lying on my desk. I often need to wake up in the morning and, in a prayerful attitude before rising, affirm the type of day God has for me.

"Lord, today is a work today. Spirit, please give me all I need to be fruitful for the glory of the kingdom today."

Or — "Lord today is a play day. Spirit, please let me freely enter into the joy of play and not get lost or go astray in boredom. Let me live as an explorer and adventurer anticipating what new challenge you may have for me."

Today, as I make edits on this book, is a work day. I need *focus*. Yes, the sun is shining and my wife is on summer break from teaching, but the editor is waiting to get started and I am already a week past my deadline!

When God designs focus work days for me, it helps to know he has built into me the capacity to rise to the challenge. To use the Greek word, God has given all of us **epi-thumia.** There are twenty-two places in the New Testament where this word occurs. It often has a negative connotation — lustful intent, desires for other things that choke the word of the kingdom, lust leading to sexual impurity. But the same word is also used in a positive sense to mean a longing to see and be with God's people, a desire to be fed when close to starvation, and to be delightfully glad in an encounter.

Here are some of my favorite positive uses of epi-thumia:

But now, since I no longer have any room for work in these regions, and since I have longed for many years to come to you,

For in this tent we groan, longing to put on our heavenly dwelling,

… and not only by his coming but also by the comfort with which he was comforted by you, as he told us of your longing, your mourning, your zeal for me, so that I rejoiced still more.

For see what earnestness this godly grief has produced in you, but also what eagerness to clear yourselves, what indignation, what fear, what longing, what zeal, what punishment! At every point you have proved yourselves innocent in the matter.

… while they long for you and pray for you, because of the surpassing grace of God upon you.

But since we were torn away from you, brothers, for a short time, in person not in heart, we endeavored the more eagerly and with great desire to see you face to face. [25]

God has designed us to select a goal, place in front of our physical or mental vision, and then direct a great deal of inner energy to move toward that objective. WHAT A GIFT!

Can epi-thumia be polluted with our sinful attempts to discover and be truly alive without God? YES! Lust, passions, and unbridled desire have destroyed countless lives. But God's design is not to castrate our capacity for strong desire but to bridle it and direct it as he intended for our enjoyment.

God is revealed as one who works with incredible focus, effort and energy. We are made in his image. God gives us the capacity to generate, to discover, to solve puzzles and problems, and to take pieces and make a new whole.

Therefore,
We encourage creativity.
We treasure the unique contribution of others.
We learn to appreciate and value others who are very different from us.
We suspend our first impressions or snap judgments and create a space in

our hearts that God can fill with love and compassion.
We are always adjusting our vision to see ourselves and others as God sees us.

THINK IT THROUGH

1. How do you practice collaboration with the Spirit in your leadership?
2. Revisit John 13-17 and summarize the gifts Jesus has provided so you may live a kingdom life while the king is residing off planet.
3. How does the idea of God wrapping up his gifts in people make a difference in your leadership?
4. In the list of ten ways the Spirit impacts your leadership, select two to apply to your current leadership situation.
5. Which of the listed elements that squash creative collaboration are ones you need to change?
6. Do you play well? What would four hours of exploring and unstructured play look like for you this week?
7. Do you have a godly goal you are intensely pursuing in your life?
8. In what aspects of your life does intense desire need to be bridled by the Spirit?

RECOMMENDED RESOURCES

1. Reggie McNeal. *Missional Renaissance: Changing the Scorecard for the Church.* San Francisco: Jossey-Bass, 2009. (While aimed at the North American Church, it has broad application to any missional work)
2. Robertson McQuilkin. *The Five Smooth Stones: Essential Principles for Biblical Ministry.* Nashville: Broadman & Holman, 2007 (Provides more detail on how to detect, develop, and deploy the Spirit's gifts)
3. Robertson McQuilkin. *Life In the Spirit.* Nashville: Broadman & Holman, 2000. (A practical guide to the work of the Holy Spirit)

PART TWO

A LIFE-GIVING LEADER'S HEART

If only it were all so simple! If only there were evil people somewhere insidiously committing evil deeds, and it were necessary only to separate them from the rest of us and destroy them. But the line dividing good and evil cuts through the heart of every human being. And who is willing to destroy a piece of his own heart.
—Aleksandr Solzhenitsyn, *The Gulag Archipelago 1918-1956*

THIS SECTION IS a major shift in the book. We will go from examining critical tools in the toolbox of leadership to taking an inward journey into the heart.

Leadership is an outward work of influencing others, so why begin the work of leadership by looking inside?

Because God does. God places a centrality on our hearts.

As you work through this section, let me encourage you to examine your own heart carefully. But also consider how you make sure your leadership cooperates with God's heart level work. I have observed that too often leaders become so goal and behavior focused that they neglect, not only their own hearts, but the hearts of those they are leading. We are always seeking to motivate them to DO more and fail to call them to BE more. And, if leaders do focus on the heart, they often lack clarity on the WHAT and HOW of God's desired work in the heart.

CHAPTER FIVE

WHAT IS THE HEART?

THE HEART IS the source of the motivations, goals, values, and desires (inner drives) of an individual. God has given us a capacity for thinking, feeling, and choosing, and these actions are carried out by the heart. The heart is also the residence of my self-awareness. Self-awareness is what the Psalms call "inner meditation". I know it as the constant running dialogue of inner conversation in my heart. The heart is the "me" that lives inside this earth suit. As we brought out in the last chapter, the heart is the dwelling place of God on planet earth. The Spirit inhabits the heart of every Jesus-follower.

JESUS SPOKE OF THE CENTRALITY OF THE HEART

- ➤ Those with a pure heart see God.[1]
- ➤ We can think and meditate deeply on truth in our heart.[2]
- ➤ The heart can process what one takes in visually and create adulterous fantasies.[3] There is also heart blindness and deafness which Jesus describes as being "dull".[4]
- ➤ God in his mercy allows one to end a marriage because of the

capacity of the heart to become "hard".[5] This allowance was not God's best design for us. Jesus was grieved by the hardness of heart and even challenged the heart condition of the twelve when he witnessed their unbelief in feeding the crowd.[6] Even after witnessing the resurrected Christ, the disciples struggled with hard hearts. Unbelief and heart hardness go together.[7]

➤ Whatever one treasures reveals the focus and location of the heart.[8]

➤ Jesus has a gentle and humble heart. Since I am changed into his image, I am becoming gentle and humble from my heart.[9]

➤ The heart is the seed bed for all actions, words and attitudes.[10] A person can put on a mask so they outwardly look godly, but it fails to match their heart. Jesus sees who we really are; our heart is our true identity.[11]

➤ Forgiving another person must not end with words but, in order to be accepted by God, forgiving must come from one's heart.[12]

➤ To love with all we have in us engages our heart, soul, and mind.[13]

➤ The heart can be accessed by the evil one to snatch away the truth of God that was sown there.[14]

➤ The motivation to endure in believing prayer and not lose heart was a priority concern of Jesus.[15]

➤ Jesus knows we will pass through seasons of a troubled, fearful and grieving heart, but he is committed to filling our hearts with JOY. A joy filled heart is a major work of grace. Joy in the heart is not only a gift, it is a goal of Jesus.[16]

We all live with three spheres of influence and responsibility around us. The outer circle is our *public world*. People touching our public life usually see only what we plan for them to see. We control what is known about us. Our middle circle is our *personal world*. Family, friends, and close associates see us in more unguarded moments. They observe more of our life, so they know more of who we really are and what our heart values. But even in our personal world, we hide and determine levels of disclosure. Our inner circle consists of our *private world,* with only ourselves and God in the audience.

We may choose to let parts of our private world show into our personal or public worlds, but we can also close out aspects of it—even to our spouse.

When God works in the human heart, he touches all of these circles. However he is never content to only work in the public or personal world. He is always aiming at the private, the heart, the intimate place where he lives and connects with the real us. Effective organizations understand God's target for activity is the heart and actively participate in the process.

MANY DIFFERENT FORCES INFLUENCE OUR HEART

When I travel outside my passport country, it is not unusual for workers to share with me that in the course of one day they engage in intimate dialogues, through technology, with people all around the world. Just twenty years ago, a worker, because of limited communication access, could be isolated for large amounts of time within one web of relationships. Letters would take weeks to be exchanged and the limited depth of dialogue and interaction allowed separate and somewhat distinct orbits of life and ministry. Now the sending church pastor can participate in a planning workshop with national and mission leaders via web cam six time zones away. We live in "real time" with people around the world and this can challenge the heart.

This level of interaction has many benefits, including up to date intercession and emotional support. But it also creates tremendous tensions and challenges as cultures, backgrounds, and values overlap and collide. Some cross cultural workers tell me it is difficult to put roots down in the culture where they are serving because they still have one foot planted in their passport culture via the new technologies. Global connectedness tends to encourage a divided heart.

A major theme in this study is that God mercifully works to expose our hearts so we can see what is really going on inside of us. We can so easily live with a primary focus outside ourselves as we bump into events, people and circumstances. The pace and the number of touches by others makes it easier to ignore our own heart. Once God helps us see our heart, he then exchanges interdependent humility for our independent pride. Deep life-giving community begins with knowing one's heart.

It takes a measure of courage and personal strength to move out of one's birth culture. That same strength can become a weakness when it isolates us from dependency on God and others. The Bible is clear—God resists the proud but pours out his grace on the humble. Pride is the stubborn child who refuses to acknowledge the need for help. How often does God see me as a four year old glaring up at him saying, "**I can do it by myself!**"

God will often build in help to get at the pride that keeps us from being what God created us to be. Uncomfortable cross-cultural, multi-ethnic and socioeconomic interactions are ways to face and know our hearts, which can hide more easily in our comfortable homogeneous settings. In so many ways, living outside our passport culture, or any comfort zone, takes us back to being like children who must desperately depend on others for basic needs. And what really helps to humble us is when our preschooler has learned more of the language than we have (despite months of language study) and corrects our grammar with the taxi driver. Oh, the faithful hand of God! He knows what each of us needs to get at the deadly pride stuff growing in our hearts.

SEEING CHANGE IN ME AS GOD SEES IT

We all show up for God's service carrying two suitcases in our heart. One is our LIFE suitcase packed with experiences from our family of origin, educational background, and other accumulated experiences. The other suitcase is our CULTURAL suitcase. Since culture is the accumulated values, beliefs and expectations of a defined people, every culture preserves some of the image of God and some of the contamination of the sin in every person. To use computer language, these family and cultural bags become our "default setting" for responding to change. We assume our perspective and view of the choices are the correct ones. We carry around definitions for everything from "success" to "respect". We have packed our bags with the expectations we use to measure every experience.

When you relate within the circle of your "passport" culture, you learn the cultural rules for keeping the bags closed and taking out the right items at the right time. You carry them around without causing much trouble. Your definitions and expectations are shared by most people around you and give you a common ground for relating. You know when to arrive for a special event and what to bring with you. You know when to stand and when to sit down. You know when to speak and when you should ask a question. You know when to make eye contact and when to show respect by looking away.

But as one moves into cross-cultural or multi-cultural settings, the bags will easily explode and spill out all around our feet. We often experience more than the minor embarrassment of a spilled suitcase when these relational explosions occur. These cultural misfires can even occur within groups of people who have very similar culture and family backgrounds but span different generations. One person says, "Your music sounds like noise!" and the other person replies, "Your music should only be endured in a short elevator ride!" You get the idea.

The protection of our own comfort and preference narrows our vision, limits our points of view, and creates blind spots in our attempts to know ourselves. In turn, this priority on protecting our comfort zone hinders our capacity to love those different from us. Is this what happens when some Jesus-followers insulate themselves in a church culture, and are not willing to bring their heart into the "foreign" lands where they work or live?

The church is a NEW family

We have been adopted into God's family. We are exchanging some of the "stuff" in our LIFE suitcase for the lifestyle, values, and attitudes of our new family. In 1 Thessalonians 2: 7and 11, Paul's vision of leadership as "mothering" and "fathering" pictures how God uses leadership in the church as a means for Christians being re-parented by our heavenly father.

There is a song echoing from heaven and earth. From heaven God sings, "You are my people!" and from the earth people respond, "You are our God!" This becomes a responsive chorus that weaves through the Bible. The Bible is one large story of how God secures a people who willingly, joyfully, and lovingly declare him to be their God. This God reveals to his people a bottomless love delighting in being their God. The church is called the "household of God" in 1 Timothy 3:15. Leadership will often look more like a dysfunctional family where the children are adjusting to being adopted. Can they really trust they won't be abandoned or abused? Is this God parent really good? And why do his house rules seem so weird and different from our former home?

This Genesis to Revelation song that sounds out from God's heart and ours, because we are made in his image, reveals a God designed longing for a family. There is a desire for home. There is a clear vision that family is to be a place of acceptance, security, learning, celebration, sacrificially giving and freely receiving. The more our earthly families are like God's family, the more we say — "this is good." The more our earthly families are destructive opposites of these values, the more we cry out — "this is not good; and beyond that it is evil and unjust." All people are thirsting for family and God understands family. He knows it takes mercy, forgiveness, grace, and truth to establish a family. He understands the price and challenge of adoption.

Coming into God's family is also radical. It is a new birth. It is being adopted off the street. It is being redeemed from bondage. And since we are already part of a biological and spiritual family; surely in some ways a dysfunctional one, we will require reparenting and bonding with God as our new parent.

Images of servant, warrior, friend, priest and many others all express important aspects of our identity. But they all fall beneath, are subheadings under, the main heading of **Child of God**. These other "hats" point out the adventure that flows from being in his family. But every other title or role is just a facet; a part of who we are or what we do. Being his child defines us now and for eternity.

Here are a few items from my baggage that God is working on to re-parent me.

How did your family members control situations or people?

In my case, I learned to control situations and others with WORDS. Win the argument. Flood the room with words. Make the sales pitch and if that fails, use guilt, manipulation, and other verbal rocks to stone the competition.

How did those around you respond to rejection or the risk of rejection? Some counselors think rejection by one we expect to love us may be the deepest emotional pain. I learned to do whatever it took to convince and win over those around me to avoid their rejection. Learn the score card for school, Boy Scouts, Mom, Dad, my peers, etc., and whatever mask I needed to construct to win their approval, get it in place.

How do you respond when you are threatened? If they use words in their offensive attack, I can use louder and more words. If they use a stick, grab a bigger stick. Blow the enemy away. Go for nothing less than a decisive win. Unconditional surrender is the only way to eliminate the threat.

How do you view purchasing possessions? Buy quality and then protect it. Put plastic covers over the furniture and the car seats. Seek to make your valuables safe and to last as long as possible. And never give anything away. It can probably be reused in some way so hold on to everything.

How did your determine the value of people? Worth was linked to hard work that you and others benefited from. So many relationships were based on the same results based status. If a friendship offered opportunity for mutual giving and receiving, then it was probably worth the relational investment. If it stops being useful — ignore it and move on.

God is committed to this re-parenting of his adopted children. I have some friends who are being challenged deeply in seeking to parent an adopted child who is struggling with Reactive Attachment Disorder (RAD). This pastor and his wife spent weeks in Eastern Europe working to exercise the privilege of adopting these children. Now each day the fight continues, but now it is for the heart of one of their sons. You can Google it if you want details of this disorder, but they have shared with me the daily frustration of a child who cannot seem to open his heart and receive the love being offered.

I wonder if my heavenly father is constantly responding to my Reactive Attachment Disorder to his sacrificial loving toward me. Praise him for his mercy in showing up every day. He can customize comfort, conviction, clarity, and encouragement for each of his adopted children. His supply of what his children need is not limited.[17]

THE CHURCH IS ALSO A NEW CULTURE.

We are also called to live out a kingdom culture. Our citizenship in his kingdom holds priority over all other allegiances. Every culture will align with kingdom truth and values in some areas; and every culture will have aspects that demand repentance and an embracing of the Spirit-produced expression of kingdom citizenship (Philippians 1:27-2:18). We are his people and he is our God and that makes us citizens of his tribe with a new loyalty.

Living in the Joy of the Kingdom of Heaven

And James and John, the sons of Zebedee, came up to him and said to him, 'Teacher, we want you to do for us whatever we ask of you.' And he said to them, 'What do you want me to do for you?' And they said to him, 'Grant us to sit, one at your right hand and one at your left, in your glory.' Jesus said to them, 'You do not know what you are asking. Are you able to drink the cup that I drink, or to be baptized with the baptism with which I am baptized?' And they said to him, 'We are able.' And Jesus said to them, 'The cup that I drink you will drink, and with the baptism with which I am baptized, you will be baptized, but to sit at my right hand or at my left is not mine to grant, but it is for those for whom it has been prepared.' And when the ten heard it, they began to be indignant at James and John. And Jesus called them to him and said to them, 'You know that those who are considered rulers of the Gentiles lord it over them, and their great ones exercise authority over them. **But it shall not be so among you. But whoever would be great among you must be your servant, and whoever would be first among you must be slave of all. For even the Son of Man came not to be served but to serve, and to give his life as a ransom for many.'** [18]

Notice how Jesus took on the culture of his disciples and challenged them with a new kingdom culture. This was not a case of just being different. God's kingdom culture is perfectly consistent with God's truth, and therefore, it always "trumps" our fallen cultures.

The law of God is the outline of the kingdom culture to which I now belong. It helps me to read the Bible out loud. I need to have my Western-culture-shaped-heart HEAR from my own voice my pledge, my affection, my affirming of the goodness of my King's law. I have taken on too much of the shape of a culture which praises doubting the law, mistrusting authority, or fighting against anything or anyone seeking to limit my unrestrained individual freedom.

How does your culture define a person's worth?

In the East Tennessee mountain culture where I grew up, respect for someone is not related to education or wealth. Blue-collar working class people made fun of those who walked around the plant carrying a clip board but did not have a clue how the operations really worked. Worth was connected to making a difference; getting the job done right. An ultimate compliment of a person was to say, "No one needs to come behind him and redo his work or clean up his messes." The ultimate curse was to call someone lazy and point out how they spent more energy avoiding work than doing it.

I remember my kin saying about someone, usually when they were not present (but occasionally in anger to their face), "he is not worth the gun powder it would take to shoot him." I think this goes back to the time when a farmer needed to put down an old, worn out farm horse. Isn't that an encouraging way to assess the people around you?

What is the value of the elderly and the young? My culture had low tolerance with carrying "dead weight". At a funeral, the highest praise would be, "she cooked dinner, washed the dishes and then went to her room, laid down and died. She worked until her last breath."

How did your culture instruct you to respond to strangers? Again, from my culture we operated by keeping our distance. We justified it by telling our self to not ask them questions. You do not ask them questions. You do not violate their space. If they look lost or in need, don't approach them and inquire if they need assistance. The offer would be like saying to them, "You can't do this by yourself; you must need my help." That would be offensive. Every person has a right to control their own space and decide if they require assistance. If they do not ask, do not offer.

Your perspective changes when you move out of your known culture. As you move out to intersect with other cultures, you encounter places which are different from your norm. You can also see your cultural values in sharper detail when you contrast them with those that are different.

If we seek to develop a biblical foundation of leadership, we must we willing to honestly explore our "suitcases". Don't be surprised by God *exposing* what is contrary to his design, *disrupting* some of our long held beliefs and reactions, and *enticing* us into the adventure of kingdom living.

⏱ PAUSE — TRY IT OUT!

Taking an honest look at your heart

Take at least 2 hours to reflect on these questions and write out your findings in a private place. This is not stuff for Facebook!

> **Is your heart close to DEATH?** Do you go through your day reminding yourself to not expect anything and then you won't have to endure disappointment?

> **Is your heart DIVIDED?** Do you have idols like a man with multiple wives? Dallas Willard says, "The body makes a good servant but a lousy master." Are there aspects of your life where many days you're in bondage to your body?

> **Is your heart DILUTED?** Daily life is so crowded with stuff and worries. Do you always feel you are in survival mode? Do you sense that you do not have the energy or the capacity to make wise changes but instead are just reacting and bouncing around like a marble in a box?

> **Is your heart DEVOTED and DANGEROUS to God's enemies?** Your heart is whole. You live abiding, seeking, asking, treasuring, and thanking the Father. You rest in knowing his goodness is true and consistent. Are you filled with grace and truth and often experience him creating moments where you can sow his grace and truth in others?

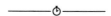

I am not proposing that you can reach a point of sailing through life with no death, division, or dilution challenging the health of your heart. I am also not asking you to come forward and rededicate your heart one more time to trying harder. But, I do believe God meets us with grace and truth when we honestly confess where we are in our journey. If I can honestly come to him, like the Psalmist often sings, with a true perspective of my heart, the God who saves us comes to us.[19]

How God works in the heart and WHAT he is doing there

The heart of the Christ-follower is the residence of the presence of God on planet earth.[20] It should not be surprising that his earthly home is very important to him. We will examine God's will for the heart by using six verbs. These words are my attempt to summarize the work of God IN the heart of a leader.

PLACING THE HEART BEFORE GOD	PRIORITIES OF GOD FOR THE HEART
Seeing	Trusting – FAITH
Hearing	Enduring – HOPE
Bowing	Giving – LOVE

These six verbs may also be used to examine how we instruct those in our circle of influence. The major fruit of our life can be modeling and guiding people into God's heart surgery to find abundant, glorious life.

The first three verbs focus on the PLACEMENT of the heart—how we live before God in a relationship, responding to his work of grace and truth, loving him with all of who we are. The second three are the fruit of a heart being made alive by God. This will be our outline for the next several chapters.

THINKING IT THROUGH

1. Write out what shows up from your family background that either supports or goes against the values of God's family.

2. How about your cultural baggage? What lines up with God's kingdom culture and what needs to be adjusted?

3. How would you describe the current state of your heart?

4. Maybe you need to stop and go take a walk with God. Open up your family luggage and cultural baggage before him. Tell him about the competing voices and the complexity that clouds your focus on him. Read Psalm 131 and remind your soul of the invitation to place your hope and trust in him.

CHAPTER SIX

SEEING AND HEARING

To be blind is bad, but worse is to have eyes and not see. —Helen Keller

Bless you prison, bless you for being in my life. For there, lying upon the rotting prison straw, I came to realize that the object of life is not prosperity as we are made to believe, but the maturity of the human soul.
—Aleksandr Solzhenitsyn, The Gulag Archipelago 1918-1956

When we look at life through God's eyes, we become lost in wonder and convinced of God's astounding generosity, marvelous mercy, and gigantic grace. Sin causes us to look at life through the lens of entitlement — that we deserve salvation without repentance, wealth without work, accolades without self-denial, health without personal discipline, pleasure without sacrifice. Biblical truth reminds us that, in reality, we deserve hell. —Gary Thomas

SEEING

ONE MORNING I WAS going through my e-mail and a short note from a good friend simply said, "How are things in your world?" Now I know he expected me to reply that everything was fine or to list some problems or challenges he could pray over for me. But the question has rattled around inside of me for several days and has become, "How do I decide how are things in my world?" How am I going to measure my moments and my days? How will I size them up, give them a grade, label them good or bad?" The real question is, "How do I perceive how my world is going?"

1. Do I measure the state of my world by my circumstances?
2. Do I measure how it is by my feelings?
3. Do I measure how it is by my progress in completing tasks or attaining goals?

4. Do I measure how it is by the perception of other people?
5. Do I measure how it is by comparing myself to the state of others?

OR

Is there a different starting point? Maybe I need to start with what is true of God.

1. My world is good because God is good and God does good for his children.
2. My world is good because Jesus is as alive today and the work he did on the cross is as vital today as it was the moment it occurred.
3. My world is good because I have the same inheritance of grace, the same indwelling Spirit and the same identity as those who followed Jesus over 2,000 years ago.

Maybe how it is in my world is more about the one who walks with me and lives with me than any other assessment I can perform.

My view of life should include joy for God providing the capacity to see and hear him. A spiritual birth includes spiritual eyes and ears. These are abilities given at the new birth. New eyes are the faith-sight Paul describes, the new ears to hear his whispers are an inheritance to every child God adopts into his family.

For to the one who has, more will be given, and he will have an abundance, but from the one who has not, even what he has will be taken away. This is why I speak to them in parables, because seeing they do not see, and hearing they do not hear, nor do they understand. Indeed, in their case the prophecy of Isaiah is fulfilled that says: "You will indeed hear but never understand, and you will indeed see but never perceive. For this people's heart has grown dull, and with their ears they can barely hear, and their eyes they have closed, lest they should see with their eyes and hear with their ears and understand with their heart and turn, and I would heal them." But blessed are your eyes, for they see, and your ears, for they hear. For truly, I say to you, many prophets and righteous people longed to see what you see, and did not see it, and to hear what you hear, and did not hear it. [1]

No one understands; no one seeks for God. All have turned aside; together they have become worthless; no one does good, not even one. Their throat is an open grave; they use their tongues to deceive. The venom of asps is under their lips. Their mouth is full of curses and bitterness. Their feet are swift to shed blood; in their paths are ruin and misery, and the way of peace they have not known. There is no fear of God before their eyes. Now we know that whatever the law says it speaks to those who are under the law, so that every mouth may be stopped, and the whole world may be held accountable to God. For by works of the law no human being will be justified in his sight, since through the law comes knowledge of sin.[2]

But I can lose my vision or let it decay. Here are examples of what will keep leaders from *seeing* God:

The Activities and Schedule of the Moment

We can attempt to invite God in to bless our activity instead of seeking to be a part of his activity. Jesus models for us a lifestyle of making sure the Father is leading in our dance through our days.

So Jesus said to them, 'Truly, truly, I say to you, the Son can do nothing of his own accord, but only what he sees the Father doing. For whatever the Father does, that the Son does likewise. For the Father loves the Son and shows him all that he himself is doing. And greater works than these will he show him, so that you may marvel.'[3]

Perhaps I set my focus on the wrong measurements and fail to see as God sees because I am not expecting God to show up in the ordinary events of my life.

And the angel of the LORD appeared to him in a flame of fire out of the midst of a bush. He looked, and behold, the bush was burning, yet it was not consumed. And Moses said, 'I will turn aside to see this great sight, why the bush is not burned.' When the LORD saw that he turned aside to see, God called to him out of the bush, 'Moses, Moses!' And he said, 'Here I am.'[4]

I agree with Richard and Henry Blackaby's wise counsel on SEEING God. "God usually speaks out of the ordinary experiences of life. Often, it is not while you are worshiping at church. Many of God's most profound and history-changing encounters come during the ordinary experiences of life. When you see the unusual in the midst of the mundane, don't continue business as usual. It may be that God has ordained that moment to be a life-changing time for you and those around you."[5]

Accomplishing or Winning with My Agenda

A distraction from leaders seeing God is when they are seeking a win for their agenda, or as they seek to win over other people.

> *In problem situations seek SOLUTIONS not VICTORIES.*
> —Robertson McQuilkin

Don't create enemies or make others losers when what you really need is a team unified around a solution. When I am seeking to "win", I lose the valuable perspective of holding two truths in tension or seeing through the eyes of the opposition. Often these other perspectives help me correct deficiencies in what I see. In a "win at all costs" mentality, all of life becomes one playing field with one goal and only one direction to push for a score. Tom Varney, in an article on the importance of a dual vision, calls it an essential "sacred discontent":

I have chosen the phrase 'sacred discontent' to encompass several ideas that are pertinent to one's effort to revision the church and his or her involvement in it. Basically, sacred discontent entails a deep commitment to 'realism' that does not, but rather releases one to engage in plodding, messy community. Sacred discontent is a godly, productive disillusionment that richly accepts both the reality of sin (the fall) and the future hope of God. It is not to be equated with cynical despair or nihilism, which says, 'Nothing works, so why bother?' and refuses to receive the mystery, meaning and full hope of the gospel. Nor is sacred discontent a more sophisticated, philosophical version of credulity (believing things too readily), which closes its eyes to suffering and evaluates life in an innocent, pious way that strips life of realism and makes God and community always congenial and safe. Instead, sacred discontent is a 'holy dissatisfaction' which is reflective of the heart of God. God is pained by the way things are, but

He remains passionately involved with an eye on redemption (Genesis 6:7, 8:21, 9:1-17). There is one major axiom out of which I want to draw several thoughts that further illuminates the nature of sacred discontent and how it can help adjust our vision of the church and our involvement in it. The axiom is simply this: Sacred discontent is nurtured by the ongoing choice to both acknowledge and accept the dual nature of the church.

First, what is this dual nature we need to acknowledge and accept? Basically, the 'dual nature' of the church is the theological reality that the church is both glorious and grotesque; it is both a masterpiece and a mess. As Eugene Peterson puts it, 'I don't deny that there are moments of splendor in congregations. There are. Many and frequent. But there are also conditions of squalor. Why deny it? And how could it be otherwise?' Much of the cynical discontent one feels toward the church is fueled by 'both sides of the dual nature of the church as an instrument of God's work and, at the same time, a culturally bound monument to human fallenness.'[6]

I often use Psalm 2 to teach on this idea of the importance of getting the right point of view.

⏱ PAUSE — TRY IT OUT!

Don't miss seeing the throne room

Below you will find Psalm 2 with some of my own observations inserted. After reading it over, paraphrase what it teaches you about SEEING in a prayer to the Lord.

Psalm 2:1-12 (ESV)

Why do the nations rage and the peoples plot in vain?

The kings of the earth set themselves, and the rulers take counsel together, against the LORD and against his Anointed, saying, Let us burst their bonds apart and cast away their cords from us."

The scene has been repeated countless times by whole groups of people as well as by the individual wrestling against acknowledging and submitting to the God who rules over all.

He who sits in the heavens laughs; the Lord holds them in derision.

God does not seem threatened by the rebellious spirit. He laughs at it like one might laugh (without the child seeing) at a two-year-old throwing a tantrum.

Then he will speak to them in his wrath, and terrify them in his fury, saying, "As for me, I have set my King on Zion, my holy hill." I will tell of the decree: The LORD said to me, "You are my Son; today I have begotten you. Ask of me, and I will make the nations your heritage, and the ends of the earth your possession. You shall break them with a rod of iron and dash them in pieces like a potter's vessel."

This is prophetic exchange between the Father and the Son. When Jesus claims in Matthew 28:18 to possess all authority in heaven and earth it was true. The Father had already made it so.

Now therefore, O kings, be wise; be warned, O rulers of the earth. Serve the LORD with fear, and rejoice with trembling. Kiss the Son, lest he be angry, and you perish in the way, for his wrath is quickly kindled. Blessed are all who take refuge in him.

This Psalm is written to leaders and is one reason I use it in my leadership courses. The God who we are to bow down to and serve in fear is also a cause of rejoicing. When leaders lay down their arms and surrender, they discover a goodness and a refuge for which their heart was longing.

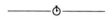

It seems it is important for leaders to have both perspectives and hold them in tension:

The EARTHLY reality

And

The HEAVENLY certainty.

With only a vision of the rebellion against God on earth, leaders can lose heart and go on the defensive. If holding only the heavenly perspective, leaders can forget the reality of the earthly war. Perhaps you have to been a prayer meeting where you came out more depressed than when you went in. The focus was so set on the needs, pain, losses, sickness, death and defeat of the world that we forgot to stand in the throne room and look around. We need a dual perspective. Use both eyes to hold on to the earthly and heavenly viewpoints.

Robert Coleman presents both viewpoints well.

The discerning English journalist Malcolm Muggeridge sees Western civilization in 'an advanced stage of decomposition, and that another Dark Age will soon be upon us, if indeed, it has not already begun.' Apart from divine intervention, the future is taking the shape of a nightmare from which there is no waking. No wonder multitudes grope in despair. Cynicism seems to permeate the air, especially on the campus. . . . We need to be reminded that usually it is in times of momentous crises that great revivals are born. Periods of human weakness accentuate the need for divine grace. If it were not for the hardships of life, most of us would never learn much about the faithfulness of God. Human nature being what it is, only when the night closes in are we prone to look up and see the stars.[7]

Looking Short Term and Failing to look Long Term

Since our seeing is taking place in the present moment we also need God's perspective of seeing over time. The Bible is full of remembering the past to learn from it and being given glimpses of the future to encourage hope and endurance. Life-giving leaders live in the present, but they also place the present within a timeline of all past and future moments held securely in God's hands. Here is an example from the last week of Christ's life.

Truly, truly, I say to you, unless a grain of wheat falls into the earth and dies, it remains alone; but if it dies, it bears much fruit. Whoever loves his life loses it, and whoever hates his life in this world will keep it for eternal life. If anyone serves me, he must follow me; and where I am, there will my servant be also. If anyone serves me, the Father will honor him. 'Now is my soul troubled. And what shall I say? 'Father, save me from this hour'? But for this purpose I have come to this hour. Father, glorify your name.' Then a voice came from heaven: 'I have glorified it, and I will glorify it again.' The crowd that stood there and heard it said that it had thundered. Others said, 'An angel has spoken to him.' Jesus answered, 'This voice has come for your sake, not mine. Now is the judgment of this world; now will the ruler of this world be cast out. And I, when I am lifted up from the earth, will draw all people to myself'.[8]

Notice the powerful use of an everyday item—a seed—to present the choices facing the heart of every follower. Also see how Jesus' impending sacrifice is cast in the light of the past and future. C.S. Lewis reminds us, "It is since Christians have largely ceased to think of the other world that they have become ineffective in this one. Aim at heaven and you will get earth "thrown in". Aim at earth and you will get neither."[9]

Seeing is the ability to capture pictures in our mind and then derive meaning from them. We use the meaning to shape our attitudes, choose our words and step out in action. That makes the pictures we focus on with our spiritual eyes very important.

Here are some of my proverbs or axioms that help me decide which mental pictures should capture my attention and are worthy for meditation.

1. Don't go with your first thought or feeling. Seeing often takes time. When I choose to not trust my first "seeing", I have to step back, not to hide or avoid, but to seek to see as God sees.

2. Look at the picture from different angles and lighting. Walk around a mental picture. Do not just view it from the perspective of the goal it may accomplish, or the passion of a person who first shared a picture. Work hard to see what it will cost everyone touched by the picture.

3. Our perspective is just our perspective.

4. Frame a picture with your life purpose that God has already made clear in the Bible. Does it fit?

5. Enlarge the picture. I do this by looking past the present short-term sacrifice to see the ripples or waves of impact it will produce.

Failing to See God's Hand in Painful Moments

Ron Dunn has a series of sermons I have listened to several times, and he also wrote on the same idea. He called the series, "God's Strange Ministers". [10] Ron's list included: Silence, Suffering, Darkness, Disappointment,

Circumstances, Failure, Weakness, Temptation, Chastisement, Trouble, Discouragement, and Depression. Through these messages I found myself going through a revolution in *seeing*.

When any of these "strange Ministers" come knocking on the door of my life, my first response is to lock the door and pray against the visitation. Surely this painful "thing" has its source in spiritual warfare and God wants me to join him in prayer to see it packing up and gone! I pray, begging God to send them away. But God would allow these unwanted guests to move in and stay for some time, bringing waves of adversity into my life. Only when I saw the "strange Ministers" as surgical tools in the hands of a sovereign God did I begin to look past the visitor and see the God who demanded my attention.

God himself explained his uses of stranger ministers in the lives of his people.

And you shall remember the whole way that the LORD your God has led you these forty years in the wilderness, that he might **humble you, testing you to know what was in your heart,** *whether you would keep his commandments or not. And he humbled you and* **let you hunger** *and fed you with manna, which you did not know, nor did your fathers know, that he might make you know that man does not live by bread alone, but man lives by every word that comes from the mouth of the LORD.*[11]

God orchestrates various hungers in my life and uses them to bring to the surface the sense of entitlement and demanding spirit which is crippling my heart and keeping it from trusting in my God. This experience also provides an opening for me to see God as greater than my hunger. And not only is he greater than my hunger, he also wants me to learn to rest in his care and awareness of my needs. But this manner of seeing only comes through experiencing hunger in a desert.

We are not citizens of this world trying to make our way to heaven; **we are citizens of heaven trying to make our way through this world.** *That radical Christian insight can be life changing. We are not to live so as to earn God's love, inherit heaven, and purchase salvation. All those are given to us as gifts; gifts bought by Jesus on the cross and handed over to us. We are to live as*

God's redeemed, as heirs of heaven, and as citizens of another land: the kingdom of God... We live as those on a journey home; a home we know will have the lights on and the door open and our Father waiting for us when we arrive. That means in all adversity our worship of God is joyful, our life is hopeful, our future is secure. There is nothing we can lose on earth that can rob us of the treasures God has given us and will give us. —The Landisfarne, via The Anglican Digest

When one reads the journeys of the men and women in the Bible who were adept at seeing God, it is clear the benefit and growth that came out of their pain and loss more than offset the cost. *"Nearly all the great examples of faith and victorious grace which we find in the Scriptures came out of situations of extremity and distress. God loves hard places, and faith is usually born of danger and extremity."*[12]

The chart below lists some examples of the Strange Ministers. We often use a variety of names to label the pain we are experiencing.

GOD'S STRANGE MINISTERS

Out of death God brings life (John 12:24-26 Matthew 26:26-29, Romans 6:1-5)

PERCEIVED DIRECTION	WHAT WE NAME THE MINISTER	CHARACTERS VISITED	KEY PASSAGES
EXTERNAL CIRCUMSTANCES RELATIONAL – ENEMIES, AUTHORITIES OVER	Failure, Testing, Trials, Difficulties	Paul, Peter, 1st century church	2 Cor 1, 2 Tim 3:10-12
	Losses, Afflictions	Jesus, Joseph, Daniel and friends	Col 4:3-6, Acts 14:27, 1 Cor 16:9
	Closed Doors		1 Tim 5:3-16
	Injustice, Unfairness,		2 Cor 6, Rom 13, James, 2 Tim 4:10, 14, 18
	Death of men in church and many widows		1 Tim 4:12-16
	Disappointment, Betrayal		
	Judged by age		

INTERNAL DESIRES LIMITS (FRAILTY)	Depression, Anger, Lust, Worry Fear, Fatigue, Depletion Weakness	Elijah, David, Sampson, Saul, Paul, Jesus	2 Cor 12, Eph 4-5
SPIRITUAL RESISTANCE WORLDLY POLLUTION DECEPTIONS	Evil teaching Attacks, Blocks to answering prayers, misunderstood motives, judged wrongly, temptations and lures toward evil Leader in Sin	Jesus, Daniel, Paul, Jeremiah	1 Tim 4:1-11, Titus 1:9-14 Titus 3:1-11 1 Cor 10, Eph 6 1 Tim 5:17-21
PARENTING BY GOD DARKNESS CORRECTIONS	Distance from God's perceived presence, dryness, exposure, disruption Corrections with anguish and many tears	Isaiah, Jeremiah, Church	Prophets, Heb 12 2 Cor 2:1-4, Heb 13:17, Col 1:24, 28-29

There are two ways of getting out of a trial. One is simply to try to get rid of the trial, and be thankful when it is over. The other is to recognize the trial as a challenge from God to claim a larger blessing than we have ever had, and to hail it with delight as an opportunity of obtaining a larger measure of divine grace."— A.B. Simpson[13]

Life-giving Leadership is about Perspective

In a Fuller Seminary doctoral leadership course Bobby Clinton said, *"Leadership is about perspective and the difference between good leadership and great leadership is about better perspective."* Over and over in this book

> Leadership is about perspective and the difference between good leadership and great leadership is about better perspective.
>
> —Bobby Clinton

you will see me referring to "seeing" or "perspective". Life-giving leadership is about *seeing* as God sees and that vision informing our priorities and choices.

Seeing as a Leadership Contribution

As we introduced in chapter four, a value leaders bring to a group is God letting them *see* what others in the room do not yet see. This contribution does not make them better than anyone else. It is simply what God gives them to bring and to offer to the group. See this example from Elisha's life:

When the servant of the man of God rose early in the morning and went out, behold, an army with horses and chariots was all around the city. And the servant said, 'Alas, my master! What shall we do?' He said, 'Do not be afraid, for those who are with us are more than those who are with them.' Then Elisha prayed and said, 'O LORD, please open his eyes that he may see.' So the LORD opened the eyes of the young man, and he saw, and behold, the mountain was full of horses and chariots of fire all around Elisha.[14]

This is simply one way leaders help those they lead. They serve through their "seeing". One caution here: I am not restricting seeing to those in formal leadership positions. God may wrap the leadership gifting in someone who is just viewed as a godly influence but who holds no titles.

Seeing as God sees, whether it is the big picture, one's own life, or as a leadership contribution, is a critical state of the heart because seeing and faith are linked. When we see with faith-vision we see differently than we see with self-vision. What leaders *see* determines if they can *receive* and *live out* of God's provision. Otherwise, we limit ourselves to what we can produce.

> ➤ Do we see only the enemy or God's protection?
> ➤ Do we see only the attacking army or do we see God's power?
> ➤ Do we see only the bread we have and the almost empty purses we carry or do we see that Jesus has asked us to feed them all?
> ➤ Do we see the waves or do we see Jesus walking on them?
> ➤ Do we see Jesus asleep and assume he does not care or do we see him at rest because of his rule?

We, just viewing our meager accumulation of experiences and skills, are often inadequate for the assignments God has given to us. But, we, as his children, are more than adequate. Do we see the overwhelming needs and challenges around us through eyes of faith and hope in God? Our leadership confidence is not drummed up self-hype, it is a realistic response to how God sees our situation. I learn a great deal by looking back over journal entries written during times of great change in my life. During my first year as pastor, I made two entries a few weeks apart.

Here is how I described the congregation I had come to serve:

1. The leadership and congregation have no vision.
2. There is a lack of unity between the leaders.
3. There is evidence of mistrust between some members of the congregation and the leadership.
4. There is a shortage of finances.
5. There is little global outreach (missions) and no local outreach (evangelism).
6. The facilities are without debt but in very poor condition. They were "70s green ugly" in the 90s.

A few weeks later I described the same group of people very differently.

1. There is an open door to design, train and launch global and local outreach.
2. The opportunity exists to start with a clean slate and forge vision with the people.
3. There are creative ways communication can be enhanced.
4. The facilities provide opportunity for expansion.
5. There is financial and growth potential.
6. Leaders are very open to individual discipleship ministry.

Both descriptions of the church contained some truth. The first list sees through the eyes of what is NOT present. It is a vision of scarcity. It is a perspective of unbelief. It is leadership believing that God is holding out on us and not doing things right!

The second list sees the church through the eyes of faith, hope and love.

It is a list filtered by a God centered confidence. It is not a list that is denying weakness but recasts the negative in a vision of God's powerful grace.

How much of what goes on in leadership team meetings is actually group complaining? I have participated in many problem solving sessions that turned out to be justifying what we are not attempting because of focusing on what we do not have available. If you find yourself in that downward spiral of a scarcity mentality, read the first few chapters of Exodus, Daniel, Esther and Nehemiah, and revisit the cross and let God's way of responding to pain, loss, problems, opposition, and weakness transform your perspective.

HEARING

Be a good listener. Your ears will never get you in trouble. —Frank Tyger

Talents are best nurtured in solitude: character is best formed in the stormy billows of the world. —Goethe

To go as I am led, to go when I am led, to go where I am led . . . it is that which has been for twenty years the one prayer of my life. —Dr. A. T. Pierson

*All these things my hand has made, and so all these things came to be, declares the LORD. But this is the one to whom I will look: he who is humble and contrite in spirit and **trembles at my word**.*[15]

I confess I am guilty of not trembling enough. I pick up my Bible looking for a message for others before listening for his word to me. I go to prayer and spend most of the time talking, forgetting to ask him what he wants to say to me. I think I am afraid of what he might say, so I fill the space with my words and then rush back out into the day where I can use the noise of life to distract me from listening to him. And hear is a passage that scares me. *"But they refused to pay attention and turned a stubborn shoulder and stopped their ears that they might not hear. They made their hearts diamond-hard **lest they should hear the law and the words that the Lord of hosts had sent by his Spirit** through the former prophets. Therefore great anger came from the Lord of hosts."*[16] My God does not force himself on his children. He will not get in my face and scream at me. But he is a companion to those who want to be with him.

I want there to be a constant thirst to actually be experiencing walking with him and hanging on his every word. I pray I can anticipate the impact of his words on me as this question implies. "If Jesus could speak and raise the dead, calm a storm, cast out demons, and heal the incurable, then what effect might a word from him have upon your life?"[17]

The Life-giving God is a Speaking God

Our God speaks often and with clarity and power. There is a confidence when he speaks that any expert public speaker or salesman would envy. There is a power in God's words and an authority to bring into reality what he states or promises. It is logical to believe the Creator who thought up speaking and hearing would be adept at both.

And they were astonished at his teaching, for he taught them as one who had authority, and not as the scribes.[18]

God speaking to a leader includes illuminating biblical teaching inspired by the Spirit and a personal and specific word for a situation. I use the term "whisper" for these specific words God speaks. It is a term used by Bill Hybels and others.[19] Here are some biblical promises and examples.

Behold, I am sending you out as sheep in the midst of wolves, so be wise as serpents and innocent as doves. Beware of men, for they will deliver you over to courts and flog you in their synagogues, and you will be dragged before governors and kings for my sake, to bear witness before them and the Gentiles. **When they deliver you over, do not be anxious how you are to speak or what you are to say, for what you are to say will be given to you in that hour. For it is not you who speak, but the Spirit of your Father speaking through you.** *Brother will deliver brother over to death, and the father his child, and children will rise against parents and have them put to death, and you will be hated by all for my name's sake. But the one who endures to the end will be saved. When they persecute you in one town, flee to the next, for truly, I say to you, you will not have gone through all the towns of Israel before the Son of Man comes.*[20]

And everyone who speaks a word against the Son of Man will be forgiven, but the one who blasphemes against the Holy Spirit will not be forgiven. **And when they bring you before the synagogues and the rulers and the authorities, do not be anxious about how you should defend yourself or** *what you should say, for the Holy Spirit will teach you in that very hour what you ought to say.*[21]

God will give assignments that are beyond our capacity in some way. They reveal our weakness, our lack of resource, or our lack of knowledge to figure it out.

Now there was a disciple at Damascus named Ananias. **The Lord said** *to him in a vision, 'Ananias.' And he said, 'Here I am, Lord.' And* **the Lord said** *to him, 'Rise and go to the street called Straight, and at the house of Judas look for a man of Tarsus named Saul, for behold, he is praying, and he has seen in a vision a man named Ananias come in and lay his hands on him so that he might regain his sight.' But Ananias answered, 'Lord, I have heard from many about this man, how much evil he has done to your saints at Jerusalem. And here he has authority from the chief priests to bind all who call on your name.'* **But the Lord said** *to him, 'Go, for he is a chosen instrument of mine to carry my name before the Gentiles and kings and the children of Israel. For I will show him how much he must suffer for the sake of my name.' So Ananias departed and entered the house. And laying his hands on him he said, 'Brother Saul,* **the Lord Jesus** *who appeared to you on the road by which you came* **has sent me** *so that you may regain your sight and be filled with the Holy Spirit.' And immediately something like scales fell from his eyes, and he regained his sight. Then he rose and was baptized.*[22]

Notice how a minor character, Ananias, plays a critical role in the story of a major character, Paul. Again this is something God often does. Notice Paul's brokenness as he regains his sight by the touch of grace of God through someone he had been planning to arrest.

Expect God to give you assignments like he did with Ananias. They may not come every day, but be alert for your moment. If you come into a position of some influence, do not miss the people God may send to you to give you a word from Him.

Be ready and when you hear his word to:

Step out of the boat

March around a city

Step into a flooding river
Stand in front of opposing leadership toe to toe
Go to prison, or . . .

Can you imagine Ananias retelling this experience to the other Jesus-followers at Damascus? Were they thrilled God had heard and answered their prayers for deliverance? Were they surprised at how God involved Ananias to save them from imprisonment and stoning? Could any of them have imagined the fruit that would come from Paul's life?

Hearing God is being alert and accessible but not demanding. As I begin and go through my day, I am working at consistently inviting the Spirit to whisper, and if I don't sense a word, then I operate on obedience to revealed biblical truth. If I do hear what may be his whisper, I check it against the Bible. The Spirit will never lead contrary to the Word. Satan is the liar; deceiver.

⏱ PAUSE — TRY IT OUT!

A prayer for hearing

Want to read some of the saddest words in the Bible?

Behold, the days are coming," declares the Lord GOD, *"when I will send a famine on the land— not a famine of bread, nor a thirst for water, but of hearing the words of the LORD.*[23]

After I read the verse in Amos I wrote this prayer in my journal.

"Spirit, There is an energy, a life, and a joy when I hear your whispers. I am so sorry for creating mental static that drowns out your presence. Why is the hunger in my flesh so consuming it covers over your voice? Show me what I need to do today to tune my ear to be straining to hear from you."

—Roy, June 21, 2015

Now write out your own prayer.

What Prevents Our Hearing God?

Much of what stops up our ears are the same things we covered in the section on "seeing". But let me add one more here.

I will take you to be my people, and I will be your God, and you shall know that I am the LORD your God, who has brought you out from under the burdens of the Egyptians. I will bring you into the land that I swore to give to Abraham, to Isaac, and to Jacob. I will give it to you for a possession. I am the LORD.""Moses spoke thus to the people of Israel, but they did not listen to Moses, **because of their broken spirit and harsh slavery.** [24]

Years of having one's humanity attacked, debased, and devalued may lead to hearing loss. One can lose the capacity to listen with a sense of hope, anticipation and confidence. It may take a whole series of experiences when God speaks and then keeps his word before the heart breathes in life and is able to trust and tune in as God intended. God uses strange ministers to work on our hearing. Strange ministers of fear and threat often isolate us from our normal lifestyle and routines and offer us a very different context in which we can hear God more distinctly.

Here is an example of what I mean.

REFLECTIONS FROM DAD BEING IN ICU — by Mark King
November 2011 (with Reply from Roy King April 7, 2015)
INTRODUCTION:
My son, Mark, recently sent me some thoughts he had recorded a few years back, which he found when cleaning up his Google Drive. They are his honest processing of an event that took place in my life in November 2011 that included over a week in ICU, then a few days in a step down unit, and then more days in a rehab facility followed by almost two years of outpatient physical therapy. My medical adventure stemmed from a very serious reaction to a blood pressure medicine I had taken for several years. After reading Mark's thoughts, I have written a reply to him which follows his reflections. —Roy King, April 7, 2015

MARK KING:
ICU smells funny. I have spent a little over a week watching my father lie in a bed. There are cables and tubes everywhere. Sometimes I worry that my size 13 shoes are going to hook around my dad's catheter, loosely attached to

the bottom of his bed, and tear it out; sending two liters of stale pee gushing to the floor. This week I have a done a lot of worrying, a lot of waiting, a lot of trying not to acknowledge my worries and fears, a lot of getting upset with nurses that don't seem to be moving quickly enough, a lot of being annoyed with doctors that never come by and a lot of thinking about my family. My life this week seems summed up best by the following list.

1. Go to hospital and wait. Try to use my cell phone to look at comics for sale on eBay.
2. Wait some more and greet all of Dad's co-workers and church friends. This involves me trying to be nice as someone else offers to pray and I have to hold their hand.
3. Wait for answers that never come quickly enough.
4. Go find fast-food.
5. Go back to hospital and wait. Try to stream Netflix which is blocked by the free Wi-Fi at the hospital. Hulu works but as usual, nothing good is on.
6. Go home and dream about hospitals and funerals.
7. Repeat the next day…

As I am trying to process what it means to see my father in a hospital, I keep coming back to three thoughts.

1. Lists are stupid. I don't ever want to live my life going by a list.
2. My greatest fears are steeped in losing people I love.
3. Waiting makes you think.

I know that these three thoughts seem random and overly simple, but they keep running around over and over and over and over and over in my mind. I think they tie together and might be a piece of what God is trying to show me this year.

Let's go backwards:

3. Waiting makes you think.

I have had a lot of time to wait. I am naturally not good at waiting. Just ask my wife how I am with Christmas presents. November 25th is just as good as December 25th. I have tried to distract myself in every way possible while waiting on my dad. I go do the meal runs for my sister and mom. I roam around the hospital and ride the elevator. I download applications on my phone and then delete them. I even played a game with myself where I would try to find a different bathroom every time I needed to go. Hospitals have a million bathrooms and none of them are clean. The point is that despite my high propensity to find joy in distraction, there was just too much waiting. Eventually I had to think. My thoughts, which I had been really trying to avoid led me straight to where I knew they would go. My worries and fears.

Some of my fears are stupid and some I won't even give voice to because they might overwhelm my entire being.

2.   My greatest fears are steeped in losing people I love.

This week I feared that I might lose my dad. This week I feared that I might have to spend another week or two in the ICU looking at him hooked up to tubes, watching him move from looks of extreme pain and discomfort to looks of raw fear and confusion born from heavy sedation and a ventilator. This week I feared I might not have been the best son I could be. This week I feared that I would see my mother, who is the strongest woman I know, break down.

This is where the blessing comes in. It is in the fears and worries that are wrapped around my heart and brain that I was reminded of how much I love my family. The love I have for my wife and parents and sibling, is a love that is deep and real. The thought of separation from that love is one of my greatest fears. I think that sort of love must be the love that Jesus talks about when he sums up the second greatest commandment,

The most important one," answered Jesus, "is this: 'Hear, O Israel: The Lord our God, the Lord is one. Love the Lord your God with all your heart and with all your soul and with all your mind and with all your strength.' The second is this: 'Love your neighbor as yourself.' There is no commandment greater than these."

As I think about it, that same love that I first experienced from my parents I can now not only reflect back to them, but also give to my wife and some friends. My father and mother were the first two people on this planet to love me in a truly second commandment way. No wonder the thought of being disconnected from the supply of that love is so scary. It's also amazing to think that through their love and the love of God I learned how to love others.

1. **Lists are stupid. I don't ever want to live my life going by a list.**

This waiting led me to thinking about my fears, and leads me to my last thought. Lists are dumb. I want to stop thinking about life in terms of lists and focus instead on thinking about my life in terms of who I care about. Do I get to spend today being loved by God and loving him? That's a great day. Do I get to love my wife today? Count that as a highly productive day. If I truly believe that the two most important things are the love of God and loving others then my true focus and measuring rod of success for a day should be did I get to receive and give love today?

I want my life to be surrounded by what I truly care about.

If I, when lying in a hospital, wake up to find money, security, a completed check list, a well-organized calendar full of finished meetings and neatly crossed off successful programs but have not love, I have missed the greatest gift both my earthly and heavenly fathers have given me.

MY RESPONSE TO MARK

Mark, how can I thank you for this gift? Mom and I have read it but I was afraid to bring it up when I saw you recently. I did not think I could make eye contact with you to respond to your words in a group setting of church and Easter without breaking down and crying in front of others who would not understand.

I cry even as I work on this written reply because:

You honestly describe me during those days and yet I have no memory of the events. I feel I somehow was present but lost out on the experience. Now that I am out of the ICU I don't want to be choosing to drift through time with loved ones, by being in the room but not really present.

I feel your pain, confusion and great love in your words. It is a tender place in your heart and it feels like you opened a gate to a quiet hidden garden in your soul and invited me in. Thank you . . .

I am so thankful we worship a God big enough to take dark moments and bring good lessons and growth in our lives through it. I don't talk as much about those days as I did the first year after they happened but there are few days that go by that they do not come into my thinking at some moment in my day.

Since my adventure in the ICU, hospital and Health South rehab I have observed that I still get weird, almost panic type feelings, when I go to visit someone in those medical settings. I have been back to Providence and other hospitals and even visited Steve Bradley who was just down the hall from my room at Health South. I almost have to push my feet forward and it feels like the air is leaving the room. I think it has made me a better visitor. I listen more, ask a few questions, and don't push to hold hands when I pray. And I keep it short. I am not sure that will fade or even if I want it to evaporate.

I am deeply touched and cry every time I read your perspective on your Mom's strength and our attempts to be loving parents. Somehow seeing my wife and our role as parents through your eyes felt very rewarding and satisfying. So often all I can see are my mistakes. I agree with your respect and view of Mom's strength. I had always doubted myself and assumed my view was colored by my deep love for her. I heard Jesus whisper to me as I read your words, *"See, Roy, what a treasure you have been given in Pandora... Rest in peace and in joy. You both have loved your children well, not perfectly for sure, but you did it well."* That comforts my soul.

I so rarely see anything in my life as having been lived well. This blindness and deafness shows my own sin and pride. My tears are deep, coming from a choked-up heart, knowing that my son knows I love him. I can die in peace whenever it is God's time for me.

Love,

Dad

CONCLUSION

*He was still speaking when, behold, a bright cloud overshadowed them, and a voice from the cloud said, 'This is my beloved Son, with whom I am well pleased; **listen to him**.*[25]

Life-giving leadership becomes something we can offer to others if we are receiving life through seeing and hearing God. Seeing and hearing are closely linked to obedience in the Bible. If I expect to hear from God, I must have my shoes on and be ready to obey what he tells me. Visions are only valid if I throw myself on God's faithfulness and step out. I must not limit hearing to gaining knowledge. Seeing and hearing are God's ways of giving his children his life-giving leadership.

THINKING IT THROUGH

1. Describe a time when you were confident you were seeing as God wanted you to see. What difference did make in your life?

2. List some of the "strange ministers" who have visited you. What are some lessons you learned from them?

3. Could you create your own two lists of seeing with eyes of unbelief or with eyes of faith for your ministry context?

4. What can you do to consistently see your ministry from God's perspective?

5. What questions do you ask of God to help you be an attentive listener?

6. What contribution does hearing from God make in your leadership?

7. How do you start your day or end your day so you are ready to hear from God?

CHAPTER SEVEN

BOWING

If you plan to build a tall house of virtues, you must first lay deep foundations of humility. —Augustine

More of Thy presence, Lord, impart, More of Thine image let me bear; Construct Thy throne within my heart, and reign without a rival there. —John Newton

There is no respect for others without humility in one's self. —Henri Frederic Amiel

No one really knows why they are alive until they know what they'd die for. —Martin Luther King Jr.

ONE OF THE GIFTS "strange ministers" leave on the table of our heart when we learn to embrace their visit is humility and meekness.

Now the man Moses was very meek, more than all people who were on the face of the earth.[1]

Yet Moses did not start out meek. He was a take-charge, do-it-his-way kind of guy with a hot temper and a willingness to kill to enforce his sense of justice. Throughout his journey as leader of the people, God would use a variety of strange ministers, including being overwhelmed by the task of leadership to the frequent whining and complaining of the followers.

We bow down when we are aware of who we really are

And I said: 'Woe is me! For I am lost; for I am a man of unclean lips, and I dwell in the midst of a people of unclean lips; for my eyes have seen the King, the LORD of hosts!'[2]

Humility should be the normal default setting for a human being. We were created by God to stand before him and have a correct assessment of God and ourselves. Because of sin, God has to break through the heart blinded by pride to show us who we really are.

I do not know what I may appear to the world, but to myself I seem to have been only like a boy playing on the seashore, and diverting myself in now and then finding a prettier shell or a smoother pebble than ordinary, whilst the great ocean of truth lay all undiscovered before me. —Isaac Newton

One of the greatest assets a life-giving leader offers to God is knowing one's weakness and limits. Both grow from living out an attitude of humble interdependence with God and others. Weakness is what God looks for in our resume. We learn more from our failures than our successes.

Many of us hold wrong perspectives about the look of a humble person. Humility is NOT letting others dictate the agenda for your life. Jesus was the ultimate servant, yet he never allowed those being served to set his agenda or strategy. He knew the danger of letting the proud religious leaders set the agenda for his ministry.

It is also wrong to envision humility as a passive response to the desires of others or our own heart. As C.S. Lewis explains, "Telling us to obey instinct is like telling us to obey "people". People say different things: so do instincts. Our instincts are at war. Each instinct, if you listen to it, will claim to be gratified at the expense of the rest."[3]

DEFINING HUMILITY

I tend to be a visual learner and the visual image that defines humility for me is, "Truly, truly, I say to you, unless a grain of wheat falls into the earth and dies, it remains alone; but if it dies, it bears much fruit. Whoever loves his life loses it, and whoever hates his life in this world will keep it for eternal life."[4]

The path to being the life-giving and fruit bearing person God intended for me lies through the doorway of humility. You choose. Lose your life or give it away, but you cannot keep it. To humble myself is to make an intentional turning from "my will" to "his will". Life-giving humility is an active reliance on God instead of my limited self. Notice in the verse the consequence of being alone if we refuse God's breaking us open for the bearing of new life. An image of a proud person in my mind is the lonely leader towering over everyone else with no one to stand alongside.

Humility is NOT. . .

Then Jesus told his disciples, 'If anyone would come after me, let him deny himself and take up his cross and follow me.[5]

What does it look like to deny our self and take up our cross? It is not a self-destructive lifestyle clothed in spirituality that we justify by calling it humble.

Here are some examples of unbiblical self-denial:

> ➤ Dying to one's delight and love for the outdoors
> ➤ Dying to enjoying good friendships which are not in the current place of ministry
> ➤ Dying to a need for silence and solitude
> ➤ Dying to quality time with the extended family
> ➤ Dying to intentional personal growth
> ➤ Dying to consistently investing in our marriage and parenting
> ➤ Dying to ever being extravagant in showing love to another person

And all of these wrongful "deaths" are often justified in the name of being committed to the Lord and the ministry he has called us to serve.

Geri Scazzero captures what I am seeking for leaders to understand so well when she writes:

But we are to die to the sinful parts of who we are—defensiveness, arrogance, hypocrisy, a judgmental spirit, finding our worth and value apart from him—as well as the more obvious sins such as gossip, lying, stealing, coveting and so on. . . . For example, I needed to die to defensiveness and social shame, to a critical spirit, to the need to be right, to my fears of vulnerability and weakness, and to people's approval. . . . The illusions of what it meant to be a good, loving Christian crumbled before me. Now I could begin to die to the right things—my self-protectiveness and fears of rejection. It was like being born again, yet again.[6]

Life-giving humility is placing all of myself in God's hands for his purposes to be accomplished. When this is taking place the prideful stuff described in the above quote from Geri Scazzero is what God wants to kill out in our heart; sinful stuff I can easily excuse through denial, justify through blaming others, or bury it from awareness to my sight. Humility is the heart living with integrity; it is not in a war or division of loyalty. Humility is authenticity; what you see is what is really there and it stands as faithful, trustworthy, and truthful. Humility is vulnerable; an open heart free to risk giving and receiving without conditions.

How do we become Humble?

Seasons of isolation or circumstances where we have lost control and experience a sense of powerlessness may be the "strange minister" God uses to transform one from a reliance on self to a reliance on God and other believers.

For we do not want you to be unaware, brothers, of the affliction we experienced in Asia. For we were so utterly burdened beyond our strength that we despaired of life itself. Indeed, we felt that we had received the sentence of death. **But that was to make us rely not on ourselves but on God who raises the dead.** *He delivered us from such a deadly peril, and he will deliver us. On him we have set our hope that he will deliver us again.* **You also must help us by prayer**, *so that many will give thanks on our behalf for the blessing granted us through the prayers of many.*[7]

Embrace the isolation. Be cautious of shortcuts or fads. Do not buy into any promise of a quick, clean or easy escape. Expect your heart senses to sharpen your ability to see and hear God. Perhaps you have experienced being in total darkness, like we did in a cave in New Zealand. I will never forget how my vision strained to see anything. New insight often comes to the person God is creating you to be when God places you in the dark.

Humility also grows in the soil of selfless service. I once had the honor of walking out of the chapel at Columbia International University after Dr. Stephen Olford had spoken. He was considered one of the greatest preachers of the 20th century and trained thousands in handling God's word. As we were making our way down the aisle, a student asked him, "Dr. Olford, what is the key to effective ministry?" Without pausing, he turned and locked eyes with the student and said, "Bent knees. Broken heart. Wet eyes." Then he turned on his heels and continued to the luncheon. All of us walking with him were stunned into silence. That was not the key we wanted to add to our key ring of experiences. But I have never forgotten that moment, and after many more years of service, I can agree with his sage advice.

Humility is Christ-like

The teaching of Christ turned many of the accepted definitions for living upside down, including the vision of leadership. He described leaders as servants. This was contradictory to everything in the culture which described leadership as the power to gather and then control a stable of servants for the leader's sake. Jesus modeled a leader using power to love and bless others. One crossroad moment came as he stood with Satan and rejected the invitation to rule over all by coming under Satan's rule.

If Jesus had only taken the power to rule the world offered to him by Satan during the wilderness temptation, then we would be at peace and not caught in the heartache of life. . . The temptation for all leaders is to encroach on human freedom and take away the suffering of humanity through some form of authoritarian order.[8]

Jesus would instead rule by laying down his authority. The sacrifice of his life would result in destroying the bondage to sin, Satan and death. Liberating power through humble service is the Jesus model of leadership. Jesus took it even further by not just sacrificing himself for a friend but also sacrificing himself for his enemies. In his leadership, he served by blessing and offered payment by forgiveness to those who intended his destruction.

Jesus was free to be the humble servant because of his greatness. E. Stanley Jones writes:

Conscious of being great with an ultimate greatness he could afford to be humble. Real humility is not rooted in a sense of humiliation; it's rooted in a sense of being inwardly great. The little person [read "insecure"] dare not be humble; it would give away his littleness. He has to act a part, a part of being great in order to compensate for being small. The one who is truly great doesn't have to act a part; he has nothing to keep up. He is great and therefore is released to do the lowly.[9]

I once did a word study on the Hebrew word often translated as "merciful" or in the NIV as "loving kindness". It is used to describe God over thirty times in the Psalms. It means to bow down in loving service. Most of the people groups around the nation of Israel bowed down to serve their idols. But Israel worshiped the God who bowed down to them in loving service. What a contrast. God, surely the greatest, is free to bow down in humility to his creation. If he did not take that posture, we would be lost forever.

So both the teaching and actions of Christ, and a broader look at the character of God, reveal to us the nature of our God; he is the humble servant. This moves humility from a preferred character quality for a leader to the essential core of being like Christ. Pride is not just harmful — it is *un*godly. And while humility is to shape those in leadership because they are granted authority and power over others, it is *the* character trait that sets *all* Christ-followers apart.[10]

Humility Submits to Rightful Rule!

Humility is living with everything we are, desire, or have, joyfully offered in submission to God. Humility is placing all of my life in an open hand held up to God. The humble cry out with Job, "The Lord gives and the Lord takes away, but blessed be the name of the Lord." How we respond to the flow of things and people moving in and out of our life reveals our humility. Humility submits to God's rightful authority.

Humility is living with an open hand

Joseph is a good model of the open-handed life. The one who rose from prison to being the second most powerful man in Egypt did not use his power for revenge but instead brought powerful reconciliation to his family. Also, Esther did not use her power as queen to protect herself but put her life on the line for her the life of her people. Humility uses personal power to serve others.

DEFINING PRIDE

The Lord sends no one away empty except those who are full of themselves.
—*Dwight Moody*

That which of all things unfits man for the reception of Christ as a Saviour, is not gross profligacy and outward, vehement transgression, but it is self-complacency, fatal self-righteousness and self-sufficiency. —Alexander MacLaren

Humility is willing submission to rightful authority. Do not buy into the world's definitions; humility is not weakness. It takes great strength to place ourselves, from the inside out, under the will of another. Pride is rebellion against any ruler exercising authority over our self-rule. Pride is almost always joined by its friends, disunity and impurity. Be alert. This gang often wears clever masks, to remain hidden in our own hearts, and are very subtle in their expression. While these three can have very obvious expressions, they are often clothed more deceptively, especially in Christian leadership. We can easily describe the obvious expressions of these three sins. The pride filled bully or lord who is out to use others to meet his or her needs. Or, the couple who feed on creating division and spreading rumor. There is also the leader who has been living a double life and is suddenly exposed. But perhaps the greatest danger to our souls lies in the more subtle expressions. To get at the more subtle forms of these sins, Jim Mellado, former President of the Willow Creek Association, compares them to athletes using performance enhancing drugs.

I am still tempted to use artificial means of enhancing my performance in ministry. Maybe you've felt the same temptation. They may not be drugs, but they are even more powerful and insidious. It's fuel sources like pride, envy, unresolved hurts and wounds, proving myself to others, people pleasing, and many more. ***Ministry on steroids is using any form of artificial, unnatural sinful sources of fuel to make you come off better than you would otherwise.*** *We all deal with temptation, don't we? We do it every time we're tempted to shave off the truth or exaggerate a bit in a sermon to help God along. We do it when we use other people's material without giving appropriate acknowledgment. We do it when we spend more time and energy protecting than we should. . . To what extent are you "fueled by steroids" in ministry? And, to what extent are you being energized by the appropriate sources of fuel — love, gratitude, obedience, mercy, and compassion. The scary thing about asking this question is that as you become more self-aware of what drives you on the inside, you will discover spiritual steroid use.* [11]

Detecting the Relational Wreckage of Pride

Since our God is humble and we are made in his image; we are made to operate best in relationships with God and people when acting in humility. Pride offends God, casting doubt on his rule and devaluing those we touch in a prideful manner. Yet pride filled relationships are such a common characteristic of the fallen hearts that make up every culture that the effects are often minimized or undetected.

A pride filled heart can wear many different masks.

> ➤ Do you submit to the ones in authority over you including God and any human rulers to whom he has delegated authority?

> ➤ Do you use your power or strength to serve others or to get service from them? Jesus made this a major defining point contrasting the kingdom of God leadership to the rulers of this world. (Matthew 20:24-28; Mark 10:41-45; Luke 22:24-27)

While response to authority and our use of our power defines prideful versus humble choices, it often takes a closer examination to really detect if pride is present. How do we recognize the subtle prideful weed deeply rooted in our soul?

⏱ PAUSE — TRY IT OUT!

Checking my pride gauge

Read through the questions and reflections below and then write out what the Spirit reveals about areas of your heart where pride is the cancer eroding your life.

UNACCOUNTABLE to those above, to those below

> ➤ **In your daily "small" choices are you living for a cause bigger than yourself or is your cause for yourself?** It surely takes courage and tenacity to make a good cross-cultural or multi-cultural worker. But are these strengths unbridled pride when a missionary refuses to provide those in charge of emergency exit plans accurate

information on how to contact them or even choose to ignore a call to move to safer ground?

> **Do you bend easily to the rule of God and those to whom he has delegated authority over you?** When does confronting a person on your team about their weakness, failure or sinful struggle move into being unwilling to forgive and holding their fault as a weight over them? Humility has courage to confront with a goal of restoration, but pride pollutes the goal and makes it about my right for payback.

UNAPPROACHABLE, especially by the unempowered who raise questions

> **Are there certain people who do not count when considering ministry decisions?** Does pride say, "It is easier to ask forgiveness than to get permission"? Doesn't that result in lower levels of trust and freedom in the future? What happens when those under your authority practice what they have seen you do?

> **Are you open to admitting your needs and receiving help, or do you refuse offers of assistance with an attitude of "I can do it by myself"?**

INACCESSIBLE, especially to the "little" people

> **Do you move into relationships with God and others with a DEMANDING manner?**

> **How many people touch your life that you fail to see?** Cab drivers, shop keepers, street sweepers, beggars, police or government officials, etc. I am not saying that humility means we say, "Yes" to every request made of us. But on what basis do we refuse? How can we value the person, even if we refuse to be manipulated by their behavior toward us?

INFALLIBLE, reluctant to consider alternative opinions

> **How often must you be the one to prove you are "right"?**

> **Do I use the excuse of being too tired to excuse forbidding my**

children from questioning a parental choice? I do not mean letting children wear us down by constantly questioning our decision. We had a "family rule" that was, "Because Mom and Dad are not perfect, you can question any decision we make — *one time.* We promise to hear your concern, and rethink the decision. But only once. Do not think you will wear us down. And if you don't like one parent's decision, don't go to the other one. What one of us decides we both support."

IMMUTABLE, finding it difficult to change, especially if the issue is with a decision of the leader or with a tradition of the church or ministry

➤   Where does your flexibility end and resistance begin?

➤   How far will you go to "win"?

God helps me see that I am still under reconstruction as I observe my response to those who interrupt me. "Indicative of a capacity to serve others through availability is a willingness to be interrupted in the midst of a busy schedule. . . . Typical of Christ's availability in the midst of a hectic schedule is the episode described in Mark 1:32-39."[12] Interruptions are perhaps God's most frequently used device to expose my pride. A friend of mine reminds me from time to time, "We want to be servant leaders, but few of us want to be treated like one."

Often we detect what is false by focusing on what is true. A behavior found frequently in humble people but rarely in the prideful is vulnerability. Pastor Don lists it as a core value of his personal life and the church he leads. Here he defines and describes the value of vulnerability:

Vulnerability means being honest and transparent about the journey we're on. It's about telling the great stories, but not only the great stories. It's the willingness to disclose the darker parts; the broken regions; the parts that we are tempted to skillfully manage and present like a spin doctor might, rather than simply telling the raw, unflattering truth. Vulnerability allows us to acknowledge, up front, that we're not perfect or problem-free. Every person's journey has good and heroic parts, and dark and cowardly episodes.

There are no experts in this journey, just some who have been covered by grace for longer than others.

Patrick Lencioni, in his book *The Five Dysfunctions of a Team* observes that trust is the most powerful trait in shaping a positive culture. 'When there is an absence of trust', he says, 'it stems from a leader's unwillingness to be vulnerable with the group. . . leaders who are not genuinely open with one another about their mistakes and weaknesses make it impossible to build trust.'[13]

Three Faces of Pride

How we respond to God's authority over us determines whether we are cultivating a heart of pride or humility. Basically the humble see God as their only help and source for their life. Joy for the humble is found in trusting God as the provider of life and seeing God's life flow through them to others. They truly believe their blessing is greater in giving than in receiving. The humble can only be satisfied with blessing flowing in and then flowing through them. The humble one's vision is childlike— they depend on another to provide life for them, and they are thrilled with delight at giving it.

In contrast, pride and lust are close siblings. Hoarding and measuring, and sequestering away what one has describe the prideful heart.

The humble believe, *without faith it is impossible to please him, for whoever would draw near to God must believe that he exists and. . .* they wake up each day confident *that he rewards those who seek him.*[14] God clearly states that the only way to please him is the faith life; believing that *he is and he rewards* those seeking him. Pride cannot flourish in this faith based relationship.

There are three circumstances that can substitute for humble submission to Jesus as Lord of our heart.

Intentional Choice

If we choose replace God with an idol, we are rewriting Hebrews 11:6 in our heart. The Self-Perverted Version (You don't buy the SPV translation in the bookstore but most of us have a copy) reads, *"And without faith in your idol it is impossible to please yourself, for whoever would draw near the idol must believe the idol IS and the idol REWARDS those who seek it."*

Rebellion is an expression of the pride of intentional choice because I want to choose my own God. I don't want to live according to his laws.

Be alert to a specific conviction by the Spirit as he exposes whatever is replacing God in your heart. Pride chooses idols (who promise power or protection) or self (many idols are simply masks for the ultimate idol of self-worship) over God. Even good things, like ministry goals, can become idols in the hands of a pride filled person.

The trouble with goals is that they so easily, so imperceptibly, so subtly, so irresistibly, become gods! [15]

Unintentional Choice

We get distracted, busy, and overwhelmed; we forget about God. If a hurried person wrote Hebrews 11:6 to fit how they live, it would change to, *"I forget GOD IS— and I think I must EARN his reward".*

At least one deeply rooted sin in the busy life is pride. Pride drives us and demands of us a sacrifice of our self to the busy life. **Drifting** is the expression of the pride of unintentional choice. I ignore my need for pace and rhythm and experience fatigue. I basically live as an atheist, not in my beliefs, but in my efforts to live life and conduct ministry in my own strength.

Nothing happens in the proud heart. It is disconnected from the flow of God's grace and the presence of God. Humility is multi-dimensional. A humble heart is humble toward God. All else is abandoned to a preference for him and his will to be done. A humble heart is a patient, enduring, peacemaker with others. A humble heart is aware of the weak. [16]

An unhurried life reflects the deliberate chosen pace of a humble heart. Why? Because, as I live with humility, I am bowing my knees to God and live only to please him. Simplicity to rest at God's command and to work at God's command involves me running my life with only one person in the audience—God.

Pride pushes me to live in the past and continually rehearse my decisions, not with a motive of learning from them, but with a deep sense of regret over a failed performance. Pride also pushes me into the future. I create multiple scenarios and prepare for a response that feeds my desire to be in control. All of that time travel in my mind is fatiguing. In contrast, humility is connected to living, trusting, and obeying in the PRESENT moment. We learn from the past and lean into the future with hope, but we can only love and trust and seek God in the present moment. The only place where you can live by faith is the present.

Unbelief

Hebrews 11:6 by the heart filled with unbelief would be rewritten as, *"I don't believe he is or that he rewards."*

My faith is shaken and shrinks before my FEARS. Fear seems logical in an unsafe world, but faith seems childish, foolish, and naive. What feeds our fears? Do we fear disappointing others? What is the difference between respecting others by valuing their concerns and convictions and letting other people's opinions erode a risk taking faith in God? Humility is a friend of faith while pride has fear as a mate.

Unbelief is pride covered over with fear and worry. Pride rewrites my job description to include the line, "Always please everyone; never disappoint yourself or anyone else, and you must take on everyone's expectations for your life." Unbelief leaves me standing alone with the world on my shoulders. Will you accept the job?

SPIRITUAL PRACTICES THAT TRANSFORM PRIDE INTO HUMILITY

I have chosen to write this section with your involvement. How can you only TALK about spiritual practices? Instead, let us PRACTICE together. Let us reflect on living in a place of tension between my responsibility and God's grace filled acceptance. Let us explore that space between our choosing and God's doing.

⏱ PAUSE — TRY IT OUT!

Trusting in my performance is fertile soil for growing pride fruit

If possible, read this parable out loud and change your voice to sound the way you think the two men would sound. Come on… get into it. But not if you're sitting in a coffee shop; that would be too embarrassing.

*He also told this parable to some **who trusted in themselves that they were righteous, and treated others with contempt:** 'Two men went up into the temple to pray, one a Pharisee and the other a tax collector. The Pharisee, standing by himself, prayed thus: 'God, I thank you that I am not like other men, extortioners, unjust, adulterers, or even like this tax collector. I fast twice a week; I give tithes of all that I get.' But the tax collector, standing far off, would not even lift up his eyes to heaven, but beat his breast, saying, 'God, be merciful to me, a sinner!' I tell you, this man went down to his house justified, rather than the other. **For everyone who exalts himself will be humbled, but the one who humbles himself will be exalted.***[17]

Reflect on these questions.

1. Am I trusting in my own behavior to justify myself?
2. Am I treating others with contempt? (Even if you don't say it—are you thinking it?)
3. What do I hold up to God as evidence for God to bless me?

I seem to remember that the Bible says something about, "God resisting the proud but giving grace to the humble." It is very important that a group of Christ-followers develop a common heart of seeking God in humility together. We are also instructed to humble ourselves. (James 4:10, 1 Peter 5:6) When we consistently engage in activities that unleash God's grace and truth in our hearts, we are more likely to develop a humble spirit.

Spiritual disciplines help cultivate humility and pull up the weeds of pride. Yes, spiritual disciplines can also be the best friend of the prideful Pharisee. But that does not make prayer or fasting bad. It is another example of my proverb, **"Anything powerful can also be dangerous."** So, how can spiritual disciplines be used from a right motive and help stimulate us to humility?

One's character does not remain static. It is either developing or decaying. The indwelling Spirit of Christ will patiently and mercifully expose where God wants to work next. Thankfully, God's Spirit does not deal with every sinful attitude, word or deed at our conversion. A way of describing these changes as we grow in Christ is we are "*being* transformed" (notice this change is an ongoing process) to a higher degree of glory (more and more reflecting the glory of God).

And we all, with unveiled face, beholding the glory of the Lord, are **being transformed** into the same image from **one degree of glory to another.** For this comes from the Lord who is the Spirit.[18]

God, in mercy, exposes an attitude, a way of speaking or an action that has been a part of us— sometimes for years. In that moment, the Spirit will use the Bible, another person, or a circumstance to get our attention and say, "Today, for your good and the glory of God we are going to begin to convict you at this point and bring glorious change and freedom." Our first response may be, "But God, I have always _____ (fill in the blank)". But the Spirit will not back down. To enjoy full fellowship, we must confess, repent, and in faith embrace this new aspect of obedience. Sin has created such pollution in the very core of our soul that God gently works in us like peeling down through the layers of an onion. He does not target everything in us that needs to change at one time. I am not sure we could emotionally handle it.

God uses commitments and relationships to bring to light what we cannot see prior to that setting. I thought I was really mature and had dealt with the sin of demanding my own way—and then God gave me a wife. As a married man, I saw sin that had gone undetected in me when single. Then when I thought I had dealt with most of my character sin, God gave me children to parent. The Spirit began to use my attempts to parent to reveal new areas of sin which I was blind to B.C. (Before Children).

God will use moving outside your passport culture and living with people who have very different family and cultural backgrounds to bring new levels of conviction to change you into new levels of glory. God sent me to Russia, where I stood for six hours in a cold Moscow airport hoping to board a plane…. Well you get the idea!

God will not work through PRIDE. He will blow it up! I have tried to arm wrestle with God, wanting to win the right to live my way. I always lose, thank God. There is only one LORD and KING.

⏱ PAUSE — TRY IT OUT!

God's Counsel to those wrestling with pride

Read these passages over slowly and prayerfully. After you complete each passage, write out what you sense the Spirit teaching you from the passage. Where is God in a wrestling match with your heart? Anticipate the Spirit bringing to light something you have been thinking, saying or doing for years now and calling you to "wise changes".

Proverbs 16:5-6 (ESV)

*Everyone who **is arrogant in heart*** (sounds like pride) *is an abomination to the LORD; be assured, he will not go unpunished. By steadfast love and faithfulness iniquity is atoned for, and by the fear of the LORD one turns away from evil.*

Psalm 16:7-8 (ESV)

***I bless** the LORD who gives me counsel; in the night also my heart instructs me. **I have set** the LORD always before me; because he is at my right hand, I shall not be shaken.* (Notice my action is a good description for many of the spiritual disciplines. "I bless" — praise, worship, thanksgiving, sing, etc., "I set" — meditation, journaling, study, prayer, etc.)

2 Timothy 2:19-26 (ESV)

*But God's firm foundation stands, bearing this seal: 'The Lord knows those who are his,' and, 'Let everyone who names the name of the Lord **depart** from iniquity.' Now in a great house there are not only vessels of gold and silver but also of wood and clay, some for honorable use, some for dishonorable. Therefore, if anyone **cleanses himself from what is dishonorable**, he will be a vessel for honorable use, set apart as holy, useful to the master of the house, **ready for every good work**. So **flee** youthful passions and **pursue** righteousness, faith, love, and peace, **along with those** who call on the Lord from a pure heart. **Have nothing*** *to do with* *foolish, ignorant controversies; you know that they breed quarrels. And the Lord's servant* **must not be quarrelsome but kind** *to everyone,* **able to teach, patiently enduring evil, correcting his opponents with gentleness.** *God may perhaps grant them repentance leading to a knowledge of the truth, and they may come to their senses and escape from the snare of the devil, after being captured by him to do his will.* (What a great word for Jesus-followers. Look at the actions to pursue and prideful actions to avoid. Notice too, this person is now prepared for "every good work" and to be used as a witness to those who are being blinded by the devil. The person Paul is describing sounds like someone receiving and giving the life of God!)

⏱ PAUSE — TRY IT OUT!

Pride polluting my relationships

Pray and ask the Spirit to make you aware of how pride shows up in your relationships by thinking through these descriptions and questions. Start with your relationship to your spouse and children, and then move out to fellow workers from the same organization, other workers, nationals, etc.

Read:

1. Proverbs 11:2
2. Proverbs 29:23
3. Luke 18:9-14
4. James 4:6
5. 1 Peter 3:8
6. 1 Peter 5:5

Reflect on how these faces of pride show up in relationships. What do these passages offer that might help:

➤ Intentional choosing of idols to displace my submission to God
➤ Unintentional choosing that comes from ignoring God; forgetting he is there
➤ Unbelief that produces fear and worry

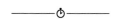

Roy King

⏱ PAUSE — TRY IT OUT!

Reconstruction in the leader's heart

Examine carefully 1 Peter 5:1-11.[19] In the first column, list the attitudes and practices of humble leaders. In the second column, list those qualities that should not be present. In the third column, list the blessings of God that help cultivate the positive and weed out the negative traits. I have listed one in each column to get you started.

Ten Character Qualities +	Three Character Qualities -	Eight Gifts From God (Seeds that grow character)
Willingly (5:2)	Not under compulsion (5:2)	Will receive the unfading crown of glory (5:4)

The correct answers are: Ten Positive Character Qualities

1. Willingly (5:2)
2. Eagerly (5:2)
3. Being examples (5:3)

4. Clothed w/ humility toward one another (5:5)
5. Humble yourself under God (5:6)
6. Casting all your anxieties on him (5:7)
7. Sober minded (5:8)
8. Watchful (5:8)
9. Resist the devil (5:9)
10. Suffered a little while (5:10)

Three Negative Character Qualities

1. Not under compulsion (5:2)
2. Not shameful gain (5:2)
3. Not domineering (5:3)

Eight Gifts from God

1. Will receive the unfading crown of glory (5:4)
2. Gives grace (5:5)
3. Exalts you (5:6)
4. He cares for you (5:7)
5. Will himself restore
6. Will himself confirm
7. Will himself strengthen
8. Will himself establish you (5:10)

List some people who are good examples of this humble leadership.

Give an example when leadership became toxic and destructive because some of the negative qualities from 1 Peter were dominant.

What about you? How do you let the gifts (third column) from God grow the positive qualities?

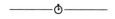

Group Exercise: Confessing Pride and Seeking Humility

In leadership we need to develop the skill of bringing others on the same journey we are taking. Here is one exercise I have used with groups in churches and organizations from many different settings to help them detect how the heart that is not bowing down in humility is at the root of many relational and ministry problems.

Instructions for a Group (1 hour)

Have the participants form groups of three, men with men and women with women. Do not give out the handout at this point.

Explain how essential humility is to the work of God in and through a congregation. Prepare for this introduction by studying all of the passages that are variations on this idea: "God resists the proud but gives grace to the humble" (Proverbs 3:34; 18:12; James 4:6, 1 Peter 5:5). Explain how healthy spiritual community is filled with coming together to practice spiritual disciplines, which open our lives to God's transforming grace. Other examples include sharing testimonies in thanks to God, singing, sharing communion, and financial giving. Each of these touches different parts of our lives with God's grace. Now we are going to practice one that has often not been practiced; we are going to confess sin and seek humility.

Distribute the handout. In groups of three they are to engage in a time of prayer. But this is a special time of prayer.

Instructions:

➤ Person 1 will read the first statements describing a proud person contrasted to the broken person. (Example: "The proud focus on the failure of others but the humble are overwhelmed with their own spiritual need".)

➤ After he/she reads softly, let the group be quiet in prayer.

➤ If the Spirit convicts someone in the group that they need to confess, they should quietly confess in prayer to God how that expression of pride has been true of them.

➤ After the confession, anyone else in the group can quietly pray a simple prayer acknowledging God's forgiveness and cleansing. Something like, "Lord Jesus, I thank you that your blood has cleansed my brother's sin he has brought to you."

➤ After a few moments, Person 2 reads the next line in the handout and process continues.

➤ If no one offers a confession after a few moments, Person 3 reads the next line.

➤ You might not complete the entire sheet in the time we have for this exercise, but it will help introduce us to seeking godly humility together.

➤ Remind the Christ-followers that the details of a sin need not be disclosed beyond the people directly impacted by it. We should be sensitive to balancing transparency about God's work in our hearts with sharing inappropriate information with those who do not understand the context or have no involvement with the situation.

After the prayer time discuss what they learned from this experience.

Discuss various ways this type of honest confession could be practiced in small groups and other settings. Also discuss possible dangers or abuses that should be avoided.

CONFESSING PRIDE & SEEKING GOD'S GRACE OF HUMILITY[20]

Proud, Unbroken People	Broken People
Focus on the failures of others	Are overwhelmed with their own spiritual need
Are self-righteous; have a critical, fault-finding spirit; look at own life/ faults with a telescope but others with a microscope	Are compassionate; have a forgiving spirit look for best in others
Look down on others	Esteem all others better than self
Are independent; have a self-sufficient spirit	Have a dependent spirit; recognize needs of others
Maintain control; must have their own way	Surrender control
Have to prove they are right	Are willing to yield the right to be right
Claim rights	Yield rights
Have a demanding spirit	Have a giving spirit

Are self-protective of time, rights, reputation	Are self-denying
Desire to be served	Are motivated to serve others
Desire to be a success	Desire to be faithful to make others a success
Desire for self-advancement	Desire to promote others
Are driven to be recognized and appreciated	Have a sense of unworthiness; are thrilled to be used at all; are eager for others to get the credit
Are wounded when others are promoted and they are overlooked	Rejoice when others are lifted up
Think "The ministry is privileged to have me!"	Think, "I don't deserve to serve in this ministry!"
Feel confident in how much they know	Know that they have nothing to offer God; are humbled by how much they have to learn
Are self-conscious	Have no concern with self at all
Keep people at arm's length	Risk getting close to others; are willing to take risk of loving intimately
Are quick to blame others	Accept personal responsibility; can see where they were wrong
Are unapproachable	Are easy to be entreated
Are defensive when criticized	Receive criticism with a humble, open heart
Are concerned with being respectable	Are concerned with being real
Are concerned about what others think	Know all that matters is what God thinks
Work to maintain image and protect reputation	Die to own reputation
Find it difficult to share their spiritual needs with others	Are willing to be transparent with others
Want to be sure no one finds out about their sin	Are willing to be exposed; know once broken, there's nothing to lose
Have a hard time saying, "I was wrong. Would you forgive me?"	Are quick to admit fault and to seek forgiveness
Deal in generalities when confessing sin	Deal in specifics when confessing sin

Are only concerned about consequences of their sin. Are remorseful for being caught.	Are grieved over the root of their sin; are repentant over sin and forsake it
Wait for the other party to come and ask for forgiveness in a conflict	Take the initiative to be reconciled; get there first
Compare themselves with others and feel deserving of honor	Compare themselves with God's holiness; feel desperate for mercy
Are blind to their true heart condition	Walk in the light
Don't think they have anything of which to repent	Have a continual heart attitude toward repentance
Don't think they need revival (think everyone else does)	Continually sense their need for a fresh encounter with the filling of the Spirit

A community of people who live out of brokenness instead of pride are ready to be life-giving people. When this occurs, it is often followed by a revival that accelerates a renewal and advance of the church. Robert Coleman describes it in this way:

Those of us who have seen this happen have learned anew that God's power shines only through broken and contrite spirits. Self-disclosure in one person encourages honesty in another troubled heart. And by sharing our weaknesses we are drawn closer to each other for strength. That is why it can be said that revival begins when we quit confessing other people's sins and start confessing our own.[21]

CONCLUSION

The incarnation of Christ made visible, in flesh, the heart of our God. The almost unbelievable character quality at the center of his life was his HUMILITY. Once we see humility as godly, we can begin to see pride in all of its destructive ungodliness. We can also see how pride grows in a heart that is rebelling against God, forgetting and failing to acknowledge God, and not believing in his goodness towards us.

Individuals and a community of Christ-followers can practice spiritual practices that unleash God's grace and truth to grow humble disciples.

Those living humbly under Christ's lordship have a fearless boldness.

The commission of Christ to make disciples among all peoples was sandwiched between his claim to possess all rule and authority and the promise of his presence with his disciples throughout all time. The humble know they bear his name and therefore exercise his authority over enemies and each day they rest securely in his presence.

This poem by a missionary pictures this godly fearless humility. This poem was sent by John Stam to his family shortly before his martyrdom in China. It was written by J.W. Vinson; a fellow missionary.

AFRAID?

Afraid? Of What?
To feel the Spirit's glad release?
To pass from pain to perfect peace?
The strife and strain of life to cease?
Afraid? Of That?

Afraid? Of What?
Afraid to see the Savior's face?
To hear His Welcome and to trace
The glory gleams from wounds of grace?
Afraid? Of That?

Afraid? Of What?
A flash — a crash — a pierced heart?
Darkness — light — O heaven's art!
A wound of his counterpart!
Afraid? Of That?

Afraid? Of What?
To do by death what life could not —
Baptize with blood a stony plot,
Till souls shall blossom from the spot?
Afraid? Of that?

Are you seeing God's hand in your world? Are you hearing God's voice through his word and by the Spirit in our heart? Are you bowing down as humble servants before our great and holy God? These are the activities going on continually in a heart receiving life from God.

The actions of seeing, hearing and bowing down position our hearts to be life-giving leaders.

RESOURCES FOR LIFELONG LEARNING

1. Nancy DeMoss. *Brokenness: The Heart God Revives.* Chicago: Moody Publishers, 2002. (Nancy spoke at Campus Crusade for Christ staff training in Colorado and God visited them with several days of deep revival and awakening. All meetings were canceled for several days after she spoke, and instead, staff stood in lines to confess sin and be prayed over. This book is based on that experience.)

2. Robertson McQuilkin. *Five Smooth Stones: Essential Principles of Biblical Ministry.* Nashville: Broadman & Holman, 2007. (See Unit V for chapters on leaders living under the lordship of Christ).

3. Alan Nelson. *Broken In The Right Place: How God Tames the Soul.* Nashville: Thomas Nelson, 1994. (This book and his books entitled *Spirituality & Leadership* and *The Five Secrets of Becoming a Leader* are excellent, practical and biblical guides to godly leadership).

4. Henri Nouwen. *In the Name of Jesus (Reflections on Christian Leadership)* Chicago: Crossroad Publishing, 1992. (I read this once a year. His reflections on the three temptations of Christ applied to the Christian worker are very helpful)

CHAPTER EIGHT

GOD'S PRIORITIES FOR THE HEART: TRUSTING, ENDURING, GIVING

Faith is taking the first step even when you can't see the whole staircase.
—Martin Luther King Jr.

Faith sees the invisible, believes the unbelievable, and receives the impossible.

—Corrie Ten Boom

USE YOUR IMAGINATION. Go to this place with me.

As far as we know there are no living Christ-followers among this people group. You are praying and pursuing "zero to one", the first convert. There is a search for the "man of peace" that will open doors for the gospel and validate your voice as one deserving a respectful hearing. As you move among the people where Jesus wants to be known, you are aware of the challenges and a feeling of resistance that slowly grind on you and the other helpers around you.

How do you define how God is working INSIDE of your own heart in this challenging place?

Turn the page in your imagination to another chapter.

It is your home town. Over coffee, a young woman on the edge of "crossing over" to faith begins to ask questions of the Bible she started reading recently. She asks you to explain how a loving God could allow the people he loves to suffer and struggle. It is an honest question, not a smoke screen.

The question beneath her questions is, "Can I really give my heart to this God of the Bible? Can I trust his heart?"

Travel with me to another time and another place.

A new believer is in a study with you on baptism. You describe the imagery of coming out of the water as being a picture of a new birth in Christ. He asks what this "new life" will be like. What does he have to give up if becomes a Christ-follower? What can he expect to change in his life?

How do you give a clear summary of the glorious new life in Christ?

In each of these different scenarios, the question is, "What is a life-giving leadership contribution?" How do I help myself and others understand what God is doing? One definition of leadership is to find where God is working and join him—where do I look and how do I know what God is doing?

If I focus on a list of Christian beliefs, I suspect that almost every person attending a church would affirm them as truth. Yet many of these church-going Christians fail to look like those described in the book of Acts. The church in my passport culture is filled with nominal cultural believers whose faith does not measure up to the faith I have discovered when visiting places where believers are a small, and often persecuted, minority of the population. While beliefs are important, I do not sense this is the place to begin.

I could share a list of behaviors that are commonly practiced in churches, but I know the danger of defining the Christian life as a checklist of good and bad choices. I do not want to grow the church by adding more Christians who are worn out from trying to work hard enough to please God and earn his favor.

Disciples often tell their journey by recounting certain experiences. A moving emotional surrender at a retreat, a hunger for God triggered by someone with a contagious spirit, a desire to have one's life count after an evening of missionary testimonies are all valuable. Life changing events are a part of most journeys, but there is a danger of building our vision of the Christian life around them. We begin to seek to copy someone else's moments with God, or we are constantly searching for the next experience that will finally break us free or take us to the next level of maturity.

How can we really understand and then cooperate with what God is doing in us?

I wonder if the answer can be found in the first generation of believers who were trying to make disciples when Christ was no longer physically present to follow around.

What was the center of the target for those followers of Christ?

How would they describe the dynamic process and outcome of the Christian life?

How did they define growth or detect a failure to mature?

I decided to start with Romans and read through to Revelation looking for clues. After several weeks I got to the end without a clear answer so I went back and started reading again. I then switched translations and started reading again. My third time through I thought I was finally seeing a pattern. So as I read Romans through Revelation for the fourth time, I marked every occurrence of what I suspected was the center of God's activity.

What was that one overarching story line for the Christ-follower? Here are some of the passages I uncovered. Join me in the discovery.

⏱ PAUSE — TRY IT OUT!

What is a biblical description of God's work in the heart?

Read them all and then see if you can list the three repeated words:

1. Romans 5:1-8
2. 1 Corinthians 13:13
3. Colossians 1:4-5
4. 1 Thessalonians 1:3
5. 1 Thessalonians 5:8
6. 2 Thessalonians 1:3-4
7. Hebrews 10:22-24

AND THE ANSWER IS: The New Testament writers witnessed to God growing **faith, hope and love** in the heart of every Christian.

The only thing that really counts is **THE HEART growing in faith, hope and love**. To describe these characteristics as active verbs: the heart is **TRUSTING, ENDURING AND GIVING**. God working in the heart by the Spirit transforms a fearful, despairing, lustful heart into a heart filled with faith, hope and love.

In the New Testament letters I believe we are observing healthy leadership supplying the three resources that God uses to develop faith, hope and love in the hearts of all those in the community:

> ➤ **DIRECTION** (critical to growing faith). Direction includes clearly counting the cost and knowing both the ultimate, *long term destination* and *the next step*. After taking a step, direction includes pausing to revisit and formulate the plan for the next step.

> ➤ **DEVELOPMENT** (seeing potential and enduring in hope). Development believes in *growth, maturity, and the persevering spirit* required to achieve it. Development also sees potential that others may not see. If I listed all of the problems in the church at Corinth, we would all question if it could ever make a Jesus glorifying impact. But Paul saw the potential because the Spirit of Christ was in them.

> ➤ **DEVOTION** (vibrant, giving love). Giving is praised in the letters. Giving is encouraged and expected. Gratitude for giving is in several letters. The essence of God's love is he gave his son.

Show me leadership consistently calling a community to live from a sense of clear direction, positive perseverance and giving from love, and I will show you people who are growing in faith, hope and love.

TRUSTING = FAITH

Hebrews 11:6 clearly states that without faith it is impossible to please God. God pleasing leadership will always lead God's people into places where they have never been before, stepping out to pursue outcomes they cannot control or guarantee. Leadership often requires, by faith, pruning the good to invest in what we see to be God's best. Life-giving leadership sees God inviting us to be part of an advance that shatters the gates of hell. Show me any leader in the Bible whom God called to play it safe. Jesus' incarnation clearly models a leadership strategy of costly sacrifice crying out for the Father's will to be done in the face of incredible risk and loss. Was that part of what Paul meant by joining in fellowship with the suffering of Christ?

Abraham is considered the father of the faith. He is held up as a model of faith, but he had to grow his trust with God. As Abraham grew in faith, he always had to let go of something in his life to receive the blessing God had for him. Let's survey three of Abraham's critical faith tests that were used to grow his trust in God.

1. In Genesis 12, Abraham first encounters God. God asks him to leave his land and go to a place he had never been. He was giving up his SECURITY and trusting God to be the source of his security.

2. In Genesis 17, twenty five years have gone by since Genesis 12. Abraham has fathered Ishmael with Sarah's handmaid. He assumes God's promise of a son is in place. God confronts Abraham and he has to give up using his own STRENGTH to carry out God's plan.

3. In Genesis 22, God has provided Isaac through the "dead" womb of Sarah and he has grown into young manhood. Now the test involves Abraham giving up God's BLESSING, the fruit of his life with Sarah.

Abraham was learning to cling to God and to not lose focus. Faith had to be in God alone— he could not even trust in the beloved blessing God had provided.[1] Abraham had a word from God and he had to trust God for resources that he could not supply himself. Faith was expressed as Abraham took steps of obedience in light of God's promise. Faith always calls for trust, risk, and turning "from" in order to turn "to". When we move by faith we have an intentional DIRECTION for our choices. Faith is our response to God's adventure for our lives. A step of faith is God's way of taking us outside our comfort zone (which is too often trusting in ourselves rather than hanging on to God). Our adventure can be as close as stepping out to love an enemy next door by faith. Or it may involve a greater sacrifice.

⏱ PAUSE — TRY IT OUT!

Images of trusting

Read the following passages and describe how the images used help us picture the faith God is working to grow in our lives.

1. Psalm 131
2. Psalm 56
3. Luke 7:1-10
4. 2 Timothy 2:1-13

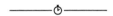

Life-giving leadership happens in the present life where we make choices. We can make choices based on the past work of Christ and the present reality of Christ indwelling.

I have been crucified with Christ. It is no longer I who live, but Christ who lives in me. **And the life I now live in the flesh I live by faith in the Son of God,** *who loved me and gave himself for me.*[2]

We can place our faith in hoping to do enough to please others. Or we can place our faith in a self confidence that is supplied with our own strength. Where will we look? Here is what God says about our other options.

Thus says the LORD: 'Cursed is the man who trusts in man and makes flesh his strength, whose heart turns away from the LORD.'[3]

⏱ PAUSE — TRY IT OUT!

Examination of my faith

How can you know if your faith is not truly in God? Spend some time in reflection on these questions.

1. Where do I turn when I experience a crisis?
2. When I am hurting or afraid, to whom do I go?
3. When I have a financial problem, whom do I want to tell first?
4. Where do I seek comfort when I am under stress or discouraged?[4]

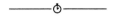

Faith is often seen in our movement toward a destination or a step of obedience. The faith stories of Hebrews 11 are often consulted to understand the dynamics of trusting God. *Faith was most often expressed in obedient action, which often involved a journey into a place where one had never been before.*

If there is no grand adventure before you right now, maybe your journey is simply taking the next step in obedience. The place you have never been before may be a new lifestyle that is shedding the sin the Spirit is touching and helping you to see. My friend, Pastor Robert Morgan writes:

To measure your faith, pull out the dipstick of obedience. Does God tell us to build up others with our words? To be kind to one another, tenderhearted, forgiving one another? To do the work of an evangelist? To avoid sexual immorality? To keep our eyes from vanity? To meditate on Scripture? Scottish novelist George MacDonald said, 'You can begin at once to be a disciple of the Living One—by obeying him in the first thing you can think of in which you are not obeying Him. We must learn to obey him in everything, and so must begin somewhere. Let it be at once, and in the very next thing that lies at the door of our conscience.'[5]

When I was a high school basketball player (who sat on the bench most games) one of our exercises was for the coach to surprise a player. "Think fast!" he would say, and then throw the ball to a player who was looking somewhere else. The goal was to sharpen our reflexes, but the frequent result was the air knocked out of us. Jesus says, "Obey fast!" Then watch faith, hope and love grow.

THE OPPOSITE OF FAITH IS FEAR

Faith is confident belief that we put our weight on. Fear is a paralysis or retreating because we do not believe God is up to the challenge of caring for us.

Fear shows up dressed in many scary costumes:

1. Fear of failure
2. Fear of rejection

3. Fear of not having the right answer
4. Fear of being alone
5. Fear of pain

When you are afraid remind yourself that the power of fear, like your faith, depends on its object. Faith has no value if the object of one's faith does not have the power or desire to come through. The same is true of fear. And remember the words of Jesus—we should not fear the one who can only destroy the body in light of the God we worship who can destroy the soul.[6]

Fear tends to paralyze us and stop our forward progress. Now we begin to see a connection between faith and enduring, persevering, hope. Have you ever been to a hospital "waiting room"? I believe we spend most of our life in various "waiting rooms". We are waiting for the answer to the prayer. We continue on while waiting for the resources that would push the project across the finish line. We wait for a friend to come apologize, a family member to offer forgiveness, an adult child to repent and return home. It is in the waiting rooms of life where those full of hope shine like light in darkness.

Count it all joy, my brothers, when you meet trials of various kinds, for you know that the *testing of your faith produces steadfastness.* And let steadfastness have its full effect, that you may be perfect and complete, lacking in nothing. [7]

Steadfast is a good word for hope. Let's examine biblical hope more closely.

ENDURING = HOPE

We must meet the uncertainties of this world with the certainty of the world to come. —A. W. Tozer

Many Christians don't fail; they just quit before they get ripe.[8] —Gary Thomas

What is biblical hope?

To them God chose to make known how great among the Gentiles are the riches of the glory of this mystery, which is **Christ in you, the hope of glory.**[9]

Our hope of being able to endure to the end and make it home, is based on one truth. Jesus has already made the journey that led through suffering and death back to the Father. He has promised to be with us as we make the journey. We are even going to run a victory lap with him when he returns to establish the new heavens and the new earth.

The Lord is not slow to fulfill his promise as some count slowness, but is patient toward you, not wishing that any should perish, but that all should reach repentance. But the day of the Lord will come like a thief, and then the heavens will pass away with a roar, and the heavenly bodies will be burned up and dissolved, and the earth and the works that are done on it will be exposed. **Since all these things are thus to be dissolved, what sort of people ought you to be in lives of holiness and godliness.**[10]

The writer of Hebrews 11 reminds us that the characters listed there were looking for the King to come. We are looking for the King to complete the victory he has won. What will be the nature of the completed kingdom? Earlier we mentioned living daily with a present kingdom mentality. The kingdom mentality also includes a future climactic finale!

Would you be comfortable living in a kingdom of:

- Universal Joy - Isaiah 61:2-3 Jeremiah 31:12.
- Universal Social Justice - Isaiah 65:21-22
- Worldwide Reclamation of Ecology - Isaiah 61:4; Psalm 72:16
- International Governing Authority - Isaiah 2:2,4
- Universal Language - Zephaniah 3:9
- Worldwide Agricultural Productivity - Joel 2:21-24; Ezekiel 34:26; Isaiah 30:25; Isaiah 35:6-7; Ezekiel 47:1-12; Zechariah 14:8; Isaiah 35:1-2; Psalm 72:16; Isaiah 32:15
- Total Providential Control of Accidents - Ezekiel 34:2,25; Isaiah 11:6-8; Psalm 91:10-12; Isaiah 65:23
- Global Center for Worship - Zechariah 14:16
- Personal Rewards for Kingdom Citizens - Revelation 19:9; Matthew 26:29; Matthew 5:5; Romans 8:17; Matthew 19:28-29.
- Eternal Stability of the Kingdom - Hebrews 12:28

Life-giving hope makes present choices in light of an anticipated future.

⏱ PAUSE — TRY IT OUT!

Choosing today in light of tomorrow's certainty

Read the following passages asking yourself how much the second coming of Christ influences your perspective. Write out a prayer that would express biblical hope.

And the glory of the Lord shall be revealed, and all flesh shall see it together, for the mouth of the Lord has spoken.[11]

As for that in the good soil, they are those who, hearing the word, hold it fast in an honest and good heart, and bear fruit with patience.[12]

May the Lord direct your hearts to the love of God and to the steadfastness of Christ.[13]

For the grace of God has appeared, bringing salvation for all people, training us to renounce ungodliness and worldly passions, and to live self-controlled, upright, and godly lives in the present age, ***waiting for our blessed hope, the appearing of the glory of our great God and Savior Jesus Christ****, who gave himself for us to redeem us from all lawlessness and to purify for himself a people for his own possession who are zealous for good works. Declare these things; exhort and rebuke with all authority. Let no one disregard you.*[14]

Besides this you know the time that the hour has come for you to wake from sleep. For salvation is nearer to us now than when we first believed. The night is far gone; the day is at hand. So then let us cast off the works of darkness and put on the armor of light. The night is almost over and daylight is on the way.[15]

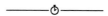

When teaching on faith, hope and love with groups of Jesus-followers I ask them to list their favorite passages on each. Hebrews 11 always comes for faith and 1 Corinthians 13 for love. Often there is only silence on hope passages. Why? I am not really sure. One guess is that many of the hope passages speak of endurance and perseverance in light of the certain hope of Christ's return. Maybe we don't teach the hope passages because we are not presently facing persecution or attack. Or maybe we do not want to get into some of the ambiguous details of eschatology. Whatever the reason, I am deeply burdened by the loss of hope in many parts of the church. That is one reason I tend to preach on hope when I have opportunity.

To not be full of hope is a tragic loss for us. I meet leaders who have lost hope and are ready to walk away. I meet former Jesus-followers who have closed the chapter on hope and moved on. I, myself, struggle to keep a hopeful, anticipating, positive spirit. I have met hope filled followers, who radiate joy and perseverance in China and Egypt. Persecution and impeding or real loss in the present often purifies, matures, and deepens hope. (There are those "strange ministers" again!)

The opposite of *hoping* is *quitting*. Hope is defined by the weight of the challenges it is enduring. I saw it last year in a former missionary who had served in China for many years and was now home to die from breast cancer. The doctors were surprised by how long she lived when the cancer reoccurred in her spine, an eye and then her liver. Her focus was to receive each day as a gift from God and to use it to love with very little focus on her own needs.

Suffering and loss in this life are described by Paul as weights on a scale. Paul concludes that the weight of glory makes the weight of suffering, in contrast, to be almost nothing. Coming glory outweighs present loss like the weight of a truck compared to a balloon.[16]

Hope helps us live for long-term value over short-term relief. Hope calls out endurance, faithfulness, and a persevering heart.

Hope is the antidote to being addicted to the next wave of fads or a continued quest for the perfect painless short cut.

Hope embraces growth as the anticipated result of being touched by God.

Hope pursues the process of transformation into the image of Christ, and is watchfully prepared for his return.

Hope says, "It is not a matter of IF we will change, but HOW we will embrace change to stay aligned with our God."

Hope says, "God gives and God takes away. Blessed be the name of the Lord."

Hope declares, "God is good all of the time, yes, all the time God is good."[17]

There is a time to let go. There are endings in this life. There are moments when some may say we have quit or failed to endure, but we know God has given us freedom to prune or move on. Please do not hear me saying that life-giving hope is being a stubborn bulldog. I am saying hope with Jesus in its center never loses heart. We will devote a study to processing losses later in the book.

GIVING = LOVE

Agape is disinterested love. Agape does not begin by discriminating between worthy and unworthy people, or any qualities people possess. It begins by loving others for their sakes. Therefore, agape makes no distinction between friend and enemy; it is directed toward both. —Martin Luther King, Jr

Darkness cannot drive out darkness: only light can do that. Hate cannot drive out hate: only love can do that. —Martin Luther King Jr.

Three times Jesus asks his #1 disciple, Peter, if he loves him. Each time Peter affirms his love. I believe Jesus asks three times to give Peter a chance to recant the three denials he made a few days earlier on the eve of Christ's crucifixion.[18] The question is not, *does Peter love Jesus*, but *does he love Jesus more than "these"*? As we begin this section on love, or in its verb form giving, the question is not, *do you love Jesus*, but *what are your "these" that may compete for your love*. Perhaps for Peter it was his love for fishing displacing the call of Jesus to be a fisher of men.

God's call to a loving life will always be a giving life. And the giving that includes a giving of our self is the better love. Just like a gift made with the giver's own two hands, or carefully selected with great thought for what the recipient would most enjoy, is better than a gift card. Our loving is defined by how God loves us.

I know "being a loving person" is held up as a value in many cultures but often the definition of loving has been corrupted by sinful culture. Often giving is polluted by:

1. A desire to call attention to the generosity of the giver (self-love)
2. An expectation of pay back from the beloved (selfish love)
3. Only being granted if the beloved performs or deemed deserving (judging love)

The more my needs, wants, or expectations become entwined in a love relationship the harder it will be to offer grace, acceptance, freedom, and space to the one I am seeking to love. Perhaps that is behind Christ emptying and then serving with his life for us. Perhaps that is behind his command for his followers to deny self and take up a cross DAILY in order to be free to love.

Peter learned to keep his eyes on Jesus, hear his assignment and then focus on giving away the love Jesus had given to him. He was not to be looking around comparing or controlling the work Jesus would have for anyone else. Later in this same scene, Jesus tells Peter that, near the end of his life, he will lose control over how he lives and there will be suffering and loss. The disciple who had denied Christ three time to avoid pain was going to face other tests. Peter looks at John and asks Jesus what will happen to him. Jesus corrects him, "If it is my will that he remain until I come, what is that to you? You follow me!"[19] John called himself the disciple whom Jesus loved. Perhaps Peter is thinking, "If my journey is going to be hard maybe Jesus does not love me as much. I am not the prized child." Perhaps, Peter thought he was not loved as much by Jesus because of his past failures.

I confess that, at times, I have thought, "Lord, if *you really* loved me you would have spared me from this thing or that situation." That is very much a false premise and if we seek to measure God's love by our experience we will also be unable to love others well. I have also believed Satan's lie that God has stopped or reduced his love for me because of my sin. As a parent, you often have to decide not to spare your child from some pain for a greater good. Jesus will direct each follower in his/her journey. It will be unique to his design for them. Do not measure, compare, or judge; just focus on Jesus.

Faith, Hope and Love grow in our heart as we connect our story of the present moment to God's eternal kingdom story. Spiritual practices (Scripture, Prayer, Listening, Giving, etc.,) all have their starting point in an ongoing daily love story. We must receive, as a fresh supply on a frequent basis, God's love that assures us of his faithfulness, hopefulness and delighting "lovefulness". Those who receive the gift of his presence deepen their capacity to gift others.

Love can be measured. It is not by counting words or little chills or exciting feelings — it is much more observable. Love may be birthed in the heart, the very core of our being, but it shows up in obedience. The fruit of loving Jesus is to obey him.

Whoever has my commandments and keeps them, he it is who loves me. And he who loves me will be loved by my Father, and I will love him and manifest myself to him.[20]

Obedience is a form of giving. When I obey Jesus, I am giving him myself, including my preferences and my right to choose. I am giving him respect and honoring his word as a better plan for my life than my own designs. In most cases, obedience, like giving, costs something. Maybe not money, but time and energy that could be invested in loving myself.

To be a giving person requires I become a receiving person. Here is an example of how I seek to receive the reality of God's love for me and then see it flow through me.

⏱ PAUSE — TRY IT OUT!

Feeding the heart on God's love and truth

After reading this personal example of the four steps, write out some examples for each step describing opportunities in your life.

1. FEED
2. FILLS
3. FOCUSES
4. FRUIT

Feed — Through my day my body and mental activity interact with the world around me. I make choices to filter the comments from others, media inputs, expectations from culture, etc. **Illustration**: I open an exercise program article and in the sidebar are ads for sexually enticing articles or photos. I must choose: will I *filter out* or click and *feed on*?

Fills — What I feed on begins to fill my thinking with images, ideas, and stories (true and made up), and mix with my past experiences and God created desires. **Illustration:** Reliving a painful relational encounter over and over with people we interact with can actually sow bitterness and make forgiveness more challenging, even if we close a conversation asking for prayer.

Focuses — What fills my thinking begins to focus and direct my motivation. Motivation is an energy, a strong desire, to reach a goal. So my focus glues me to pursuing a certain goal.

Fruit — My goal begins to show up in real time throughout my day in my attitude, words and actions. Fruit of flesh or Spirit grows from the seeds I sow into my thinking.

Illustration: I am singing through the Baptist Hymnal (2 songs per morning on most days) as part of my morning wake up with God time. If I don't know the tune I make up one . . . no one but God is listening and I think he appreciates my creativity. Often the ones I do know stir up childhood memories of being in church services with my grandparents or my mother. **Feeding** on old familiar music goes well with my favorite morning coffee.

The songs on the cross of Christ **fill** my thinking with thankfulness for his sacrificial gift and also seem to wash me in joy and peace to know that the Spirit is there with me.

My energy level comes up and the desire to use my hours to love Jesus is kindled like a newly laid fire. My day's plans have a clear **focus** and an overarching goal that will impact phone calls, e-mails, meetings and writing.

Fruit will be revealed as a feeling of peace as I move from task to task. I know I am loved, and the Spirit of Jesus is able to whisper and empower me because of his cleansing blood. No matter the outcome, I can lay down at night with thanks, trusting that his grace and truth have been seen in my frail flesh.

☉ PAUSE — TRY IT OUT!

Growing good fruit from a good heart

Read this passage reflecting on the four steps you just read. What does this passage add to your understanding of how God desires to make you a loving giving person?

For no good tree bears bad fruit, nor again does a bad tree bear good fruit, for each tree is known by its own fruit. For figs are not gathered from thorn bushes, nor are grapes picked from a bramble bush. The good person out of the good treasure of his heart produces good, and the evil person out of his evil treasure produces evil, for out of the abundance of the heart his mouth speaks. Why do you call me 'Lord, Lord,' and not do what I tell you? Everyone who comes to me and hears my words and does them, I will show you what he is like: he is like a man building a house, who dug deep and laid the foundation on the rock. And when a flood arose, the stream broke against that house and could not shake it, because it had been well built. But the one who hears and does not do them is like a man who built a house on the ground without a foundation. When the stream broke against it, immediately it fell, and the ruin of that house was great.[21]

––––––– ☉ –––––––

LOVING IS FREEDOM TO BLESS GOD AND OTHERS WITH WHAT GOD HAS GIVEN

But all of us are obligated — perhaps better to say, invited — to be freed from the endless pursuit of accumulation and become instead profoundly thankful and uncommonly generous people. Ultimately, it is to our own advantage to receive this spirit from God. 'A heart at peace gives life to the body, but envy rots the bones' (Proverbs 14:30). Do we really believe Jesus when he says, 'Watch out! Be on your guard against all kinds of greed; a man's life does not consist in the abundance of his possessions' (Luke 12:15).[22]

Love gives UP in order to be giving TO. The lover seems almost unaware of the cost of what is being given UP because of the passionate devotion and desire to give TO. Any needs in the life of the one loved simply create concrete opportunities for the lover to show love by giving. "Our humanity comes to its fullest bloom in giving. We become beautiful people when we give whatever we can give: a smile, a handshake, a kiss, an embrace, a word of love, a present, a part of our life...all of our life."[23]

The opposite of love is to lust. Love is about giving and lust is about getting. Lust is the seed of every consumer. "We often live as if our happiness depended on having. . . . A happy life is a life for others."[24]

George Verwer stood years ago in chapel at CIU and began his message with these words, "Let me give you a definition of a missionary. A missionary is someone who gives up everything for God and then spends the rest of their life complaining about it." Complaining is evidence of a "taking" spirit residing in my heart. God wants to displace such a spirit with a one of "giving" open handed love.

Any discussion of giving will naturally include financial giving. I have put to death the idea that my giving of my money to God should be a tithe. I won't go into the details of how I made this journey but instead will refer the reader to the writings of David Croteau, a fellow professor at Columbia International University. What I will do is share the summary of the principles of giving that should be obeyed by every Jesus-follower, as presented by David in my leadership course.

Categories of Application

The Driving Force of Giving

Principle	Description	Location
Grace-Driven	Giving is a response to the grace of God shown to believers	2 Cor 8–9
Relationship-Driven	Giving is based upon one's relationship with the Lord and the receiver of the giving	2 Cor 8:5
Love-Driven	Giving is a demonstration of a Christian's love	2 Cor 8:8–9

The Motivations for Giving

Principle	Description	Location
Thankfulness	Giving expresses thankfulness to God	2 Cor 9:12
Spiritual growth	Giving causes one to grow in good works	2 Cor 9:6, 8
God's Praise	Recognize that God praises sacrificial giving	Mark 12:42–44; 2 Cor 8:2–3
Rewards	Not storing up for rewards here, but for eternal rewards	Matt 6:19–21

The Details of Giving

Principle	Description	Location
Universal	Every believer should give	1 Cor 16:2; Rom 1:20–21
Systematic	Give on a regular basis, that is, weekly, bi-monthly, or monthly	1 Cor 16:2
Precautions	Proper precautions should be made with the handling of money	2 Cor 8:20–21

The Attitude of Giving and Possessions

Principle	Description	Location
Voluntary	Giving ought to be done out of one's free volition	2 Cor 8:3; 9:7
Intentional	Seek opportunities and give deliberately in order to meet a genuine need, not out of guilt merely to soothe a pressing request	2 Cor 8:4; 9:2
Cheerfully	God loves a cheerful giver	2 Cor 9:7
Willingness	All of a Christian's possessions should be at the Lord's disposal	Matt 19:16–21

The Amount of Giving

Principle	Description	Location
Income-Based[25]	The value of the gift given is expected to be related to the income of the offerer	Deut 16:16–17; 1 Cor 16:2; 2 Cor 8:3, 12
Needs-Based	Meet the needs of those ministering and of fellow saints	1 Cor 9:1–14; 2 Cor 8:13– 14; 2 Cor 9:12
Generous	Give generously, but not to the point of personal affliction	2 Cor 8:2–3, 13; Phil 4:17–18
Heart-Based	Giving is based upon the amount determined in one's heart	Exod 25:1; 35:5, 21–22; 36:6; 2 Cor 9:7 [26]

Prayer:

Lord, may I be known for generosity with all I have received from you. May I be one who sows the right seed in large quantity with a vision of an abundant harvest. Lord, you are the owner of the field. Send me and many other laborers into your harvest. Lord, you are one who gives the increase to the seed.

Water it by your Spirit. Amen.

⏱ PAUSE – TRY IT OUT!

Being loved by the God of love

Read the following passages with my comments inserted. I have included the references so you may choose to look up the passages and read in a larger context.

After reading over these passages prayerfully, write out what else you have learned about the definition of life-giving love.

Hosea 3:1 (ESV)

And the LORD said to me, 'Go again, love a woman who is loved by another man and is an adulteress, even as the LORD loves the children of Israel, though they turn to other gods and love cakes of raisins.' **Have you tasted God's relentless love? Do you know the reality of rejecting him and then seeing him buy you back out of adultery to bring you home?**

1 Thessalonians 3:12 (ESV)

And may the Lord make you increase and abound in love for one another and for all, as we do for you. **God intends for his children to keep growing and abounding in love all of their days. It is one course you never complete.**

1 Thessalonians 4:9 (ESV)

Now concerning brotherly love you have no need for anyone to write to you, for you yourselves have been taught by God to love one another. **God is a teacher. And what he teaches is how to love.**

1 John 2:27 (ESV)

But the anointing that you received from him abides in you, and you have no need that anyone should teach you. But as his anointing teaches you about everything, and is true, and is no lie—just as it has taught you, abide in him. **Our very core has been changed in the new birth. We dwell in the life-giving love of God.**

1 Corinthians 13:4-8 (ESV)

Love is patient and kind; love does not envy or boast; it is not arrogant or rude. It does not insist on its own way; it is not irritable or resentful; it does not rejoice at wrongdoing, but rejoices with the truth. Love bears all things, believes all things, hopes all things, and endures all things. Love never ends. As for prophecies, they will pass away; as for tongues, they will cease; as for knowledge, it will pass away. **Love may well be the most powerful and enduring aspect of his creation. Interesting to consider that love can only exist where relationship exists.**

————— ☼ —————

CONCLUSION

Are you starting to see a pattern?

The object of our faith is God. We rest in his promises and his presence in us. Faith is growing as we are letting go of other objects and focus our vision clearly on God.

The object of our hope is Jesus in us. We long for his return as a bride looking for her husband to return from battle. We have a pure, faithful devoted longing, knowing his presence will complete all he has started.

And the focus of our love? We love because he first loves us. We give as one who is abundantly, graciously, mercifully blessed.

A life-giving leader has God as the central focus of his or her life. Please do not read over these words too quickly. One of the dangers of leadership is the powerful spotlight and visibility most leaders experience. Life in the spotlight can shift the focus so that our faith, hope and love are really resting on ourselves, not on God.

Spirit, help us see!

Roy King

THINKING IT THROUGH

1. Write out your definition of life-giving faith.
2. What god substitutes are you tempted to let replace trusting God?
3. Study and determine at least 3 hope passages you can meditate on and share with others.
4. What is an aspect of your life, right now, where you need to see hope in Jesus realized?
5. Write out your own definition of life-giving love.
6. What dangers or lies can pollute or decrease your loving?
7. How would you assess your generosity?

CHAPTER NINE

HOW GOD GROWS FAITH, HOPE AND LOVE IN OUR HEARTS

THE BIBLE TELLS US to have faith, practice endurance, and choose to love. And the Bible teaches that God grows these character traits as fruit in us. As I step out and trust God to show up and be with me, my heart develops an increased capacity for faith, hope and love. It may seem to be circular reasoning to say that practicing faith, hope and love brings a greater ability to practice faith, hope and love, but this is how God works in us.

An illustration of the means and the end being the same can be seen when Jesus asks Peter to do some fishing.

And when he had finished speaking, he said to Simon, "Put out into the deep and let down your nets for a catch.[1]

There are no promised rewards, only Jesus implying, "Peter, trust me." Peter was tired from fishing all night and catching nothing. (Nothing happening makes the clock crawl and gives you time to consider a career change.) Then in the early morning sun, Peter had washed and repaired the nets. But as he exercised faith in Jesus, he began to learn that with Jesus anything could be accomplished. "God does not want you to merely gain intellectual knowledge of truth. He wants you to experience His truth. There are things about Jesus you will learn only as you obey Him.[2]

When one actually takes the step of trusting, hoping or loving (the means), then the person actually gains a heart filled with faith, hope and love (the end; the goal). One benefit to the means God provides and the goal God intends being the same is a simple child-like, what the Psalmist calls an "undivided heart".[3]

Can you remember listening to several voices blending in perfect harmony? The actions of trusting, hoping and loving open the heart to it becoming a heart of faith, hope and love. The heart and the abilities of the heart (thinking, feeling, and choosing) are then singing one song.

FAITH, HOPE AND LOVE GROW

But we do not simply turn some inner switch to activate faith, hope and love. So the question becomes, how do they grow? God gives us people, events, and circumstances as exercises. I understand how to get in shape physically. It is the same with developing one's heart. God is the trainer and life is the gym. Physically, I set up an exercise plan. The first week of doing one set of ten repetitions of twelve exercises leaves me exhausted. Amazingly, after just a few cycles I can complete that same circuit without breaking a sweat.

The only way I will gain additional strength and endurance is to:

1. Add more repetitions (lengthens the time)
2. Increase the weights (increases the intensity)
3. Add different exercises that target slightly different muscle groups (targets different aspects)

God, in his sovereignty, uses every person, every event, and every circumstance as part of his customized workout routine to grow faith, hope and love in you.

Example:

It is clearly his will for me to love my enemies. How does God grow that in me? He gives me a few to practice on! As I look across the street at that "enemy" who lets his children pick on my children I pray something like, "God you know I do not love that person. But I believe I am the body of Christ and you want to love him through my 'earth suit' (body). I choose to step out in faith to bless this person and trust your Spirit will change my heart as I go."

Illustration: Ray Rising, an alumnus of Columbia International University, was held captive in Colombia, South America for 810 days several years ago. I will never forget him recounting his story in our chapel. Ray spent most of his captivity chained between two trees. A couple of times a day he would be released and allowed to have a toilet and meal break before returning to his chains. Around day 180 he was sitting there waiting for the next break and using the time to complain to God about his situation. Suddenly, in his spirit, Jesus spoke as clearly as if it had been an audible voice. Jesus whispered, *"Ray, I love these people. I want to be among them and I am letting you be here with me."* Ray's perspective for the rest of his days was different. His heart began to grow in faith, hope and love once he saw the privilege of being on this adventure with Jesus. His attitude change removed a hindrance to what God wanted to grow *in* him and place on display *through* him.

I have learned you do not commit to a physical exercise plan when you arrive at the gym. You have to think about it the day before. You lay out your clothes, pack your towel, locate your membership card, and set the alarm earlier. You cultivate a good mental attitude by saying to yourself, "I will probably not feel like getting up when the alarm goes off, but the reward of a healthy start to my day and the long term health benefits are my extra push to get up and go".

In a similar manner, God commands us to do the mental meditation on aspects of beauty, truth and goodness that will motivate us to want a heart of faith, hope and love. I cry out for the help of his Spirit as I step out and go for it; trusting, hoping and giving.

Finally, brothers, whatever is true, whatever is honorable, whatever is just, whatever is pure, whatever is lovely, whatever is commendable, if there is any excellence, if there is anything worthy of praise, **think about these things.**[4]

Remember, because God is sovereign, EVERY person, event, and circumstance he allows to touch your life he can redeem and use as exercises for trusting, hoping and loving which grow the heart God intends for you to enjoy; a life-giving heart.

Faith, Hope and Love grow best in a Community of Support

Faith, hope and love are like an ongoing conversation between good friends who are on a long journey together. As you read Paul's missionary letter to his sending church in Corinth, you will find his perspective on how God was using his suffering in ministry to strengthen his dependence on God and his interdependence on the prayers of the Corinthian Christians. When I read about messed up and struggling Corinthian church, I am not sure I would have chosen them to be my prayer warriors!

For we do not want you to be unaware, brothers, of the affliction we experienced in Asia. For we were so utterly burdened beyond our strength that we despaired of life itself. Indeed, we felt that we had received the sentence of death. But **that was to make us rely not on ourselves but on God** *who raises the dead. He delivered us from such a deadly peril, and he will deliver us. On him we have set our hope that he will deliver us again.* **You also must help us by prayer**, *so that many will give thanks on our behalf for the blessing granted us through the prayers of many.*[5]

Faith displacing Fear

If you smell fear in a room full of leaders you can count on poor decisions as a result. There is only ONE way to please God—living by faith.[6]

For God gave us a spirit not of fear but of power and love and self-control.[7]

And they went and woke him, saying, "Save us, Lord; we are perishing." And he said to them, "Why are you afraid, O you of little faith?" Then he rose and rebuked the winds and the sea, and there was a great calm.[8]

Faith is not based on a vacuum. Faith grows from a foundation of trustworthy commitment. Faith rests on past promises kept.

➤ Am I at a place of confident peace because I know God has rescued me and brought me into his family?

➤ Am I playing "offense" or only "defense" in my goals and choices to act?

➤ Are my life investment choices motivated by FEAR or FAITH?

Hope Replaces Despair

Endurance, perseverance, and living with an awareness of potential and growth is the best description of Christ and his followers. Our most effective witness to non-Christians is often found when we model how a Christian faces suffering, loss and death. God grows HOPE in my heart as I seek to see what he is doing and remind myself what he is going to do.

But we do not want you to be uninformed, brothers, about those who are asleep, that you may not grieve as others do who have no hope.[9]

➤ How does death impact my hope?

➤ What causes my hope to diminish?

Love Replacing LUST

God is a giving God. We reveal his image most fully when we become givers instead of takers. Biblical love joyfully sacrifices in order to give what is most needed to the one being loved. Jesus-followers are to be contributing, not consuming.

To be truly alive is to know I am perfectly LOVED and to be LOVING.

What then shall we say to these things? If God is for us, who can be against us? He who did not spare his own Son but gave him up for us all, how will he not also with him graciously give us all things? Who shall bring any charge against God's elect? It is God who justifies. Who is to condemn? Christ Jesus is the one who died—more than that, who was raised—who is at the right hand of God, who indeed is interceding for us. Who shall separate us from the love of Christ? Shall tribulation, or distress, or persecution, or famine, or nakedness, or danger, or sword? As it is written, 'For your sake we are being killed all the day long; we are regarded as sheep to be slaughtered.' No, in all these things we are more than conquerors through him who loved us. For I am sure that neither death nor life, nor angels nor rulers, nor things present nor things to come, nor powers, nor height nor depth, nor anything else in all creation, will be able to separate us from the love of God in Christ Jesus our Lord.[10]

Am I clinging to the promises of God and taking risks to love in his name?

When I think about what I pray, are my requests too small in light of who God is and what he is already doing?

> Is there anything I can do to make God love me less?

> Is there anything I can do to make God love me more?

> Do I act as if God is a good father who delights in me as his child?

⏱ PAUSE — TRY IT OUT!

Passages with faith, hope and love in close context

Practice being still and reflecting on God's truth and remembering God's promises. Take a walk or find some other way to be in alert prayer where your heart comes into alignment with God's heart.

Read the following passages out loud, and then write out what these passages teach about the PROCESS and the GOAL of God's work in our hearts to develop faith, hope and love.

These passages include faith, hope and love in close context: (In some passages hope is presented as endurance)

Romans 5:1-8	Ephesians 1:11-23	1 Timothy 2:15
Romans 12:11-13	Ephesians 2:1-12	1 Timothy 4:6-16
Romans 14:1-23	Ephesians 3:11-21	1 Timothy 6:11
Romans 14:1-15:13	Ephesians 4:1-16	2 Timothy 1:5-7
1 Corinthians 13:13	Philippians 1:25 – 2:11	2 Timothy 3:10
1 Corinthians 15:12-19	Philippians 3:7 – 4:1	Titus 2:2
1 Corinthians 16:13	Colossians 1:3-5	Hebrews 6:10-12
2 Corinthians 1:12 – 2:17	Colossians 2:1-5	Hebrews 10:22-25
2 Corinthians 5	1 Thessalonians 1:3-5	1 Peter 1:3-9
2 Corinthians 8:1-7	1 Thessalonians 3:6-13	1 Peter 1:20

2 Corinthians 10:13 – 11:3	1 Thessalonians 5:8	2 Peter 1:3-11
2 Corinthians 12:11 – 13:14	2 Thessalonians 1:3-6	Jude 17-23
Galatians 5:1-6	1 Timothy 1:3-7	Revelation 2:1

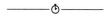

⏱ PAUSE — TRY IT OUT!

Reflecting on a mission statement

One of the most effective mission sending Southern Baptist churches in the United States is MOSAIC. Here is their mission statement:

*We are a community of followers of Jesus Christ, committed to **live by faith**, to be **known by love**, and to be **a voice of hope**. The name of our community comes from the diversity of our members and from the symbolism of a broken and fragmented humanity which can become a work of beauty under the artful hands of God. We welcome people from all walks of life, regardless of where they are in their spiritual journey.*[11]

Write out how your individual life as a leader and the lives of those in the organization would look if you were living with this mission statement. What are you doing that you would stop? What would you begin doing?

PART THREE

A RHYTHM FOR LIFE-GIVING LEADING

Our choices become our actions. Our actions become our habits.
Our habits become our character. —*Michael Hyatt*

ONE OF BOOKS I read this past year was *Slow Church: Cultivating Community in the Patient Way of Jesus* by Chris Smith and John Pattison, who are leaders in two different congregations. The title makes a connection to the global "slow movement", which advocates a slowing down of life's pace and a focus on quality instead of quantity.

If you are interested in the Slow movement, I would recommend Carl Honore's *In Praise of Slowness: Challenging the Cult of Speed.* He provides a broad exposure to the movement, which ranges from slow eating to slow cities, medicine, sex, work, exercise, leisure and parenting. He explains that slowness is not a like a slow motion scene in a film. Instead, "the slow philosophy can be summed in a single word: balance. Be fast when it makes sense to be fast, and be slow when slowness is called for. Seek to live at what musicians call the *tempo giusto* — the right speed. . . . Being slow means you control the rhythms of your own life. . . . The problem is that our love of speed, our obsession with doing more and more in less and less time, has gone too far; it has turned into as addiction, a kind of idolatry. When you accelerate things that should not be accelerated, when you forget how to slow down, there is a price to pay."[1]

The authors of *Slow Church* apply the philosophy of slowness to a biblical, theological and practical application of congregational life. Smith and Pattison borrow the term, "McDonaldization" from sociologist George Ritzer, who describes four dimensions of modern culture that reflect the fast food model: efficiency, predictability, calculability (quantifiable results) and control—or at least the illusion of control. Smith and Pattison then apply those criteria to a biblical view of church and conclude, "Following Jesus has been diminished to a privatized faith rather than a lifelong apprenticeship undertaken in the context of Christian community."[2]

I have found this book helpful in challenging my perspective on our Western, "speed is king!" approach to life. While I am still making adjustments in my own life, I hope this section of the book will encourage you to examine your pace and the effect of your leadership pace on others. I have found that to truly honor the two rhythms I will introduce, I must slow down at several places in my week. I have wrestled with feelings ranging from guilt to the fear of disappointing others when I can't respond to requests as quickly as expected. So, I do not have all of the answers to the pace of life.

For several years I have been exploring three dominant images used in the New Testament to refer to Jesus-followers: soldier, farmer and athlete. Rhythm, pace and disciplined action are required of all three. But I struggle to apply them to my own life when my cell phone notifications are grabbing my attention every few minutes.

In spite of my own learning curve with pace, one thing I am sure of— God intends for us to live by the daily and weekly rhythms in the next chapter if we want to receive and offer others his life. Let's explore them together.

CHAPTER TEN

TWO RHYTHMS OF LIFE-GIVING LEADERS

God has given us two hands, one to receive with and the other to give with.
—Billy Graham

Cheered by the presence of God, I will do at each moment, without anxiety, accord-
ing to the strength which he shall give me, the work that his providence assigns me. I
will leave the rest without concern; it is not my affair. I ought to consider the duty to
which I am called each day, as the work that God has given me to do.
—Francois Fenelon

THE DAILY RHYTHM: RECEIVING & GIVING

IN SWIMMING, we place one arm out in front and pull through as the other arm moves up and out and then repeat the cycle. In breathing, the contraction of our diaphragm expands our lung capacity and creates space for air to flow in and the relaxation of the diaphragm aids in pushing air out, over and over again. Think about running, our heart beat, eating—all around us are God's rhythm of life —Receive and Give… Receive and Give… Receive and Give!

Every time I receive anything into my life, it reminds me that I am incomplete. I cannot generate my own life apart from outside resources. Every time I give, I am reminded that anything I give I have first received. Everything I give is first received and mixed with my contribution before it is given away. I take in food and water, my body uses those raw materials to produce strength and energy, enabling me to walk across the room and offer a hug, wash the dishes, or change a diaper.

Perhaps it goes back to pride, but for most of us receiving is a greater challenge than giving. Henri Nouwen explains that, even though we have inner resistance, we need to focus on the importance of receiving:

Receiving often is harder than giving. Giving is very important: giving insight, giving hope, giving courage, giving advice, giving support, giving money, and, most of all, giving ourselves. Without giving there is no brotherhood and sisterhood.

But receiving is just as important, because by receiving we reveal to the givers that they have gifts to offer. When we say, "Thank you, you gave me hope; thank you, you gave me a reason to live; thank you, you allowed me to realize my dream", we make givers aware of their unique and precious gifts. Sometimes it is only in the eyes of the receivers that givers discover their gifts.[1]

Life Requires Navigating the Rhythms of Life

Life is filled with all sorts of rhythms that influence how quickly we move, when we rest and play and when we sit beside a warming fire in tears and deep prayer. Seasons vary with times for plowing and sowing, weeding and harvesting. It is impossible to do all of these activities at the same time in the same field. Leadership involves wisdom in pacing and in living with points of tension between the unresolved and the uncompleted. Yes, most leaders do have a bias for action, but life-giving leadership also includes waiting and seeking. Leadership often involves offering what we have AND being very conscious of resource needs and gaps.

The gifts of grace and truth flow from God into us and then through us to others. Do our lives reflect the flow of grace we say we believe in? Do we seek to stir up the blessings of life from within ourselves without taking time to receive them?

To honor the flow of life is to acknowledge that life centers on connections and relationships.

What do connections look like?

1. Taking a one hour walk with the phone turned off just to breathe the fresh air, while appreciating and celebrating the sights and sounds of our Creator's handiwork.
2. Sitting with a friend while they are waiting for a chemotherapy treatment and listening as they tell stories of their childhood memories.

3. Rising early and sitting outside as the morning fog clears and the sun breaks through and closing your eyes and feeling the warmth creep into your bones.

4. Pausing in a crowded market in a new city on the other side of the world and seeking to describe a new smell or identify a new food.

5. Taking time to ask the name of someone serving you and then using their name in your conversation with them.

6. Asking a new neighbor if there is any way you can pray for them this week and then checking back in a week to see if there has been an answer.

We are designed, created, to be connected with others. Just as God "dwells with", we were made for interacting with this world, not for blindly running through the crowd to get to a finish line. We must learn to measure our connectedness and disconnectedness with the world. We cannot receive or give if we are not connected. We must develop an alarm system that goes off in our head when our pace of life is rushing us past chances to love and be loved.

Maintaining the Daily Rhythm

For most leaders, there are two critical decisions that must be lived out consistently to maintain a life-giving daily rhythm.

Decision #1 — What are the critical non-negotiable commitments I will say "yes" to every day?

I can assess if I have made a real commitment by what I will give up to fulfill the commitment.

1. Will I give up staying up late so I can get up and exercise and spend time alone with God?

2. Will I give up multiple conversations on my social network so I can be fully present with my children the three hours we have between then end of the work day and their bedtime.

3. Will I always ask my family to understand and reschedule but never ask a church member to make the same sacrifice?

Decision #2 — What will I prune by saying "no" to, in order to focus on what God shows me is most fruitful?

1. Do I prune by taking some one-year goals and shifting them to five-year goals so I have a realistic pace of life?

2. Do I say, "no" to more activity in the short term so I can train others and develop a coaching care system for them? Can the team then take on some of the responsibilities I am being tempted to add to my life?

3. Do I prune additional opportunities to teach so I may be well prepared for the ones I have already accepted? Being well prepared includes having time to pray before the event and following up afterwards with the groups I do teach.

⏱ PAUSE — TRY IT OUT!

Two means to greater fruitfulness

Take some time to use the previous questions to review the commitments in your life right now. Be willing to make changes. It may require letting someone know now that when this three month commitment is up you won't be continuing, so they have time to locate your replacement. Pruning is not breaking your word. Realize that it may take some time to bring your pace of life into alignment.

Begin by writing down how you spend your time for three weeks. To review your time log, begin by writing the numbers 1-4, corresponding to the grid below and to the entries in your log. You may also want to add some activities that you did NOT spend time doing, but you know should, as quadrant two activities. [2]

Q1 Urgent/ Important	**Q2** Not Urgent/ Important
Q3 Urgent/ Not Important	**Q4** Not Urgent/ Not Important

Quadrant 1 — Activity with a very clear deadline and very important to accomplishing your highest priorities. (Examples: Some meetings, projects deadline events, public events with set time, etc.,)

Quadrant 2 — Activities lacking a clear deadline but very important. (Examples: exercise, devotions, and time with your family) The vitality and effectiveness of your life will be determined by your commitment to schedule and invest in these Q2 activities.

Quadrant 3 — These activities may be urgent, or deemed urgent by someone else in your life, but are not strategically important. (Most e-mail, some meetings, many expectations of others) Many Q3 activities are wrongly perceived as Q1. Often when I review the time log of someone I am coaching they have almost no activities identified as Q3 but a massive list of Q1.

Quadrant 4 — Time wasters and activities we often use to seek to refresh or do because we do not have energy for productive work. (Surfing magazines or the internet, most junk mail, TV, some social networking, etc.,) People who have failed to create good Q2 activities cycle between Q1 until exhausted and then fall into Q4 to seek to recover and go back out to more Q1.

Be intentional in your sowing and pruning. Sowing well means to be a good steward of the gifts and resources of God.

Does how you invest your time connect to the assignment or calling God has given you?

1. *Am I living my own dream or someone else's?* If we are not careful, we can unconsciously be following someone else's agenda for our lives. This usually happens because we are unwilling to take responsibility for our own lives.

2. *What is my dream?* This can get lost in the complexity of life. As a result, we need to pause and remember our own agenda. What is it that we believe God is calling us to be and to do? What is our passion? What would we do if we were brave?

3. *What can I do now to move in the direction of my dream?* The only way to reclaim our dream is to reject all substitutes and begin

moving in the direction of our dream. We don't have to do anything heroic. We can start small and take baby steps. The issue is to make sure we are making progress toward our goals.

Pruning requires the courage to say, "no." Keep a time log for 3 weeks, writing down what you actually do. Then review and make a list of changes using the following categories:

1. Things I should eliminate or reduce
2. Good things I should replace with the best
3. Tasks I can overlap (Asking a student to travel with me when I go to speak allows me to be a mentor, modeling serving others)
4. Train, delegate and evaluate with others versus doing it myself
5. Postpone for a period of time

Which of the above changes do you need to make in order to accomplish the attitude and commitment changes you desire?

We do with time what we would never do with our money. We write "checks" for future obligations without considering how we are presently spending it.[3] I have very seldom regretted any decision I have made to prune a time commitment. I have many times regretted adding a commitment. Those poor additions often came from an internal problem. In my heart I was seeking to earn God's grace, earn other people's approval, or was being dominated by an impatience in my own spirit. I have kept this quote from Nouwen close by to call me to check my heart before making commitments.

Patience asks us to live the moment to the fullest, to be completely present to the moment, to taste the here and now, to be where we are. When we are impatient we try to get away from where we are. We behave as if the real thing will happen tomorrow, later and somewhere else. Let's be patient and trust that the treasure we look for is hidden in the ground on which we stand.[4]

The elements of God's grace and his will for our character surely connect and compliment like the pieces in a jigsaw puzzle.

➤ Gratitude precedes Generosity

➤ Patience and Peace grow together

➤ Joy and Desire are close companions. Choosing to rejoice in the Lord as the Bible commands for daily life increases my motivation (desire) to seek and be with my Lord.

➤ Humility opens me to Receiving

Challenges to the Daily Rhythm

1. Lack of gratefulness — Taking time to be thankful and offer gratitude for all we receive from God and others makes us more open to receive again. Just acknowledging what we have received helps us remember the neediness we carry through life.

2. Failing to go to a mountain top — I served two church families in two cities in the mountains of North Carolina. I learned the value of getting to a high point on a ridge to gain perspective, and reorient myself when I was lost. It always helps to get a fresh reminder of the bigger picture. Whether it is done alone in a journal, or with a friend in a coffee shop, we must cultivate those places we go to gain a clearer perspective on our life. In that mountain top place we gain clarity on exactly what we need to receive and wisdom on how to best give. We get lost too easily down in the trees.

Summary

In the chapter on "seeing" we mentioned the reality of the dual perspectives so often experienced in life. Life is living in a place of tension, acknowledging and choosing to balance in the light of two or more truths. The rhythms of life are a good example of double vision.

Receiving is to live with an awareness of God making me needy. My neediness is close to the surface of my life. I do not seek to fill it on my own, or deny it, but let myself be open to however and whoever God wants to use to bring life to me. The life-giving life is full of gratitude. My leadership is richer when it is covered in thanksgiving.

Giving is to know that God will pour life through me to others. To give in Jesus' name is to give to Jesus. To see the image of God in another, and seek to honor and serve them, honors the Creator. I am made in the image of a giving God; to be like him is to join him in pouring out on others. The life-giving life is joyous blessing of others.

If I am too busy, and there is just too much to do for me to take time to listen, pray for wisdom and then contribute with faith, hope and love, the perspective and commitments that govern my pace of life must be changed.

THE WEEKLY RHYTHM: WORKING AND RESTING

Work is not always required. There is such a thing as sacred idleness.
—George MacDonald

Do not work so hard for Christ that you have no strength to pray,
for prayer requires strength. —Hudson Taylor

Working

The nice thing about a daily rhythm is that we get a fresh start every 24 hours. Today I can be more receptive to receiving and more open-handed in giving than I was yesterday. But a weekly rhythm frames my days. This larger chunk of seven days is like a larger rock going into a stone wall.

Eighty-five years of life is 31,025 days but only 4,432 weeks. God's outline for our week is six days of productive work and one day for rest. I am defining work as any productive labor, not just employment. Maintaining the home, self-care and parenting are fruit-bearing works. Intercessory prayer is work.

Life at work is an expression of purpose and value. Surely God works and we learn who he is, what he values, and see his character as we observe his labor. The same is true for his image bearers.

In the mid-1800s, Rev. Daniel Payne lifted up the value of hard work that goes beyond just physical exertion to include time invested in mental work for the Christian leader.

The Christian minister is to dedicate himself to cultivating the life of the mind. He is to feel and know that he was not a mere drone about the hive, a snail in the garden, or a lounger about the house of God — but that he had a mind, and that mind was made for thinking, investigating, discriminating—for study.[5]

Work is to be viewed in the holistic manner: Physical, Mental, Emotional, Social and Spiritual.

Life at rest is an experience of rest and renewal. Rest is an act of faith as we trust God to keep the world going until we return to our tasks. The freedom to rest is a way to practice grace. Rest is the ultimate way to know our identity is deeper than what we do.

Work and rest are meant to go together. Work without rest does not allow for meaning and fulfillment. Workaholics don't have time for reflection and course correction, and life has enough twists and turns that, without some pause, hard chargers eventually run off course. One of my hobbies is biking, and I know that if I want to survive the ride, I need to coast down a downhill after a steep climb. I can't just keep pedaling with all I've got.

On the other hand, rest without work also falls short and does not allow for peace and satisfaction. To be honest, it's not even real rest if you haven't worked beforehand. That's what makes a good sleep so good or a break so enriching. It was preceded by hard work. I sleep hard when I've worked hard, and I'm not alone. A recent National Sleep Foundation study found that exercisers sleep better than non-exercisers.

Work and rest are married. They're not like a twin-engine plane that can fly on a single engine if needed. They're more like a pair of oxen—these two concepts must be harnessed together pulling your life in the right direction. If either one is unharnessed, success is impossible; the plow either goes wildly off course or crashes altogether.[6]

Working in grace means you are free to focus fully on one thing in the present moment trusting God to handle all the rest.

Living under his rule puts us in a place of freedom, life, and peace! Our bodies serve as "contact points" between the kingdom and the surrounding world. Be aware that the body is the vehicle, the means, of our investing in, partnering with, and responding to the King of Kings. 1 Corinthians 6:12-20; John 1:51; Luke 10:18

We do not live beyond time and limits. Being in the kingdom does not remove me from the limits of the body. Remember Herod. He promised up to half his kingdom, and even though he did not want to do it, had to deliver the head of John the Baptist. We tend to promise too much, often to keep people thinking well of us, but also because of our legitimate desire to serve. Remember that we do not use the rule of God in order to bring us glory. Remember that when he rules, he is in the center of the photo and we surround, serve and respond to his initiative. Running on promises we make to others can be like living on credit cards. At the time of the purchase, pay back looks far into the future. But the future arrives sooner than we expect and the cost is more than we can deliver. All promises must be "under God", recognizing our limits.

RESTING

God made us so we leak. We deplete, drain out and wind down. We need Sabbath time to reflect, to grow and to renew energy and our creative juice. I am 13 days past my deadline for editing this book as of today. Yet, I have learned it does not help me to violate my Sabbath. Yesterday, Sunday, my wife and I experienced true rest and today I am ready to write again!

Earlier we mentioned that life-giving leadership must be holistic in its scope. A survey of full-time and bi-vocational pastors found:

1. 34% of US Protestant pastors are obese.
2. Bi-vocational pastors are twice as likely to be obese
3. For those who practice Sabbath, one in ten were obese.
4. For those who did not practice Sabbath, the hours worked per week were a factor, with five in ten being obese who worked 40 hours a week and nine in ten for those working 70 hours. Stress and lack of rest was determined to be the primary contribution, according to the Baylor University sociologists who conducted the study. [7]

Jesus practiced a rhythm of working and resting.

But now even more the report about him went abroad, and great crowds gathered to hear him and to be healed of their infirmities. But he would withdraw to desolate places and pray.[8]

Do we really think we know more of how we should invest our time in a week than Jesus does?

Even with several years of seeking to learn to work and rest well, I am still learning. I find myself going back to three words over and over: BOUNDARIES, LIMITS AND MARGINS. Notice I list my three ever present realities in alphabetical order; I will often take a few minutes in the morning to think about how I will live my day and the coming week using these words.

One major shift I have made is to move from what I am going to tell someone to what questions I am going to ask them. Maybe it is the teacher in me, but as I look at meetings, e-mails, and other relational connections, my thoughts seem to go first to what insight, information or correction I need to dish out. Instead, in my calendar or journal, I try to craft a few questions. That one simple shift often helps me clarify where my responsibility ends and theirs begins. I live my week as more of a servant than a judge and instructor.

B-Boundaries: the reality of where God has made you. You end and everyone else begins. God does not violate personal boundaries. I should not violate the boundaries of others or allow them to violate me. It is okay to say, "I am sorry this is not an appropriate conversation." Personal boundaries do not change over our lifetime.

L-Limits: These are given by God and will sometimes change throughout life. I have different physical limits at 60 than I had at 25. I have larger amounts of discretionary time to spend on my grandchildren than I had as a young parent on my own children. I see my aging parents having less financial resources than they had 30 years ago. Limits require frequent updating of inventory.

M-Margins: Margins are space I create in my schedule to acknowledge the fallen world and our lack of control, and recognize that God's Spirit delights in giving me surprises—sometimes called interruptions.

Grace is being able to give myself and others freedom as we navigate the B.L.M. of our lives. In my journal, I have recorded a whisper from the Spirit to me: "Roy, all you offer is imperfect. Don't apologize for it. I take your offering and use it for my glory. Apologize for sin. Do not apologize for an imperfect offering."

RECOMMENDED RESOURCES

1. The best book on Sabbath: Mark Buchanan. *The Rest of God: Restoring Your Soul by Restoring Sabbath.* Nashville: W Publishing, 2006. ISBN: 0-8499-1848-0.

2. Henry Cloud and John Townsend. *Boundaries: When To Say Yes And How To Say No To Take Control Of Your Life.* Grand Rapids: Zondervan, 1992. ISBN: 978-0-310-24745-6.

3. Leighton Ford. *The Attentive Life: Discerning God's Presence In All Things.* Downers Grove, IVP, 2008. ISBN: 978-0-8308-3516-4.

4. Tim Hansel. *When I Relax I Feel Guilty.* Elgin: David C. Cook, 1979. ISBN: 0-89191-137-5.

5. Archibald Hart. *Thrilled To Death: How The Endless Pursuit of Pleasure is Leaving Us Numb.* Nashville: Thomas Nelson, 2007. ISBN: 978-0-8499-1852-0.

6. Roy King. *Time Management Is Really Life Management.* Columbia, SC: LeaderSpace, 2009. ISBN: 978-1-4486-5624-0.

7. Gordon MacDonald. *A Resilient Life: Finish What You Start, Persevere In Adversity, Push Yourself to Your Potential.* Nashville: Nelson Books, 2004. ISBN 0-7852-8791-4.

8. Reggie McNeal. *Practicing Greatness: 7 Disciplines of Extraordinary Spiritual Leaders.* San Francisco: Jossey-Bass, 2006. ISBN: 0-7879-7753-5.

9. Peter Scazzero. *The Emotionally Healthy Church.* Grand Rapids: Zondervan, expanded edition, 2010. ISBN: 978-0-310-29335-4.

10. Richard Swenson. *Margin: Restoring Emotional, Physical, Financial, and Time Reserves to Overloaded Lives.* Colorado Springs: Navpress, 1992. 08910-9887.

LIFE-GIVING LEADERSHIP WITH PEOPLE

IN PART FOUR we look at how we relate to others and how we walk through change with them. Living in a healthy rhythm as described in part three is essential for us to have the margins to invest in relating well with others.

Without people you do not have leadership. I have heard leaders joke, at least I think they were speaking in jest, "Leadership would be great if it weren't for the people." But in reality, if no one is responding to your influence, you are only leading yourself. Pastor Don Barry writes:

The first basic core value that undergirds our ministry is that we choose to value people. . . . People are the ends, while structure and programming are the means. . . . Jeremiah the prophet has some chilling words for leaders who are tempted to reduce people to so much cannon fodder for the sake of institutional goals. . . . The Message renders this verse (Jeremiah 22:13), 'Doom to him who builds palaces, but bullies people: who makes a fine house but destroys lives.'[1]

Ministry flows best along lines of relationship. Churches often try to substitute paperwork and systems to compensate for the vacuum of relationship and undeveloped community. I once heard Erwin McManus, teaching pastor of Mosaic[2], say, "Only place people in leadership who leave more than they take as they relate to people." That went straight into my journal and has saved me more than once from placing someone into leadership primarily on their ability to get things accomplished. I now ask, "At what relational costs do they get results?"

Chapter eleven will focus on *relating to* people, while chapters twelve and thirteen are reflections on *changing with* people.

CHAPTER ELEVEN

RELATING TO PEOPLE

THE FIVE DIRECTIONS OF RELATIONAL LEADERSHIP

ONE OFTEN NEEDS a simple way to organize learning if it is being consistently applied to life. The five directions of relational leadership (illustrated below) provide a leader with a simple framework to help avoid leadership wrecks that often result from ignoring one of these directions. This grid helps one continue to learn how to improve in each direction.

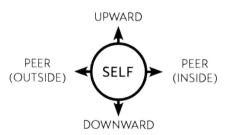

Not all positions of leadership will contain all five directions. This grid is to be viewed as a general guide to be adapted to the particular context of one's leadership. Most people who talk about the grid refer to Dee Hock, the former CEO of Visa, as the seminal thinker. He uses slightly different language than the five directions I have included here. The distinction I make is that horizontal may include those doing the same kind of work that you do, within or outside of your organization.

Example: Youth Pastor — "Peers inside" might be the worship pastor, children's pastor or outreach pastor. "Peers outside" may be youth pastors in other churches similar in size and make up.

In organizations where there is a wide range of time commitment from full-time to volunteer, the leadership directions may be a mixture of people serving at various levels of engagement.

Self-Leadership

Hock estimates 50% of leadership is SELF LEADERSHIP. That has been the focus of this book up to this point. Self-Leadership is primarily about the heart and life rhythms we focused on in parts 2 and 3. Another way of expressing trusting, hoping and giving is as aspects of self-leadership:

> Leadership is often described as getting the best out of other people, but the first job of leadership is often getting the best out of yourself.
> —Richard J. Daft

1. Character = another way of saying **faith** choices
2. Maturity = **hope**ful growth
3. Vitality = refreshing **love**.

UPWARD LEADERSHIP

Upward leadership is providing those over me with what they need to know to lead me.

Is there evidence of Leading UP among the Trinity? Jesus asked the Father in prayer. Jesus carried out the instructions of the Father, saying and doing what his Father asked. Jesus models effective upward leadership.

⏱ PAUSE — TRY IT OUT!

Study on God's use of human authority

Read the following passages, and write out what you learn about God placing you under authority.

God places people under authority.

Luke 22:24-28; John 10:28-31; 2 Corinthians 1:20-24, 2:17, 4:5, 6:16-7:1, 11:3

It is God's will for leaders to model a high value on protecting unity.

John 13-17; 1 John; 2 Corinthians 6:11-12, 7:2-4, 12:15

What do I need to keep in the front of my thinking when I am approaching those over me?

1 Peter 3:13-25; Romans 13:1-10; Titus 3:1-8; Ephesians 6:5-9

Leading UP in an imperfect world

Many senior leaders or boards have very little training or experience of leading down in a way that encourages healthy leading up. Top leadership often assumes, incorrectly, that if they hire good, competent people, it will just happen. Wrong. Leadership relationships, like a good marriage, require focus and intentional effort.

Those under others also make wrong assumptions. It is wrong to expect those over them to be mind readers and to know how to provide them with effective leadership. Never assume that those over you know how to lead you.

Leading UP is taking the initiative to share with those over you who God has created you to be, what you can contribute to the mission, and how you can be most productive over the long term. Leading up is investing encouragement, influence, creativity, and assistance to the person or persons placed over you, specifically, in helping them provide you with empowering leadership.

What if those over me are leading me or the organization poorly?

The critical question for you to answer is, "Can I trust the character/ heart of the person/s over me even when I have good reason to not trust their competence in handling the situation we are facing?"

If you answer "No", pray and ask God if you should leave the position. The Bible warns of the danger of leaders with corrupt character creating a wake of destruction. If you choose to stay, pray and be very cautious.

If you answer "Yes", realize that the poor exercise of competence can still sink the organization, wound people including you, and generally make a mess. A lack of clear communication, or a hundred other poorly executed skills related to leading, managing and empowering others still spells poor supervision.

BUT — skills can be learned and practiced and improved, if supervisors are humble and teachable.

SO — what do you think and do?

Think — I should not assume that someone over me knows how to lead me well. Your supervisor/s are not mind readers and often do not have a good feel of what you need to carry out your responsibilities. They are too concerned about their own work to know yours well. They often hired you to do what they do not have time or desire to do.

Do — Inform the supervisor/s what you need to be empowered and effective in your responsibilities. List your vital contributions to the organization. Then describe what you need now or in the near future to be effective. Sit down and discuss the list—even when it includes items such as, "Limit surprises that disrupt my day or week . . . they confuse my priorities and push me out of clarity into crisis reaction." Be honest but realistic about the nature of the workplace. Lead UP the way you want to be addressed by someone UNDER you.

Also, remember that you work *for* them. Do not assume that you know their preferred work language. Ask questions and then be diligent to lay down your own preferences, if necessary, to use their language.

What is a work language?

Examples of questions that uncover work language or style:

1. How do you prefer to communicate? (Face-to-face planned meetings, as you walk by, e-mail, text, phone, etc.)

2. How do you prefer to address conflict? (Write up summary and then ask to meet to follow-up, over lunch, etc.)

3. How do you prefer to evaluate results? (Standard reports of benchmarks, surveys, daily tasks accomplished, etc.)

4. How do you prefer to handle personal non-work issues in my life? (Leave it at home, let's have coffee, at weekly meeting, etc.)

Bottom Line — We are ALL developing competence in leading UP to those over us and DOWN to those under us. Stay humble and ask this question, "What am I doing that is making your job more challenging or difficult?" Then listen, act on what you hear and follow up in a few weeks to see if you have improved.[1]

⏱ PAUSE — TRY IT OUT!

Questions to help you lead up

Here are some questions to use to help you gain perspective on the Leading UP culture, values and challenges:

1. Stewardship — Why am I here? Do I make a positive difference?
    a. What is my contribution?
    b. Can I support this leadership with my sacrificial giving? (If you can't give joyfully and sacrificially, leave.)
    c. What are the expectations?
    d. How do you measure up?
    e. What am I doing that makes your job more difficult?
    f. What do you need me to provide so you can do your job?
    g. Are you waiting for anything from me right now?

2. Empowerment — What resources have been provided? (Example: How will financial decisions be made?)
    a. How should we be leveraging the resources God has provided?
    b. The only resources we can leverage — Compassion, Cash, Calendar, Communication (4 C's)

    c.   Is there a circle of freedom and safety?

    d.   Am I free to risk, experiment and fail, so I may learn?

    e.   Am I free to ask questions and "push back" of those over me without them becoming defensive or labeling it as disloyal? 1 Cor 10:23-11:1

    f.   What do we need to abandon or stop investing our resources in?

    g.   What do we prioritize or seek additional resources to invest in?

    h.   As we start to make investments, what resistance can we anticipate?

    i.   Conduct a decision audit: list every critical decision that needs to be made in order for the mission to advance.

3.   Excellence — These questions can help you bring your best to leading those over you.

    a.   Do I know what is expected of me?

    b.   Do I have the right materials and equipment to do my work?

    c.   Do I have opportunity to do what I do best every day?

    d.   In the last seven days, have I received recognition or praise for doing good work?

    e.   Does my supervisor, or someone at work, seem to care about me as a person?

    f.   Is there someone at work who encourages my development?

    g.   Do my opinions seem to count at work?

    h.   Does the mission/purpose of my company make my feel my job is important?

    i.   Are my co-workers committed to doing quality work?

    j.   Do I have a best friend at work?

    k.   In the last six months, has someone at work talked to me about my progress?

    l.   This last year, have I had opportunities at work to learn and grow?[2]

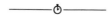

PEER LEADERSHIP

Peer Leadership (Inside & Outside the Organization Where I live)

PEER LEADERSHIP with those inside my organization (sometimes called peer mentoring)

1. Use many of the ideas presented in Leading UP to clarify responsibilities and determine effective communication loops.
2. Be sure you minimize relating as competitors and instead focus on the unique contribution each of you makes to the "wins" for the organization.

PEER LEADERSHIP with those outside my organization (often called professional development—gatherings of the like-minded)

1. Pray for God to help you develop good friendships with those who are further along in the journey who may mentor you.
2. Develop safe relationships to laugh and also share the tears of ministry together.
3. Look for ways to stay connected outside of annual conferences.
4. Share work you create for your context which may be helpful to peers in similar organizations.

Bottom line: Grow friendships with like-minded leaders.

DOWNWARD LEADERSHIP

Downward Leadership (Leading those under me)

DOWNWARD LEADERSHIP (leading those who are looking to me to exercise authority or who expect my influence)

1. Teach all of those under you the Five Directions and provide open discussions coaching them to grow in leading in each direction.
2. If they are leading UP well, you will be learning what you need to lead them.
3. Use the questions provided in the Leading UP section above to create a safe setting for them to share with you the leadership they need from you.

How we Learn as We Lead in the Five Directions

We learn almost everything with and through others. The more we have this clearly in mind, the more effective we can be as learners and teachers. Here are four visuals to help you think through effective life on life development:

1. **Mirrors** - I must be able to see myself well and measure my progress. A simple dashboard of measurements and benchmarks is a helpful guide for frequent review and to make accurate plans for development.

   a. Think of the rulers on the top and side of this computer screen. With one glance I can tell where I am on the page.

   b. I served on the board of a Missions ministry and prior to each board meeting we received several pages that summarized where the organization was on critical financial, registration and training measurements.

2. **Models** — Without a great deal of conscious effort we develop a library of examples in leadership. We compare, contrast and learn from the good and the bad.

   a. From my Boy Scout leaders to my first boss in a grocery store where I bagged groceries, I have been building a library of leadership/influencers in my life.

   b. I even add biographies I read of those long dead to my gathering of models.

3. **Maps** — A traveler uses a map to determine the present location and then set clear plans get to the destination. Often another person or organization helps provide us with a map. They have traveled the same journey and have wise perspectives to offer.

   a. I have a collection of bylaws and organizing documents from churches and organizations I respect, and I have a gained a great deal from what is often months of their thoughtful work.

   b. I ask questions of everyone I meet who is taking the same journey. "What are biggest mistakes to avoid?" "What do you wish you had known when you started out that you have learned since?" "Where are the best places to eat or stay and the ones to avoid?" "If you only have 3 days in that part of the country what is essential that you see or do or who do you want to meet?"

4. **Fixed Points (like GPS)** These are similar to a map, but based on a connection from a known point to an unknown point. I see this correlating in leadership development to principles and generalized truth that can be adapted and applied to many contexts.

    a. Ministry flows best through good relational pipelines.

    b. Never allow conflict to go underground.

    c. The first question is, "Is this a problem to solve or a tension to manage?"

    d. Fruitful ministry is messy. Embrace the ox in the stable.

I am attempting to weave some of each of these into this book.

Loving in ALL Five Directions

God's will is for us to love people. There is no "Plan B" if loving does not work out. Yet loving is complex. It is not just being nice. Love can certainly include confrontation and discipline. Love is to give what is best for the person, often at great personal loss or sacrifice, but also with great joy. Knowing what is best for the beloved requires God's wisdom.

God is always LOVE!

Does God sometimes say, "NO?"

Does he correct, judge, and discipline?

Does he allow people to reap the consequences for their choices?

We have to re-teach ourselves and those we lead what healthy relational love involves. Fortunately the Bible gives us some assistance. God not only commands us to love in the same way Jesus loves us, but he gives us twenty-five commandments in the New Testament which specifically apply to loving within communities of Jesus-followers. I have organized them into four categories:

1. TREASURING — Ways we lift up, honor and build up others. Honoring is valuing who a person IS without stumbling over who they are not.[3]

2. RISKING — We risk being misunderstood but are motivated by a higher goal of seeking the best for the beloved.

3. INITIATING — Take the first step of reaching out to lend a hand and keep our heart open to the beloved.

4. DESTROYING — There are certain behaviors that are opposite of love. They attack or wound the person loved and treasured by God.

⏱ PAUSE — TRY IT OUT!

Applying the reciprocal commands to your community

Look up each command in the four sections of the table below and read it in its context. Reflect on the questions following the list of commands.

TREASURING	RISKING
Accept one another (Rom. 15:7)	Confess sins and pray for one another (James 5:16)
Be at peace (Mark 9:50)	
Be devoted to one another (Rom. 12:10)	Forbear one another (Eph. 4:2)
	Forgive one another (Eph. 4:32)
Be kind to one another (Eph. 4:32)	Greet one another (Rom. 16:16)
Belong to one another (Rom. 12:5)	Live in harmony with one another (Rom. 12:16)
Encourage one another (1 Thess. 5:11)	
Fellowship with one another (1 Jn. 1:7)	Wait for one another (1Cor. 11:33)
Have equal concern (1 Cor. 12:25)	Wash one another's feet (John 13:14)
Honor one another (Rom. 12:10)	
Love one another (John 13:34)	
Be humble (Rom. 12:16)	

INITIATING	DESTROYING
Admonish one another (Col. 3:16)	Do not slander (James 4:11)
Carry burdens for another (Gal. 6:2)	Stop grumbling (John 6:43)
Instruct one another (Rom. 15:14)	Stop passing judgment on one
Offer hospitality (1 Pet. 4:9)	another (Rom.14:13)
Serve one another (Gal. 5:13)	
Speak truthfully (Eph. 4:25)	
Spur others toward love (Heb. 10:24)	

1. Which of the commands are praised in your culture?
2. Which of the commands are seldom practiced in your culture?
3. Which ones are done poorly and need to be modeled and taught?
4. Which commands do you want to develop and learn to do well?
5. Recall some good and bad experiences of the practice of some of the commands? What went wrong?
6. In what ways would those who are not Jesus-followers be influenced if they could see a community consistently living out the one-another commands well?

One of our graduates of Columbia International University is a counselor and Bible teacher whom I deeply respect for his effort of calling fellow Jesus-followers to true biblical community. I think most of us struggle with being God's touch when admonishing or speaking truthfully to one another. I have included Paul Tripp's advice here as a way to stir us to examine our real motives when holding back in fear or lashing out in harshness:

*Real, biblical, self-sacrificing, God-honoring love never compromises what God says is right and true. **Truth and love are inextricably bound together.***

If love wants and works for what is best for you, then love is committed to being part of what God says is best in your life. So, I am committed to being God's tool for what he says is best in your life, even if that means we have to go through tense and difficult moments to get there.

I think often we opt for silence, willingly avoiding issues and letting wrong things go on unchecked, not because we love the other person, but because we love ourselves and just don't want to go through the hassle of dealing with something that God says is clearly wrong. We are unwilling to make the hard personal sacrifices that are the call of real love.

Now, I'm not talking about being self-righteous, judgmental, critical, and condemning. No, I'm taking about choosing not to ignore wrong, but dealing with wrong with the same grace that you have been given by God.

The Cross of Jesus Christ is the only model you need of what love does in the face of wrong. Love doesn't call wrong right. Love doesn't ignore wrong and hope it goes away. Love doesn't turn its back on you because you are wrong. Love doesn't mock you. Love doesn't mean I turn the tables and work to make you hurt in the same way you have hurt me. Love doesn't go passive and stay silent in the face of wrong.

No, loves moves toward you because you are wrong and need to be rescued from you. *In moving toward you, love is willing to make sacrifices and endure hardships so that you may be made right again and be reconciled to God and others. God graces us with this kind of love so that we may be tools of this love in the lives of others.*[4]

How does love show up in our sinful fallen world? We will start with the leader's motives and perspective and then examine several reasons it is difficult to establish and maintain relationships with true intimacy. The intimacy we are aiming for is the way Jesus loves us and the way the Father and Son love each other.[5]

LIFE-GIVING RELATING IS MESSY

One of the best images for leadership is that it takes place in a messy environment. There is something very freeing when I relax and embrace the messy context of life as a leader. Can you picture these two farms from Proverbs 14:4 next door to each other? Farmer "A" has a clean stable but is left to his own strength to plow his furrows and prepare his fields for sowing. Farmer "B" has the added strength and guaranteed greater harvest of plowing with an ox but must also spend some time cleaning the stable.

> Where there are no oxen, the manger is clean, but abundant crops come by the strength of the ox. —Proverbs 14:4 (ESV)

The wrong question for a farmer is, "How can I farm and keep everything clean, controlled and predictable?" The better question is, "What contribution can I make that will produce an abundant harvest?"

Every day I am investing my time in one of two ways. I am working to attain or maintain a clean stable, or I am choosing to wade into messes where there is potential for a greater harvest. Swatting flies, shoveling manure, wrestling a yoke onto an ox, and following its backside while keeping the plow straight somehow captures at least 80% of my best leadership. This book explores those kind of days.

Here are some examples:

Do I respond to an attacking e-mail with prayerful face to face conversation or go to work on a sermon? Can something as spiritual as the study of the Bible be a clean stable that a leader retreats to avoid messy relational encounters?

Do I pray for grace and invest some time in a person who leaves me depleted or go spend time with my missionary best friend? One of my ways of avoiding the messy stuff is to convince myself I am just so busy—but that is just me, right? It takes almost no effort to make myself busy. It is hard to admit that I value cleanliness over messiness and that my busy pace is actually a cave where I hide to feel safe.

Do I include a person who asks hard challenging questions in the invitation list to a meeting or only invite those who I am sure will agree to my recommendations? The ox comes dressed in many different ways; one way can be a person who relates to me like a porcupine.

Can you see the "no ox" and "ox" in each of these decisions?

When I enter into a consulting process with church or parachurch leaders, I ask them to write down specific issues, challenges, questions, problems, and opportunities where it would be of value to have an outsider's perspective. When what comes to me could be summarized as, "Help us get our stable organized and clean; remove the mess, confusion, uncertainty, risk, and lack of control from our leadership," a yellow flag goes up in my mind and I know that the first thing that must change is the perspective and goals of the leadership.

I showed up on a Saturday evening for a first contact with church leaders. They spent the first block of time showing me around the facility.

> Parking lot paved, striped, and sealed—beautiful; hope none of the guests have a car with an oil leak!
> Entrance perfectly color coordinated and no hand prints on any of the walls or doors.
> Perfectly lined up chairs and soft lighting; like a very nice restaurant.
> AND – they showed me the chart and schedule involving many volunteer hours each week keeping the grounds and building pristine.

Is there anything wrong, unbiblical or ungodly with having a nice place to meet? Well of course, meeting environments are filled with cultural values and expectation; but, NO, I cannot make a strong case that the Bible forbids or speaks against a nice place to meet. The problem is: *has this sacrificial investment in cleaning a substitute and maybe even an avoidance of partnering with God's work of cleaning up lives?*

Turns out I could not be much help to them. They had brought me in because they wanted to see new people come into the church. They knew they were aging and in a slow decline. Yet they had voted a few months before to close down a children's ministry that reached out to children in the community. WHY? They were upset by the mess it created — they even had to repaint because of hand prints on the hallways.

Loving with sinful people is very messy. We are ALL sinful so we will all be messy to love.

Being clean and organized can have the sterile feel of an art museum. I love strolling restfully and reflectively through a museum, but it is not a conducive setting for messy work. We pick up the brochure and browse through the hallways and in and out of rooms in awe at the displays.

Growing up, my Dad's second job was auto mechanics. I have been in hundreds of garages. I worked in two shops performing small and routine work while the trained mechanics did the hard stuff. An auto mechanic often starts or ends the day by cleaning up the garage so he can find the right tools and be more productive in what will be a messy week. But if you look away from the tool bench and cabinets, you will see several cars partially disassembled. With some vehicles, the mechanic is seeking to determine the problem, with others, he is waiting on a part to be located or delivered, and still others are being reassembled. Ministry with people always has this same feel.

Read the word of Jesus like you are seeing them for the first time.

Leave your gift there before the altar and go. First be reconciled to your brother, and then come and offer your gift.[6]

Now put yourself into this scenario and tell me the truth. Who wants this kind of day? You get the whole family dressed, fed, and travel across the city by bus to join a gathering of Jesus-followers. And after being there only a few minutes, while everyone is drinking tea and eating sandwiches, and the leaders are get ready to focus the group on worship, you have to excuse yourself to leave. After handing off your children to some close friends and telling them that you will return, you travel to a different section of the city (more buses) to arrive at your friend's flat to seek to mend a relationship. Who wants to join a kingdom with those kind of rules?

But also think of the potential for good that comes from a messy moment like this one.

1. You just loved Jesus by showing him you honor his word and take it as the rule of your life.
2. You have just loved your friend by showing how important a reconciled relationship is in your life.
3. You have just loved your family and community by trusting them to support you seeking to live out the loving life.

And I am sure there many more ways love is strengthened in the messy obedience of one Jesus-follower. Will you be the one?

LIFE-GIVING RELATING CREATES A VIBRANT CULTURE

Now there is a final reason I think that Jesus says, "Love your enemies." It is this: that love has within it a redemptive power. And there is a power there that eventually transforms individuals. Just keep being friendly to that person. Just keep loving them, and they can't stand it too long. Oh, they react in many ways in the beginning. They react with guilt feelings, and sometimes they'll hate you a little more at that transition period, but just keep loving them. And by the power of your love they will break down under the load. That's love, you see. It is redemptive, and this is why Jesus says love. There's something about love that builds up and is creative. There is something about hate that tears down and is destructive. So love your enemies.[7]

We must learn to live together as brothers or perish together as fools.[8]

A loving community requires leadership give attention to crafting a healthy culture within the organization. Organizational culture is defined by the values of the group. Leadership literature in recent years has been filled with research and study of best practices on the "culture" of a business or non-profit — really any organization. Let's focus on one very important component of a group culture: How do people treat one another in this organization? The standards, expectations, and daily rituals of relating determine to a large degree whether the community is satisfying and challenging or chaotic and toxic. The relational culture either draws people in energizing them, or it pushes them away, intimidates or encourages passive consumerism. In churches and ministries seeking to be life-giving, we want our culture to be defined by biblical truth. I have quoted Dave Barry, who pastors a church in Hamilton, New Zealand, earlier in the book. Here is a summary of the values they continually revisit to shape their community.

Our core values create the culture in which we seek to work out our core purposes.

1. We value **people.** God's supreme passion is people. This being so, any endeavor that bears his name must value and love people. We are careful at Gateway to ensure that people never become "the means to the end."

2. We value **authenticity** — We value an atmosphere in which people can be honest and real.

3. We value **integrity** — We seek to function and communicate with

truth and simplicity.

4. We value **vulnerability** — We are all on a journey. There are no "experts" here. The only reason any of us are here is the grace of God. We are honest about that.

Priorities

1. We want people who are a part of Gateway to develop and deepen a personal relationship with God.

2. We want people who are a part of Gateway to be convinced of the value of, and who are developing in, a life of responsive praise and worship of God.

3. We want people who are a part of Gateway to be people who are growing in their knowledge of, and in obedience to, the Word of God, the Bible.

4. We want people who are a part of Gateway to be people who are growing in their ability to recognize and respond to the person and ministry of the Holy Spirit.

5. We want people who are a part of Gateway to be people who are on a journey of identifying, receiving training and using the spiritual gifts that God has given them so that he is glorified and his kingdom extended.[9]

One way to clarify values and begin to shape culture is found in how we pray blessings over one another.

⏱ PAUSE — TRY IT OUT!

Loving people as God loves them

Look up and read the passages in context. Help re-frame how you see the people you lead by praying blessings over them. After reading each passage, pause and think of a specific person, and then pray out loud a prayer of blessing over them.

1. Numbers 6:22-27
2. Romans 15:13

3. Romans 16:19
4. 2 Corinthians 7:4
5. 2 Corinthians 13:11-14
6. Philippians 1:3-7
7. 1 Thessalonians 2:19-20
8. Philemon 1:7
9. Hebrews 13:20-21

———⏱———

⏱ PAUSE — TRY IT OUT!

Practicing living out the King's culture

In Luke 17:1-10, Jesus describes the family rules; the culture. As you read, see my inserted notes and then write out how this teaching applies to your leadership right now.

And he said to his disciples, 'Temptations to sin are sure to come, but woe to the one through whom they come!'

Rule 1: Expect relating well to be hard!

It would be better for him if a millstone were hung around his neck and he were cast into the sea than that he should cause one of these little ones to sin.

Rule 2: Take being the source of pain to others seriously

Pay attention to yourselves! If your brother sins, rebuke him, and if he repents, forgive him, and if he sins against you seven times in the day, and turns to you seven times, saying, 'I repent,' you must forgive him.

Rule 3: When you are sinned against go talk to the person.

Rule 4: If they repent forgive them—keep forgiveness on the table.

The apostles said to the Lord, 'Increase our faith!' And the Lord said, 'If you had faith like a grain of mustard seed, you could say to this mulberry tree, 'Be uprooted and planted in the sea,' and it would obey you.

Rule 5: Repeated forgiving is beyond us and God will help!

Will any one of you who has a servant plowing or keeping sheep say to him when he has come in from the field, 'Come at once and recline at table?' Will he not rather say to him, 'Prepare supper for me, and dress properly, and serve me while I eat and drink, and afterward you will eat and drink'? Does he thank the servant because he did what was commanded? So you also, when you have done all that you were commanded, say, 'We are unworthy servants; we have only done what was our duty.'

Rule 6: This is normal family life in Jesus' family — so don't expect a bonus or a celebration for being a good family member.

Organizational culture can contain weeds that will hinder the growth of life-giving fruit. It can be challenging to deal with the weeds because for many of us there is a unstated assumption that our way of seeing is the true or correct way.

What are Four Frequent Disruptors to Life-Giving Culture?

1. Unexamined definitions and expectations
2. Failing to live responsibly in our circles of responsibility and influence
3. Distorted images of God
4. Dividing our world into secular and sacred

Unexamined Definitions and Expectations

When I was a pastor, I used to say to the people I served, with some humor in my manner but serious in my intent, ***"There are only two kinds of people in this church; those I have disappointed and those I will disappoint. If you are one of the few whom I have not disappointed you must not have been here very long."*** I wanted to prompt a conversation on a regular basis that made it okay to acknowledge our disappointments.

➤ Often anger grows out of unprocessed disappointment.

➤ Often lack of trust grows out of disappointment that we are unconsciously holding over someone.

➤ Often a slow cooling and distancing in a relationship are also growing out of disappointment.

Disappointment that is not understood and dealt with is often the silent killer in a marriage that is struck down by adultery and dies in divorce.

Disappointment occurs when a person has expectations of another person's behavior, words, dress, etc. that are not met. I heard Larry Crabb say in a message at a family conference something like, "Most people can sort out their relational problems without a counselor if they learn to closely examine the DEFINITIONS and EXPECTATIONS they are holding and using on others and self."

Why is this so hard to do? Look at Genesis 3. After Adam and Eve's disobedience to God in the garden, they hide in shame from him and one another. We have not stopped hiding. And as we hide from each other, we also lose focus on what is really going on inside of ourselves. Expectations and definitions hide in the shadows of our awareness.

Here are some of the types of expectations and definitions I have seen damage my own or others' relationships:

1. I DEFINE the truth only by what I believe it to be at the moment.

2. I EXPECT you to understand my needs and meet them in the way I need you to, but without me having to tell you what they are or how I prefer you meet them. If you really care you would *know*.

3. I EXPECT to be thanked for my serving and contribution in a certain way.

4. I DEFINE success as reaching the stated goal we had when we started the journey. Anything that falls short or is different from the starting objective is TOTAL failure.

5. I EXPECT you to remember my name because we met once a few months back. And by the way I remember your name…

6. I DEFINE anger as any increase in volume or intensity in your voice. And even if you are speaking about others, I know you are also angry with me.

7. I DEFINE excellence as an end in itself, and it really equates with making me look good.

What do some of these examples have in common? We are often not conscious that we are holding them, or even how we arrived at that definition or formed an expectation. Because we are in a fog about the definitions or expectations motivating our action or judgment toward you, we are also failing to speak openly and directly with you.

In part two on the heart of the life-giving leader, I laid out three responses of the heart that are always God's will: trusting, enduring, and giving, or to state them in noun form: faith, hope and love. Earlier we stated the opposite of faith is often fear. The opposite of hope is usually to quit or pull back. The opposite of love, which is biblically defined as giving, is lust — a desire to take from.

One helpful suggestion to encourage you to pause and see what is going on in relationships is to put *faith, hope* and *love* as green lights on your dashboard as you "drive" into relationships. Also put *fear, despair* and *lust* as red lights on your dashboard. The presence of these attitudes and the actions that flow out of them are recognizable. If the red lights begin to flash, we need to pull over and see what is going on.

How do I process and decide what to do next, once I am aware that we hold differing expectations and definitions? There only a few options.

1. **I am right and they are wrong** — If that is true then honest conversation is needed to let them adopt my definition or expectation.

2. **I am wrong and they are right** — I may know that we are at different places, but not be aware I am wrong until we start to examine the gap between us. If I honestly recognize the possibility that I *may* be wrong, it frees me to ask questions, listen, and if needed, ask for forgiveness and make some edits in the definitions and expectations I am carrying into the relationship.

3. **We are both right and just different** — This means that both of our views fall within biblical guidelines and we need to appreciate that we are different. This often occurs when we relate to people of different cultures. There are many cultural differences relating to our view of time, priorities of people vs. task, modesty, etc., that when viewed with no bias are not outside biblical lines but are a violation of each other's definitions or expectations. Learning how they formed their view and adopting tolerance, grace and an appreciation of the difference can really help.

4. **We are both wrong** — The Bible and wise counselors can assist us in sorting out where we both need to change in order to reach more correct expectations and definitions.

Failing to live responsibly in our circles of responsibility and influence

God is Sovereign over Our Responsibilities and Influence

God rules over all. He is ultimately responsible and the ultimate influence toward his story that history records.

God designed us with the capacity to think, feel and choose, and he then draws a circle around every person which he does not cross. He wants us to choose to love, obey and trust Him. But he never forces, manipulates or violates the circle of our personhood. His kingdom runs on the fuel of kingdom citizens choosing loyalty and love to the King!

> No man can think clearly when his fists are clenched.
>
> —George Jean Nathan

The implications of this truth for ministry include such practices as how we approach counseling and care. In every counseling appointment, give a homework assignment and do not schedule the next appointment. Explain that when the work is completed, then it is time to contact you and set the next appointment. There is a danger in ministry of pulling people under our "rule" instead of encouraging them to respond to God's rule.

Robertson McQuilkin is one of my mentors. When people interview him and try and draw out how he planned to make the kingdom impact that has flowed from his life, he honestly tells them he had no such plan. In his life, he never really attempted to do great things, he just **did the next thing God gave him to do**. Some of them produced little visible impact, and some have produced tremendous visible ministry. But he did not calculate or plan for "big" or "great"—he just sought to respond in trust and obedience to the next step God showed him.

The goal which shapes our choices should be to take steps of following Jesus. We are responding to his actions and movements in this world. God has designed us in his image, and at least one implication of this is that *his rule* and *relationship with him* directs our lives. Adam and Eve were given the first command, which was an act of delegation by the Creator, instructing them to be fruitful and to rule over the earth. But in the details of our creation in Genesis 2, Adam's first breath came from being face to face with God. God gives Adam life by breathing into him, and he wakes like the sleeping princess in Sleeping Beauty. Adam and Eve walk with God in the garden. They know God in oneness with him, in intimacy. They were perfectly made for fellowship with him.

As the progressive revelation of the Scripture continues, we find another man walking with God—Abraham (Genesis 17:1—"walk before me, be blameless"). This idea of a holy walk (like God) helps us understand the role of the law of God for the God-follower. Because of sin, we lose our ability to discern God's will (the good and the right). Law was a gift from God, not only to expose our sinful heart and desperate need for forgiveness by God, but also to describe God-likeness. The law visualizes the rule of God over life and the personal relationship with God, which he desires for us to enjoy.

We are made in God's image and he grants each of us a *circle of responsibility* and *circle of influence*, which is pictured in the illustration below. When this basic ground rule of relationship is ignored or violated, it causes relationships to implode in misunderstandings and disappointment.

The circle of responsibility

My responsibilities before God.

I am responsible *for* my:
➤ WORDS
➤ ATTITUDES

- ➤ ACTIONS
- ➤ THOUGHTS

Biblically, it is clear that God has placed these four items in my circle of personal responsibility (I won't take the space to make the argument here). What is more interesting is what is **NOT** in my circle:

- ➤ I am not responsible for how others respond to my words or actions.
- ➤ I cannot be responsible for the assumptions, judgments, attitudes or thoughts inside of another person.
- ➤ I cannot assume responsibility for someone's happiness. (I can be responsible to not inflict unnecessary unhappiness!)

When you take out what does not belong in my circle of responsibility, it is actually quite a small piece of real estate. The number one robber of life for me has been my assuming too much responsibility for others and failing to focus on the circle God has designed to delegate to me.

The circle of influence

My reach and influence into this world is where I can touch others.

With others, it is important to remember I am RESPONSIBLE TO them but not FOR them. I heard Ron Dunn say once in a sermon, "Most of the problems we have in our Christian life come about because we ask God to be responsible FOR what he has told us to be responsible FOR and we try to be like God for what he says only he can be responsible FOR."[10] Did you follow that sentence?

Examples:

I am responsible TO love my wife — but I am not responsible FOR her choices.

I am responsible TO my parents — but I am not responsible FOR them to be happy in their circumstances.

I am responsible TO love my enemies — but I am not responsible FOR how they respond to my loving actions.

God's Spirit empowers me to live well within my circle of responsibility and takes my obedience to lovingly be responsible TO others and multiplies the seeds I sow. The primary way a Jesus-follower influences others is through prayer in Jesus' name and acts of loving with Jesus' love.

The Foundation of life-giving relationships is:

➤ Clarity on what I am responsible FOR (These are my goals to which I answer to God)
➤ Clarity on what I am responsible TO (My desires and prayers which I offer for the sake of others).

A wife with an alcoholic husband should not have a goal of having a sober husband and a Christian home. That is surely a good desire and a great prayer request. Her only legitimate goal before God is to be a godly loving wife exercising wise and perhaps tough love to bring grace and truth to her husband. For example, she can't be responsible for his choice to drink, but she can choose to not lie to his boss for him to cover up or enable his poor choice.

Personal Responsibility and God's Rule — Where and How One Serves

➤ Are you a free agent?
➤ What does the Bible teach about God's level of influence over our choices?
➤ What does the Bible teach about our responsibility to others?
➤ What does the Bible teach about individual accountability to God for one's choices?
➤ Does trusting God for results in ministry prevent us "measuring" and making hard changes based on assessment?

The Bible does teach that God is in control of all actions and his will becomes reality. (Job 42:2; Proverbs 21:30; 2 Kings 19:25; Psalm 33:11; 40:5; Isaiah 23:8-9; 25:1; 37:26; Jeremiah 29:11; Hebrews 11:40). We live in a world where, when we increase control over a person, the person's range of freedom decreases. When we lessen influence over another, their freedom increases. It is a see-saw type of arrangement that holds true from friendship to government, from marriage to employment.

Yet God is unique. Because his power, knowledge, and presence are without limit, he can prescribe for us a circle of freedom and responsibility without decreasing his control over the outcome. There is no other relationship where power and freedom work in this manner.[11] We experience a taste of sovereignty when we stand in the circle of responsibility granted to us by God. He can overrule our plans. (Job 5:12; Psalm 64:5-8; Isaiah 8:10)

Our range of personal rule is so limited; I cannot even make my heart keep beating. Biblical scholars have been seeking understanding on God's rule and our responsibility for centuries, and I do not propose to answer all of the issues in this brief study. But I would stress that our relationship of living under the rule of God is unique. It is a one of a kind understanding of power, freedom, control, and responsibility. It is very difficult to open the Bible and read for just a page or two and not come away with two truths: **God is in charge** — the outcome of history is not up for grabs or being created as we go, and **he holds us accountable for our choices** — we do not have excuses that will stand up. That is one reason we need forgiveness as a mercy gift provided by the death of Jesus. We are without excuse (Romans 3:10-20).

Therefore,

> ➤ We are citizens in a kingdom unlike any other kingdom
> ➤ We willingly operate under the rule of God and long to see his will visible over all of creation

As his kingdom agents,
> ➤ We should be responsible TO but not attempt to assume responsibility FOR others
> ➤ We respect the circle of choice of others. We do not violate or manipulate their personhood.

God is the Relator — We have a family in heaven

We are made in his image — his will is for us to be recipients and givers of love.

Therefore,

> We love.

> We are slow to judge. We suspend our art of quick judgment.

> We look for ways to give.

> We are not here to be served but to serve.

> We do not use others to build our comfortable kingdoms.

Our actions, attitudes and speech about others reveals what we believe about ourselves and others as image bearers. How we see our self and people is rooted in how we see God.

DISTORTED IMAGES OF GOD

Our definition of God is THE foundation of our leadership. Wrong beliefs about God will produce wrong perspective on my leadership and wrong perspective on the people I am leading. Distorted images of God pollute everything else I see.

☉ PAUSE — TRY IT OUT!

Examining and correcting our view of God

Read over these six DISTORTED images of God. After each one write out a prayer to God for what is true to his nature and how he relates to you.

Six Examples of a Distorted Image of God

#1 - The Distorted God of Impossible Expectations, Psalm 103:1-14

Children have a tremendous need for approval from their parents. They want their parents to be pleased with them. Unfortunately some parents, often in a desire to develop the best in their child, withhold encouraging words and speak only to correct and criticize. When children are unable to win the approval of their parents, they take in negative messages, not only about themselves but also about God.

The result may be that God is seen as one who is never pleased. His standards are impossible, his expectations beyond reach. Biblical texts which speak of God's desire for service and obedience are absorbed as justification for self-condemnation. And texts which proclaim God's unconditional love may not be absorbed at all.

In contrast to this distorted image, the God of the Old and the New Testaments is presented as a gracious and merciful God who delights in his children and loves all that he has made. He is a God who knows and accepts our limitations far better than we do ourselves.

Read Psalm 103:1-14

1. What insights did you gain during your time of personal reflection?
2. How are the actions that God takes on our behalf described?
3. What do these verses reveal about God's character?
4. Which of God's qualities or actions described in this text are especially meaningful to you? Why?
5. What does this psalm say about God's expectations of us?
6. How does the image of a God-of-realistic-expectations compare or contrast with your understanding of God?
7. How does this biblical image of God help you to feel more accepted and loved?
8. What practical steps can you take this week to remember that God is "the Lord of Compassion"?

Prayer: What do you want to say to the God-of-realistic-expectations?

#2 - The Emotionally Distant Distorted God, Hebrews 4:14-16

Children are very emotional people. Infants experience sorrow and joy, and they express these emotions freely. As they move out of infancy, children continue to need to have their feelings acknowledged and responded to. They need to know that their sadness and happiness matters to the people who are most important to them.

It is not uncommon, however, for parents to discount or minimize the feelings which their children express. Rather than providing emotional closeness by hearing and validating their children's emotional experiences, parents often distance themselves from their children emotionally. Common family messages that minimize the emotional experiences of childhood include: "Big boys don't cry," "It's just your feelings that got hurt," "Don't come out of your room until you have a smile on your face," and "Don't be silly, there is nothing to be afraid of." These messages create shame in the child for feeling these things and result in an emotional distance between the child and the parents.

As a result of the emotional distance they experienced as children, many people develop an image of God as unsympathetic and emotionally distant. God is seen as cold and unapproachable. He is seen as interested only in facts and in performance. People who have experienced emotional distance in their families may ask: "How could God understand my problem? Does he even care about what I feel?" The image of the emotionally distant God is dramatically different from the biblical image of Immanuel, "God with us." God came and lived with us, as one of us. He felt our temptations and struggles and feelings. He offers an intimacy with himself which includes the emotional closeness for which we long.

Read Hebrews 4:14-16
1. What insights did you gain during your time of personal reflection?
2. A high priest stood before God on behalf of the people. In this passage, what qualifications does Jesus have to serve in this capacity?
3. What does it mean that Jesus can "sympathize with our weaknesses"?
4. How does the image of God-who-sympathizes-with-your-weakness compare with your image of God's emotional involvement with you?
5. According to this passage, what is now possible for us with Jesus as our high priest?
6. What encourages you about this invitation to approach the God-who-sympathizes-with-your-weaknesses?
7. Spend a few quiet minutes before God. Picture yourself approaching him confidently. Picture him sharing your feelings. Listen as he says to you, "Receive my mercy; here is grace for you in your

time of need." Describe your experience during this meditation.

8. What difference would it make to you as you face your current struggles to know that God cares about you emotionally?

Prayer: What are you experiencing at this time that you would like to share with the God-who-sympathizes-with-your-weaknesses?

#3 - The Disinterested Distorted God, Psalm 139:1-18

Parents are busy people. Their lives are full of anxieties about work, money and relationships. They work long hours. They are tired. Sometimes they are depressed. Some have learned from childhood not to talk and not to feel. So they may not be very good at helping their children talk and feel. As a result, parents often communicate a lack of interest in their children. If they do manage to show interest in their child's performance in athletics or in academics, they often fail to communicate interest in the child as a person.

Children who experience their parents as disinterested often view God as disinterested as well. God may seem to be too busy with other matters to care or to listen. As a result, it may be very difficult for them to imagine that God could be interested in the daily struggles of life.

The God of the Bible, however, is presented as being intimately involved with us. He is interested in what we need and think and feel and do. He pays attention to us.

One way of challenging our distorted images of God is to meditate on Scripture. Several biblical images which picture God as interested and attentive are listed below, along with a Scripture passage.

Choose one of these images and write a brief prayer to God which focuses on your response to that image.

1. Counselor   Isaiah 9:6
2. God with Us   Matthew 1:23
3. Helper   Hebrews 13:6
4. Spouse   Hosea 2:16
5. Mother Eagle   Deuteronomy 32:10-11

Read Psalm 139:1-18

1. What insights did you gain from your time of personal reflection?
2. What in this prayer suggests that God is interested in and attentive to you?
3. What is the author's response to God's attentiveness?
4. The author says to God that no matter where he goes in the world, "your hand will guide me and your right hand will hold me fast." What does this picture communicate to you?
5. How does the image of the God-who-is-attentive, which is presented in this prayer, compare or contrast with your own image of God?
6. How does it affect your sense of security to know that God pays attention to you?
7. What practical things can we do to help each other join the author in seeing God's attentiveness as good news?
8. Write a brief prayer, thanking God his loving attention.

Prayer: What do you need the God-who-is-attentive to pay attention to today?

#4 - The Abusive Distorted God, Matthew 20:29-34

Children silently ask their parents every day: "Do you love me?" In order to experience the answer "yes," children need attention, affection and guidance from their parents. Unfortunately many children experience abuse instead of affection, and harsh punishment instead of guidance. They hear violent words from their parents, words that convince them that they are not lovable or valuable or capable. They may also experience violent actions which leave them terrified, violated, with no safe place to hide.

Experiences of verbal, physical or sexual abuse can shatter any image of a loving, gentle God. God is seen instead as easily angered and demanding. If a person doesn't feel and think and act just right, God stands ready to punish. But the God of the Bible is not an abusive parent. He is not easily angered. God does not yell hurtful words at us or stand ready to club us. He is, rather, the Father of Compassion. He is the one who heals our brokenness. He is the one who is moved with compassion by our need, and who is ready to act on our behalf.

In order to see God as one who is gentle in his love for us, and who provides protection for us, it helps to focus on one of the many biblical pictures of him. Choose one of the following images of God from Scripture and write a prayer to God, focusing on that image.

1. Comforter   Jeremiah 8:18
2. Deliverer   Psalm 18:2
3. Father of Compassion   2 Corinthians 1:3
4. Father of the Fatherless   Psalm 68:5
5. Refuge   Psalm 9:9

Read Matthew 20:29-34

1. What insights did you gain during your time of personal reflection?
2. When the blind men called to Jesus for mercy, "the crowd rebuked them and told them to be quiet." What kinds of things do you think the crowd might have said to these men?
3. What attitudes do you think the crowd had toward them?
4. In spite of the crowd's attitude, Jesus stops. He calls to the men, asks them a question and listens to their answer. What attitude does this suggest Jesus had toward the men?
5. The text says, "Jesus had compassion on them and touched their eyes." What impresses you about his response?
6. In addition to receiving their sight, what were the consequences of the encounter with Jesus for these men?
7. How does the portrait of Jesus in this text challenge the image of an abusive God?
8. What experiences have you had of God's power to heal in your life?
9. How would it help you with your current struggles to know that God loves you and desires to heal you?

Prayer: What do you want the God-whose-touch-heals to do for you?

#5 - The Unreliable Distorted God, Psalm 145

Many children conclude from observing the adults in their lives that people are unreliable. Adults sometimes make promises they do not keep. Sometimes they get angry when there seems to be nothing to be angry about. Adults may be loving, attentive and kind at times and hostile, inattentive and unkind at other times. These changes may take place without explanation and without an opportunity for clarification. It can be very confusing.

Children need love to be reliable and predictable. When people they trust are unreliable, they experience both confusion and disappointment. Often they begin to believe that everything would be better if they tried harder to please their parents. Children do not, however, have the power to control the behavior of their parents. Eventually, they give up. They decide they cannot count on other people. Often, by extension, they conclude that they cannot count on God. They believe that they can only count on themselves. People who have experienced repeated disappointments with parents or other significant people can develop an image of an unreliable God. He is seen as a God who cannot be counted on. He makes promises he may not keep. He may be loving one day and unaccountably angry the next. People who have experienced unreliable parents may ask: "How do I know God will keep his promises? How do I know he listens to me? How do I know he will answer me or help me?"

The image of an unreliable God stands in stark contrast to biblical images of God. The God of the Bible is the Faithful One, the Rock, and the Fortress. He is the same, yesterday, today and forever.

Read Psalm 145
1. What insights did you gain during your time of personal reflection?
2. What descriptive words and phrases are used about God?
3. What phrases suggest that God is reliable?
4. What image of God comes through most clearly from this psalm?
5. How does this compare with your image of God's reliability?
6. Why is it important for you to know that God is reliable?

In order to correct distorted images of God, we need to allow our imaginations to be engaged by the biblical text. Focus on the phrase: "God satisfies the desires of every living thing." Picture God, the Faithful King, with his hands stretched out to you, wanting to satisfy your desires. Meditate on this image for a few minutes. Describe your thoughts and feelings during this meditation.

Prayer: Write a brief prayer of thanks to God for his faithfulness. What would you like to say to the God-who-is-reliable?

#6 - The Distorted God Who Abandons, Luke 15:1-7

Separation. Divorce. Death. Prolonged hospitalization of a parent. Mom or Dad's endless hours at the bar. Or at work. For a child, these are experiences of abandonment. One of their parents, to whom they look for their very survival, has left them.

A child's perspective of reality is very limited. A child asks, "Why would my parent leave me?" Often the child concludes, "It must have been my fault. If I had been better or happier or nicer, my parent would not have left." It is easy to see how a child could end up with feelings of anxiety and over-responsibility. A child experiences terrible trauma when abandoned by a parent. It can destroy the child's sense of security. And it can leave a deep fear that the other people the child loves may also leave. Out of this insecurity and fear grows an image of God as one who also will abandon. The person may try very hard to please God, hoping that God will not leave. But the fear of abandonment by God is always there.

The god-who-abandons is not the God of the Bible. The biblical image is of a God who will never leave or forsake us and of a God who will be with us until the end. Not only will God never leave us, but when we are lost, He will come and look for us.

Read Luke 15:1-7

1. What insights did you gain during your time of personal reflection?
2. How did the response of the tax collectors and sinners to Jesus differ from that of the Pharisees and teachers of the law?

3. What is the difference between hearing Jesus and muttering?
4. Why do you think the Pharisees believed it was wrong to "welcome sinners" and to eat with them?
5. Jesus told this story in response to the Pharisees' "muttering."
6. What does this story tell us about God?
7. How might the realization that God takes the initiative to have a relationship with you help you to be more secure in that relationship?
8. How does the image of God rejoicing when he finds you help you feel loved by him?
9. What difference would it make to you in your current struggles to remember that God will never leave you?

Prayer: What do you need today from the God-who-rejoices-when-he-finds-the-lost?[12]

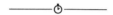

DIVIDING OUR WORLD INTO SECULAR AND SACRED

Be cautious of segregating life into boxes labeled "sacred" and "secular". The Bible instructs that everything in every place is to be done for his glory (1 Corinthians 10:31-33). Be careful of defining ministry as only service that takes place in the church building or is connected to ministry activities. The presence of the church is to be invasive in the community.

Once we begin to separate life into the sacred and secular, it is easy to create other separations. Be careful of valuing congregational activities over being part of the geographic church of a region or city. Perhaps only in the West can we accumulate such abundance of resources that an individual congregation may operate independently from the others in the same community. The impact of the church encompasses local, regional, and global strategy (Acts 1:8). Some would argue that the emphasis in the verse is on cultural difference instead of geographic distance. I encourage churches to think both ways. Within our local geographic reach, what opportunities exist to minister to a distinct cultural group requiring a distinctive group strategy?

Jesus did operate with an "all peoples" heart. Jesus clearly demonstrated a global perspective even though he targeted his ministry to Abraham's chosen ones (John 12, Matthew 28, and Matthew 9).

Life-giving relationships networks, builds bridges, and seeks unity, not separation by being so busy in our back yard we fail to ever look over the fence.

THINKING IT THROUGH

1. How could you address loving in five directions in your leadership this month?

2. How will you live out the one-another commands so they contribute to a life-giving organizational culture?

3. Are you ready for the mess of leadership?

4. The kingdom runs on personal responsibility. What are some ways you can address the four disruptors:
   a. Definitions and expectations
   b. Circles of responsibility and influence
   c. Distorted images of God
   d. Separating the secular and the sacred

RECOMMENDED RESOURCES

1. The Arbinger Institute. *Leadership and Self-Deception: Getting Out of The Box.* San Francisco: Berrett-Koehleer, 2000. ISBN: 1-57675-174-0.

2. Jim Brown. *The Imperfect Board Member: Discovering The Seven Disciplines of Governance Excellence.* San Francisco: Jossey-Bass, 2006. ISBN: 978-0-7879-8610-0.

3. Max Depree. *Leadership is an Art.* New York: Doubleday, 1989. ISBN: 0-385-26496-8.

CHAPTER TWELVE

CHANGING WITH THE PEOPLE WE LEAD

You cannot seize opportunities prompted by change if you cannot see opportunities prompted by change. —Michael G Winston

Problems are only opportunities in work clothes. —Henry J. Kaiser

Announcing a change is not the same as implementing it.
—Ken Blanchard and Dee Edington

LIFE-GIVING LEADERS PROCESS CHANGE WITH THE PEOPLE THEY LEAD

MOST OF LEADERSHIP is about processing change. Everything in the book up to this point—

A God Focus,

The Tools Focus,

A Heart Focus,

A Time Focus,

And a Relating Focus

— prepare the leader to navigate change with those they are influencing.

Leadership is a calling from God to be involved in his activity. God is into change. New births, redemption, restoration, death to life, conquering kingdom rule, new heart — all biblical words. If God, (The leader of all leaders) is into change, guess what? Your leadership in his family is going to be about initiating and responding to change.

To be alive is to be changing

We cannot be alive and avoid change. One of the skills that contributes to the sense of fulfillment and joy in life is the capacity to navigate the constant moving waters of change.

Notice these "re" words:

- ➤ Re-pent,
- ➤ Re-deem,
- ➤ Re-sist,
- ➤ Re-ignite
- ➤ Re-turn
- ➤ Re-fresh
- ➤ Re-vive

Much of our life takes place in a "changing room". We start, and then we start again at many points on our spiritual journey. Leaders invest their lives in kick-starting people into spiritual change. Leaders also guide and coach people in learning and growing from the change that God brings into their life.

In the final section of the book, we will lay out the direction and destination of life-giving leadership. So keep in mind, we are looking at some of the dynamics of change apart from the target of all our leadership. The changes we experience should always be evaluated by the way God's wind intends to blow his kingdom people. From a life-giving perspective, history judges change by how well it aligns with God's objectives for his people.

What is CHANGE?

Change is how we describe and experience movement. It can be found in a variety of types of movement:

1. Geographic (from Place A to Place B)
2. Over time (from birth to death)
3. Qualitative (from healthy to sick)
4. Quantitative (from a few to many more)

5. Way of thinking (from one value or perspective to another)

We classify change as positive or negative based on our perception of the direction and goal of the change. Previously we examined disappointment and the role of our expectations and definitions in fostering disappointment. Those relational reactions and approaches wrapped up in our values are the benchmarks we use for labeling a change as good or bad.

Change requires energy, which may be experienced as positive or negative. Energy can be a "push" or a "pull". People are energized or motivated to embrace a change process when they are touched by:

Change is an expense of energy that influences motion.

Positive influence: A compelling vision, which leads to a desire to pursue a preferred future.

Negative influence: A "burning oil platform"—leads to a desire to avoid pain and/or loss.

⏱ PAUSE — TRY IT OUT!

What does change feel like?

Read Matthew 1 and 2 and Luke 1 and 2. Focus on each person touched by the birth of Jesus. Review the accounts of the changes in their lives. Take some time and review some of the major changes God has brought into your life. What axioms are you starting to see that are true of most major changes?

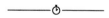

My answer: God initiates these changes, but from the perspective of the people living through the changes, it feels like:

1. Life is full of the unexplainable and the unexpected and change is the interruption of our plans.
2. People need information and inspiration during the change.
3. It is normal to experience turmoil during periods of change.
4. People's reactions to change reveal the condition of their heart.

5. Most change feels messy and uncertain.

6. God does not change— we do.

7. All change, even if it brings tremendous value and blessing, still contains losses for those involved.

GOD IS A CHANGE AGENT

God is into change. The Holy Spirit is resident in every Christ-follower as God's "change agent". God is not afraid of change; he is the author of it. God changes people by loving them. A dear friend, Pete Cannon, told me not long before he died, "It is our job to love people. It is God's job to make them lovable." Do not seek to do God's job. Trust the power of the Spirit to give you the capacity to love those that are not easily loved.

⏱ PAUSE — TRY IT OUT!

How God views change

Read the following passages and then offer God a prayer of thanks for how he views change.

Psalm 102:25-28

In the beginning you laid the foundations of the earth, and the heavens are the work of your hands. They will perish, but you remain; they will all wear out like a garment. Like clothing you will change them and they will be discarded. But you remain the same, and your years will never end. The children of your servants will live in your presence; their descendants will be established before you.

Matthew 18:3

And he said: 'I tell you the truth, unless you change and become like little children, you will never enter the kingdom of heaven.'

1 Corinthians 15:51

Listen, I tell you a mystery: We will not all sleep, but we will all be changed.

Change is normative and is part of the created design. However, the introduction of sin impacted change over time so that aging and decay leading to death serves to limit the impact of sinfulness. We were created for eternal life in a love relationship with God and each other as image bearers. Will there be change on the other side of death? I would say, "Yes!" But it is difficult to conceive what it will look and feel like. It is difficult for us to conceive of change unaffected by death, loss or sin.

How does God guide us into and reinforce changes?

It is encouraging to see how God seeks to prepare his people for change, call them into the change, and then encourage them as they change. Perhaps we can learn, as life-giving leaders, how to assist people as they process changes. Here are some samples of God's teaching tool box:

> ➤ God uses STORIES (real history and parables), "Remember Abraham...", "A farmer went out to sow his seed..."
>
> ➤ God uses PICTURES/IMAGES (creation, and word images to visualize eternal truth) "I am the vine..." "Drink this cup..."
>
> ➤ God uses PROVERBS (distilled wisdom in memorable words) Proverbs are God's bumper stickers! "Ox, Dirty Stable, Greater harvest..." Do I need to say more?
>
> ➤ God uses POETRY (The majority of poetry is set in musical form which makes it memorable and transferable) "The Lord is my shepherd..."
>
> ➤ God uses CONSEQUENCES (reaping from what is sown "letting the chips fall") "so, God gave them a king..."
>
> ➤ God uses QUESTIONS and DIALOGUE (Ones he asks and ones he lets the people ask him) "Adam, who told you, you were naked..." "Jesus, why do you say..." God listens as well as speaks.
>
> ➤ God uses GIFTS/THE BLESSING "God promises rewards..."
>
> ➤ God uses CORRECTION/THE CURSE "A father disciplines those he loves..."
>
> ➤ God uses PRESENCE/BEING AMONG "The Word became flesh..."

THE ORGANIZATIONAL LIFE CYCLE

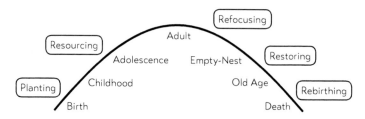

THE LIFE CYCLE

In life-giving organizations there are parties celebrating and embracing change as a good and healthy aspect of being alive. How can we read passages like 1 Corinthians 15 or 2 Corinthians 5 and fail to see that God is all about resurrection, restoring glory and new creation? God's physical world, even in its groaning with sin and death, still reflects his love for change. Movement in the organic world is one indication of life. It is the same with our created structures. Change is an indicator of life. No change — check the pulse. Similar to the biological life cycle of change from birth to death, Scripture never promises our man-made organizational structures will last forever. History tells us our structures have a life cycle.[1]

For everything there is a season, and a time for every matter under heaven...[2]

Change occurs in the life cycle of every organization. Rapid, high cost change occurring on the rapid growth side of the cycle is easier to absorb than similar type of change occurring in old age. How many times do you overhear grandparents talking about the joy of grandchildren but adding something like this, "They are so energetic! That is why God gives us children when we are young."

The life cycle is a tool to help leaders understand any organization in its development or decline. Life cycle theory helps leaders answer the question, "Where are we living"? As I coach congregational and parachurch ministry leaders, I observe that many of the wrong strategic decisions made by leaders result from failing to consider the stage of the organization. Understanding one's physical stage of life gives helpful guidance on the most appropriate care and practices to choose.

Perhaps God gives organizations a limited shelf life to prevent them from becoming idols we treasure more than Him.

A human life is more like WALKING on a journey than PLANNING with a blueprint.[3] "Whoever claims to live in him *must walk* as Jesus did." Most organizational planning processes are very different from going on a journey where God is the initiator and we are responding to his lead.

I have turned sixty. Yet I had to arrive at that mile marker one day at a time; 21,900 of them to be exact. Each of those days included thousands of steps, leading to hundreds of crossroads, and hundreds of choices. And each day placed me at a different point in my journey. Every one of those days I could say, "I am once again at a place I have never been before". This "new" place invites me to look around and approach each step in a childlike, questioning, learning mode. Daily, in my never-before-walked-path, I am discovering God's presence and power to respond to every person, event or circumstance he brings to me. Ministering to aging parents, adult children, and a seasoned marriage requires a fresh daily dose of God's grace.[4]

Yet Christian organizations have spent millions of kingdom dollars on long term planning, and most of it is a waste. Much of our planning in the church is a sad attempt to copy corporate models of planning. These models have a starting point that leaves no room for a dramatic intervention by God.

Our timelines, projections and budgets may even dull us to anticipating and hungering for Him. Long-range planning is often an attempt to extend our very limited human control into the future and "play God" when Jesus has clearly instructed us to invest in the future by how we live today. We are to always place our planning, in humility, under his sovereignty, not seeking to project an appearance of our control of the future[5].

Life-Giving Leaders Do Need to Plan

Planning for Christians is reminding ourselves what God treasures and then committing to be intentional in pursuing those same treasures, regardless of the reaction of the world around us. We are to invest in bringing God the gifts he values. And what does he treasure? People![6] This approach to planning is more like "walking with the God who is building his church" instead of a static set of predictions and goals. A "WALKING WITH GOD" planning process will parallel the biblical principles of how an individual navigates the life cycle through seeking wisdom, clinging to God, and joining him in what he is doing.[7]

I need exercise and swimming is best on my joints. If God gives warm sunny days, I swim outside. On a rainy day, I swim inside. God provides the weather, and I adjust the tactical strategy but do not give up the goal. And if I am traveling, I may need to use the machines in the hotel gym. The point being, there is a clear objective and flexible options on pursuing it. I must be willing to change.

When it comes to planning, there is good news and bad news.

The "good news" is that planning forces us to acknowledge reality and cuts through our denial of the serious issues facing us. The Bible is always calling God's people to see themselves and their world as it really exists.

The "bad news" is that planning will always leave us with a sense of disappointment. In a "fallen" world, a great deal of the dreams and desires found in our plans become just another notebook on the shelf. The "planned" destination and where we actually arrive will almost never match. And that can be discouraging. West Point teaches soldiers to always plan to re-plan. They capture the limit of planning with the phrase, "No plan survives contact with the enemy."

God's Spirit does give leaders a burden for the future. They are motivated to pursue a future different from the present.

God's grace gifts leaders with the skills and creativity to propose what those improvements would be and "plan" how to bring them into reality.

God does stir his people with a "groaning" of longing for the sinful decay of this world to be replaced by its intended glory (2 Cor. 5, Rom. 8).

God does stir up deep passion in his people for redemptive action, salt and light intervention, and justice inspired compassionate sacrifices. These biases to actions are elements of a normal walk by faith with Him.

God does choose to use leaders to see problems or untapped potential and "name the change".

But to sit down in a room with "outside experts" and the organizational leaders and map out a 3 to 10 year time line that preserves and advances the organization is often about as far from capturing the wind-like moving of the Spirit as a written program on Sunday morning can predict and orchestrate the worship God intends for his people to experience.

Life-Giving Leaders Will Often be Change Agents

Leaders move the organization toward plateau or decline if they are afraid to call for the deep level of surrender and repentance needed. When leaders fear the level of conflict will be too great because of the degree of change needed, and change goes undirected, a moment of growth has become a seed of decay. Blame and denial direct energy away from the intentional changes needed.

Leaders can also seek to avoid the cost of long term endurance and look for a "magic pill" that will suddenly (in no more than 3 months to a year) bring the organization back into vital health. In most cases, the organization did not get into an unhealthy state in a just a short period of time, and in reality, there are no magic pills.

There is no substitute for daily steps of faith. These faith steps attempt the risky journey while holding God's hand. These steps are made with a God focused hope that endures and love that gives, sacrifices for the beloved, and serves no matter the cost. The believer is like a long distance runner who keeps putting one foot in front of the other, mile after mile, to complete the race.

Most things wrong in an individual's or organization's life are the result of failing to do the right things. Life-giving leaders have learned that repentance is not an act occurring only at the moment of salvation but they know a growing Jesus-follower is a repentant follower.

Most changes God leads individuals or organizations to adopt are course corrections returning them to the essentials of what they are called to be and refocusing them on their God given mission.

Many of the changes we initiate are really steps of repenting; turning around so we can go in the right direction. Repentance is THE path of transformation with God. We never come under his touch and become more like Christ apart from a loving assault on our pride and a required submission to his will.[8] Therefore, needed organizational change is often simply part of God's way to get at deeper individual repentance; our relational conflicts are the heat needed to thaw the unresponsive heart.

In marriage one says "NO" to all other possible spouses in order to say "YES" to the one beloved. During the wedding, the man and woman are not even aware of the "NO" they are declaring to all other potential partners because his/her heart is responding to the loved one with a declaration of "YES." God is working into the hearts of his disciples that same kind of loving, relaxed, unforced obedience to his will.

> Most things wrong in an individual's or organization's life are the result of failing to do the right things. Life-giving leaders have learned that repentance is not an act occurring only at the moment of salvation but they know a growing Jesus-follower is a repentant follower.

While we have been describing the leader as driving or directing change, God frequently initiates change from several different starting points. Leaders spend more time and energy seeking to manage changes they did not initiate than launching changes. I don't find this discussed much in the reading I have done on change theory. Some articles give a false impression that being a change agent is about driving change from the top leaders downward. God's Spirit uses many creative starting points when initiating a change process:

1. Acts 1:13-26 — Leaders initiate, propose plan, pray, ask God, cast lots
2. Acts 2:1-7 — Direct intervention by the Spirit "on" those gathered
3. Acts 4:23-3 — Threatened by religious leaders, reported by leaders, prayer, Spirit fills
4. Acts 5:33-42 — A wise word from a respected religious leader

5. Acts 6:1-7 — A complaint/problem with care for the Greek widows, brought to leaders, thrown back to group to bring solution

Leaders have only been given a few tools to influence and shape changes

Regardless of the origin of change, leaders need to know what resources God places in their hands to be a wise change agent. One of the challenges in most change is the level of confusion, miscommunication and distorted expectations or wrong definitions. The solution is CLARITY. Leaders must provide clear understanding for:

1. WHY we are changing,
2. WHAT will be the cost,
3. HOW we will move from step to step through the change. Honesty helps here. You could say, "We do not have all of the answers but we will take this step, pause to pray, evaluate, adjust our thinking, re-plan the plan, take next step and REPEAT until God says we have arrived or he shows us our next major change."

What are some practical approaches life-giving leaders can use to help bring clarity to those navigating change?

Maintaining clarity will often call for the courage to prune. Change does not always mean adding new things. Often pruning is the most effective way to increase capacity. Just look at an apple tree that has been carefully pruned each year and contrast the quantity and quality of the fruit from this tree with that from an old tree which has gone many years without pruning.

Too often when I come in as a consultant, I feel like I have entered an archaeological dig with layers upon layers of life exposed.

Example

The Sunday School was evaluated and, instead of making needed changes, we left it alone and added another layer of Sunday evening small groups. A few years later small groups are exposed as having some failures in making disciples, but we do nothing that would threaten or stir up those leaders. Out of fear and maybe for the fun of doing something new, we add a Men's and Women's ministry.

You get the idea.

Twenty years down the road we have layers upon layers of mediocre ministries, which are only marginally effective in making disciples. Now we have no more margin to add anything new, and we couldn't find breathing leaders for a new layer anyway. Fear based layering also limited the personal growth of those leading and faithfully seeking to make the programs in each layer work. At some point it begins to cave in on itself.

The good thing is, because there so many confusing layers, we can find lots of stuff to blame (satirical humor here!).

A Lack of Clarity is failing to do the Right Things Well.

There are three ways for leaders to choose to invest in the life of an individual or organization:

1. Do nothing,
2. Do too many things — the distracted, busy, shallow life,
3. Do a few things — the ones placed in your path by God.

⏱ PAUSE — TRY IT OUT!

The importance of clarity and priorities

Look up these passages in context and read them over seeing the words I have inserted. Now add your own reflection on the importance of clarity and how one maintains it.

Matthew 25:21 (ESV)

His master said to him, 'Well done, good and faithful servant. You have been faithful over a little [Assessment]; *I will set you over much* [Next Action]. *Enter into the joy of your master.'*

1 John 5:2-3

This is how we know [Assessment] *that we love the children of God: by loving God and carrying out his commands. This is love for God:* [Action, Alignment] *to obey his commands. And his commands are not burdensome."*

1 Corinthians 9:25-26

Everyone who competes in the games goes into strict training. [Accountability, Alignment] *They do it to get a crown that will not last; but we do it to get a crown that will last forever. Therefore I do not run like a man running aimlessly; I do not fight like a man beating the air.* [Assessment]

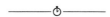

Approach change to navigate it and redeem it, but never just drift in a sea of purposelessness.

Prayer brings Clarity

Prayer is the great mysterious secret ingredient in processing change. We focused on prayer earlier in the toolbox of a life-giving leader. But prayer is also a great resource for reinforcing clarity. What we pray passionately about gets our attention and resources.

Time-Travel brings Clarity

God is a time traveler and often calls his people to time travel by using the words:

Remember — Go back to your past. Recall the works of God. Renew your mind with God's faithfulness.

You yourselves have seen what I did to the Egyptians, and how I bore you on eagles' wings and brought you to myself. [9]

Be alert and endure — Know with certainty what God promises for the future. Keep looking beyond the pain, losses and challenges of this life. See where history is headed.

Life-giving Leaders know when to time travel. Leadership is provided for a group when the leader has the gift of jumping into the past to mine lessons or redeem values from the group's history.

Leadership is leaning into the future and seeing how the present contains seeds from which the actions planned for the future can bring a fruitful harvest.

But leaders must live in the present. Leaders know how to "time travel". Leaders visit the *past* or the *possible future* but live in the *present* with the people.

When leaders are trapped in the past, they grow afraid of change and preserving the spoils of historic battles becomes the goal. When leaders are dominated by living in the future, they are so caught up in their anticipated dreams, they are blindsided by the present challenges.

> Leaders visit the PAST or the POSSIBLE FUTURE but live in the PRESENT with the people.

Leaders use tools to help others time travel with them. Tools include: assessment, inventories and any media tool possible to get God's global heart for all people before the people.

Leaders must be centered and be fully present in the present. But there are times when the best leadership action is to travel to the past or the future. Here are some ways to evaluate a leader's time as constructive or destructive to the work of God *in* and *through* the leader.

1. What is the motive for going back to remember?
2. Who is the main character in the story?
3. What will be celebrated?
4. What will be confessed?
5. What will be brought back to the present to impact your leadership?
6. How will you use what you see with others?

Major Change Often begins with Small Actions

Often dramatic change grows slowly from sowing seeds and taking small steps. Ever hear an interview with the newly rising star musician or actor? The real story is they have been working at their craft for years and have just recently gained high visibility. Miraculous massive change can occur but it is not the normal way.

How do we start small and let it grow? Throughout creation, most of what God creates, he works organically from small seed to multiplying fruitfulness. I propose what I would call a Kingdom Principle: God provides the living seed, we sow, and in time, God brings the growth.

A seed containing life is broken in humility and then it produces multiplying life.

Bread and fish are offered, broken and then feed five thousand.

The seed of the word of the kingdom falls on a good heart; it is treasured, and with patience, bring a multiplied harvest.[10]

SUMMARY

God has designed creation so life and change go together. At the core of God's work in the world today is change. Perhaps there is nothing more transformative than to give eternal life to the dead.

Change expends energy to accomplish movement. Change agents direct change and influence those experiencing change. Sometimes they drive change, but more often, they respond to change coming at them through circumstances, other people or a direct intervention of God.

Everything alive in this world, including our organizational structures goes through a life cycle. The stage of the life cycle is an important element to weigh in the strategy of a change agent.

The best form of planning is to hold God's hand and take one step at a time.

God is a model change agent and uses many different ways of communicating to help us process and achieve change. We can learn to use some of the same forms of communicating. Clarity is a desired aim of a change agent. The tools to accomplish clarity can be summed up by:

$$\text{Clarity} = \frac{M + C^3}{V}$$

Clarity = **Mission** (assignment from God) + **Communication** (horizontal and vertical) + **Calendar** + **Cash**

Our mission, communication, calendar and cash are all being pursued and invested in a way consistent with our values. **Values** are the priceless ingredients we refuse to violate as we pursue our mission.

Change agents know that pruning is an essential tool for clarity, focus and effectiveness. Prayer and time travel will also assist change agents in offering clarity to a group.

THINKING IT THROUGH

1. How quickly do you respond to upcoming change?

2. What are three ideas you can adopt to become a more effective change agent?

3. What is the stage on the life cycle for the organization where you lead? What are the implications of this stage for your leadership?

RECOMMENDED RESOURCES

1. Hans Finzel. *Change Is Like A Slinky: 30 Strategies For Promoting and Surviving Change in Your Organization.* Chicago: Northfield, 2004. ISBN: 1-881273-68-7.

2. Gary Hamel. *The Future Of Management.* Boston: Harvard Business School Press, 2007. ISBN: 978-1-4221-0250-5.

3. Alan Hirsch & Dave Ferguson. *On The Verge: A Journey into The Apostolic Future of the Church.* Grand Rapids: Zondervan, 2011. ISBN: 978-0-310-33100-1.

4. Bill Hybels. *Axiom: Powerful Leadership Proverbs.* Grand Rapids: Zondervan, 2008. ISBN: 978-0-310-27236-6.

5. John Kotter. *Leading Change.* Boston: Harvard Business School Press, 1996. ISBN: 0-87584-747-1.

6. Gordon MacKenzie. *Orbiting the Giant Hairball: A Corporate Fool's Guide to Surviving with Grace.* New York: Viking Penguin, 1996. ISBN: 0-670-87983-5.

7. James O'toole. *Leading Change: The Argument for Values Based Leadership.* New York: Ballantine, 1996. ISBN: 0-345-40254-5.

8. Everett Rogers. *Diffusions of Innovations 4th Edition.* New York: The Free Press, 1995. ISBN: 0-02-874074-2.

9. Noel M. Tichy. *The Leadership Engine: How Winning Companies Build Leaders at Every Level.* New York: HarperBusiness, 1997. ISBN: 0-88730-793-0.

CHAPTER THIRTEEN

LIFE-GIVING LEADERSHIP
PRODUCES HEAT

If one is forever cautious, can one remain a human being? —Aleksandr Solzhenitsyn

You will find that most change involves a level of pain and some level of resistance to the movement required. In most cases, there is a kind of "gravity" that works against change. This is especially true where the change involves revealing the kingdom of God on planet earth where the kingdom of darkness is still exercising influence.

Lay down this book for a moment. Place your palms together and begin to move them back and forth against each other. Your hands were created to "fit" and yet these incredibly similar parts still create friction in their movement.

Christian leaders should be those who celebrate change just like the angels in heaven rejoice over the "change" of one sinner's heart. At the same time, leaders are in tune with the reality of sin's pollution of the human heart and the basic resistance to God's will present throughout creation. Healthy leaders then are not surprised by conflict. They expect conflict to be present and approach it with both God's **truth** (fuel that drives change through asking questions, learning, and experimenting) and God's **grace** (the oil of authenticity, vulnerability, healing compassionate care, and a thankful, praise filled spirit).

A LIFE-GIVING PERSPECTIVE ON CONFLICT

Healthy leaders understand that when people show up full of questions, even if the questions are delivered with some anger, they need to receive them. The attacking manner of conversing provides a character development teaching moment; we can begin by giving thanks that they feel strongly about something. One of my pastoral mentors, Ron Barker, has often said, "It is easier to tame the demoniac than to raise the dead!" Strong emotion may not always be justified, but it does indicate passion and life, and perhaps even a deep desire for the organization to be effective. Make it a rule: NEVER ALLOW CONFLICT TO GO UNDERGROUND.[1]

Change generates the heat of conflict because:
1. Our *definitions* feel discounted.
2. Our *expectations* are in danger of falling short.
3. Our *motivations* clash with the motives driving change.
4. Our *values* feel threatened. Most people operate with a hierarchy of values. God seems to operate this way as well. We should appeal to and find common ground on higher values. We value people when we understand and appreciate their values. Change may require asking them to sacrifice and grieve the impact on their values. Trying to understand their "cost" helps them know we value them.

We have discussed some of these aspects of our inner operating system before, but now we need to revisit them because they become critical in the judgments we make concerning change. Our identity is tied up with these four. When you challenge my definitions, seek to adjust my expectations, ignore my motivation, and dismiss my values, it is very easy to take this as an attack on my person. Often this perceived attack is not an intentional act by the leader, it is part of the way the ground is shifting with a change process.

⏱ PAUSE — TRY IT OUT!

Developing the art of adopting various points of view

The scenario: The global missions team spends a year examining all of the financial support commitments of the church. They develop a plan to prioritize direct church planting work among least reached peoples. The plan also calls for reducing and then freezing, for at least five years, the support levels of those not involved in direct church multiplication engagement.

Now, put yourself in the place of a parent. Let's assume that your child grew up in the church and is involved in media and internet support for outreach to athletes. They have been supported by the church for over ten years.

1. Using some of the four items above what are some ways they may choose to process the change? Add to the case study this inside knowledge: The parents are retiring in the coming year. Their income will be decreased, and with it, their margin of available support for their single daughter. And, a supporting church the parents grew up in has gone through a split and has just announced they can no longer support their daughter.

2. What might be going on in the parents' minds in terms of their definitions, expectations, motivations and values?

3. As you think out different responses, how can the leadership assist them in processing the change?

There are, of course, many possible ways this could play out. How the missionary daughter responds may also influence how the parents respond.

The leader's response should include these principles:

1. Avoid the temptation to defend or "sell" the new policy. There is always a need for clear communication. But just more communication to present the strengths of the new approach will not resolve the pain. This is not primarily a communication problem.

2. If there is emotional hurt, anger, or sense of betrayal—a HOT situation—make sure you are listening well, asking questions, and seeking to determine which of the four aspects are perceived as being under fire. *Do not be on the defensive and do not go on the offensive. Just listen, and love well.*

3. Ask how you can assist, encourage or support them emotionally through the change. This may or may not revise the policy. But do your best to communicate that you value them, both the parents and daughter, and you value the relationship you have with them.

4. Avoid written or phone communication as soon as you sense the heat. Sit down face to face and ask to have a person they trust also be there to protect both of you from, "He said/We said" inaccurate communication later. *Never, never, never get into an emotional exchange via e-mail.*

⏱ PAUSE — TRY IT OUT!

Principles of conflict resolution

Carefully read Joshua 22. Use a blank sheet of paper and draw a visual to represent what happens in the story.

1. What was the conflict over?
2. Why did the conflict occur?
3. What almost happened that would have been highly destructive?
4. How was the conflict resolved?

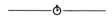

Expect some friction/conflict. It is a normal part of our resistance to change and desire to be in control. It often exposes our real motives, values, priorities and lack of trust in God.

LIFE-GIVING LEADERS WALK WITH PEOPLE AS THEY PROCESS CHANGE

People process change differently. They need various amounts of time to absorb change. They also choose different roles to contribute to or disrupt the change. I have gathered the following list from several books on change mentioned at the end of Chapter twelve. The + or − in the list represents how leaders perceive these people playing these roles. We see some as supportive and positive toward the change. They want us and the organization to survive and navigate the change well. Then there are those God allows to give us some pause, resistance, and challenge, and who, though it feels negative, also offer a valuable contribution to the change.

Roles often found in a community processing change:

1. Innovators (+) — Not invested in NOW, embrace THEN easily
2. Defenders (-) — Invested deeply in NOW, resist change
3. Allies (+) — On your side, more committed to you than the THEN
4. Potential Allies (+) — Uncertain at present but possible Allies

This next group can be either + or - depending on where they land on supporting the change. If possible, have several of them take part in planning and determining the scope of change early on in the process. Their support is critical.

5. Formal Leaders — In position NOW, want to size up the cost of change to their personal situation.
6. Influentials — May not be in position, but when they speak many listen. Many people will ask for their opinion.
7. Maintainers — Are drawn to keeping the status quo, but may embrace change if they know if won't push them out.
8. Gatekeepers — Control resources. They are vital networkers who can open or close doors.

Some of these roles listed below are often present but not wanted. It is better to be aware of these roles than to ignore what we don't want to see. Political and personal power games exist in many settings and change can become a battle ground for those seeking to be the last man standing and win the game.

9. Key Informants (+) — Are able to tell you what others are thinking, can often "read" the room.
10. Faction Leaders (-) — Are able to rally opposition and attack.
11. Compatibility person (+) — Click with you and are on the same

page, but their support capability may be limited because they are considering leaving or may have to step back because of life issues.

12. Vocalizers (+ or -) — Articulate or speak to change in positive or negative way.

13. Resisters (-) — Just do not like change of any kind.

14. Public Relation Linkers (+ or -) — Represent the group to the community.

Note that people can change roles, depending on the interplay of the four aspects mentioned earlier. And do not forget that you may play one or more of these roles in your leadership. All of these roles can be contaminated by prideful and selfish sin. All of these roles can be ruled by the Spirit and offer wise counsel. Check your own insecurity when you find yourself going on the defensive and becoming judgmental. Be sure you are operating with a heart filled with faith, hope and love.

LIFE-GIVING LEADERS ENDURE RESISTANCE TO CHANGE

Every Christian leader I know has a desire for fruitful living, and yet, every leader I know finds reaching the goal an uphill challenge. We live in a world filled with resistance to fruitful living. Resistance is an opportunity to grow life-giving HOPE.

What is resistance?

Resistance is any person, event or circumstance that hinders you from bearing fruit from your investment of energy.

> ➤ Resistance could be a child who finds a hundred ways to avoid doing his or her homework.

> ➤ Resistance could be severe weather that wrecks your plan for the week and demands full-time clean-up effort.

> ➤ Resistance could be a physical loss of vision that cannot be corrected. You may have to live with this limit for the rest of your life.

> ➤ Resistance comes through people walking with us through change who are playing some of the fourteen roles presented above.

Where did resistance start?

In Genesis chapters one through three, we find that Adam and Eve were designed to rule over creation and to be fruitful and multiply. Their labor would result in work that produced fruit and their intimacy would produce the fruit of a family. But they chose to break away and instead of living as children in God's family and citizens bowing a knee to the rule of their King, they struck out to live life apart from God. They disobeyed his law and rebelled against his rule over them. As a consequence, God created resistance. Adam would continue to work but thorns would now make work painful labor. Eve would still have children but birth would require painful labor.

Adam comes home at the end of his day complaining of how he didn't get anything done. He complains about the seeds being too small, the dirt being too hard, and these things called weeds that were choking out the good plants. Can you imagine how painful it is for Eve to listen to his whining and showing of the blisters every day? Can you imagine how hard it is on Adam to hear his wife complain about her feet swelling, her bad breath and then there is all that whining (mixed in with a little screaming) when she gives birth. Resistance is nothing new.

Why does God think we need resistance?

Trying to make a fruitful life apart from God is self-destructive. God designed hurdles, friction and painful resistance to our labor not to tear us down but to draw us back. In the first chapter of 2 Corinthians, Paul describes God using pain to move him from relying on himself to relying on God—and he says that is a good thing.

Jesus told some fisherman, "Follow me and I will make you fishers of men!" I wonder if they ever looked up as they were out fishing for people and said, "Hey Jesus, you left out some things! Your fishing is like lowering our nets and getting them so tangled in underwater limbs that it's almost impossible to pull them in to get the fish in the boat. We preach and we are stoned—to death. We preach and we are beaten. We preach and we are locked up. We preach and some respond, and then a few months later they turn and leave the faith." The disciples found that this kind of fishing was so hard that they knew they had to pray, and God was going to have to be involved by his Spirit for any people to be caught and join the Christ-followers.

Embrace the resistance God allows into your path

Never say **if** we encounter resistance this is how we will respond. **Know** that resistance will be part of the plan.

- ➤ We won't have enough money.
- ➤ We won't have enough volunteers.
- ➤ And the volunteers we do have will fail to follow through or even show up sometimes.
- ➤ We won't have enough time.
- ➤ We won't be able to communicate in ways that eliminate confusion and wrong perceptions in the mind of the listener.

But do remember that every time you feel a new blister and splinter in your hand, it is an opportunity to experience God moving your heart from pride to humility.

Perhaps we fail to value and give thanks in encounters with resistance because we do

Change is often very depleting and requires rest and restoration to stay at it for a long period of time.

not see *pride* as being as much of a problem as God does. If we did, would we lay down on the table and welcome God's heart surgery instead of trying to pray all resistance out of our life?

When I go the gym and pick up some weights, I expect there to be resistance. If there is almost none, I get a bigger weight. Why? **There is no gaining of strength apart from exercise against resistance.** High resistance speeds depletion. Rest is God's way to restore what is drained during depleting challenges. Strength is gained after rest. You must trust God to care for the organization and learn to experience physical, mental, emotional, social and spiritual rest.

LIFE-GIVING LEADERS GROW TRUST

Trust filled relationships still experience loss of clarity, conflict and resistance. BUT trust is also a blessing that lubricates and helps move along the change process.

GOD leads by BEING TRUSTWORTHY

The faithful, trustworthy character and conduct of God is our model for our leadership. The greater the trust levels between leaders and people, the easier it is to navigate the change. So every investment in relating well is a deposit in the trust account that helps when threatening change is on the horizon.

The life-giving leader *consistently makes deposits of trust with those they lead.*

> ➤ Trust involves keeping one's word — proving trustworthy
> ➤ Trust means caring for the people
> ➤ Trust means being passionate for a mission or cause the group values
> ➤ Trust means humility and being willing to apologize when wrong
> ➤ Trust means modeling sacrifice, an open heart and being fully present

These are just a few ways that God shows us he is trustworthy.

LIFE-GIVING LEADERS CONSISTENTLY ASSESS AND EVALUATE

Effective organizations evaluate everything that requires an investment of time or money in pursuit of the purposes of the organization. In short, evaluate everything you do.

What are the biblical purposes of the church?

They have been outlined in different ways by leaders seeking to focus disciples strategically.

Gene Getz, writing over forty years ago, had two purposes: edification and evangelism[2]. Chuck Swindoll used the acrostic W.I.F.E. (the church as the bride of Christ) to help us remember the purposes of worship, instruction, fellowship and evangelism.[3] More recently Rick Warren uses a baseball diamond visual for the five purposes of worship, loving, growing, serving, and sharing.[4]

One thing these various lists have in common is that they seek to describe a healthy gathering of Christians in terms of "being" and "doing".

A clear and balanced description of the purpose of the church is found in Unit Two of Robertson McQuilkin's *The Five Smooth Stones: Essential Principles for Biblical Ministry* which can be seen in the following illustration.

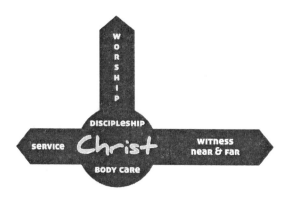

For each of these critical functions, leadership asks questions to determine if the money, time and gifting of God's people is carrying out these purposes. Leadership continually revisits the "right questions" in order to evaluate practices and strategies.

⏱ PAUSE – TRY IT OUT!

Aligning change with purpose

Here are some descriptions based on Robertson's work of bringing how we do church under the functional authority of the Bible.[5] Read these over, seeking to evaluate the organization where you serve.

1. Worship is defined biblically in terms of whole-life worship. The music ministry is God focused, not man-focused, and developed in a way that all can fully participate emotionally and spiritually.

2. The teaching ministry of the church is multi-faceted, including small group accountability, and the results in spiritual transformation and growth are evident.

3. Member care reaches beyond spiritual pastoring to full-service emotional, physical, and material responsibility for all members.

4. The congregation has programs and involvement in mercy ministries to the community at home and abroad.

5. It is assumed that every member has a Spirit given ability (gift) to minister. The church has a program and leadership in place to help every member discover, develop to the full, and deploy his or her gifting and calling.

6. People understand that talents, while not the same as Spirit given gifts, are given in creation and growth and should be invested for God's glory.

7. When some purpose of the church is less than optimally fulfilled, the leaders and members actively "desire earnestly" in prayer the Spirit gifts necessary.

8. Corporate prayer is pervasive (involving a majority of members, and in many formats), vital, expectant (faith-filled), and focused on spiritual needs of the congregation, the community and the unreached of the world, not just on the physical needs of the members.

9. The constantly articulated goal is for all members to be faithful witnesses in walk and talk.

10. Teaching and training are provided to guide and empower for effective witness. Evidence is seen in consistent "body-life reproduction."

11. Leaders are constantly on the look-out for those who might be evangelistically gifted and provide training and encouragement to make them ever more effective.

12. The church body is knowledgeable and concerned about the unreached of the world, and a steady stream of career missionaries moves out from the congregation.

13. Short-term ministry and financial provision for God's people away from home are carefully planned and harnessed to maximize kingdom effectiveness.

14. Prayer for global outreach is informed, vital, and pervasive throughout the body, throughout the year.

15. Great effort is put into in helping people progress in their level of investment in ministry. Giving is expected and honest managership is encouraged. Sacrificial love giving is celebrated.

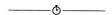

Wise change is focused on creating alignment between what we are doing and how it is accomplishing our purpose. Some changes involve simple "solve the problem" or "put out the fire" situations. But change that propels the organization forward will be change made to increase effectiveness in our purpose.

> When it comes to discussions about problems and performance, direct discussion produces honest evaluation of issues and improves challenging situations. —Dianna Booher

I debated moving this material on purpose to chapter 12 on understanding change. I decided to leave it in the context of processing conflict to underscore the need of leaders to answer two questions that critics raise:

1. WHY? Why is it important enough to disrupt our lives to make this change?
2. IS THIS THE RIGHT CHANGE? There are usually no shortage of possible changes that could need change agents to implement them. Changes flowing out of purpose driven assessment are higher priority changes and are worthy of the resistance one will encounter.

Evaluation is not always a written inventory. It should be part of the culture to ask how everything is going and how it can be improved. For example, here are four questions that could be used in a weekly pastoral staff meeting to help maintain focus on the right purposes.

1. How did you invest time with pre-Christians this past month?
2. How did you invest time developing new Christians?

3. How did you invest time in developing leaders?

4. How did you invest time in self-leadership development of your private, personal and public spheres of influence?

By the way, the pastoral staff members should not be penalized for admitting struggles in these four questions. For people to grow from facing hard questions, there must be a "safe place" where grace and truth are mixed in equal portions to empower change and growth.

> Most change looks like failure from the middle. Some people may be "purpose driven". I tend to be "failure driven". —Craig Groschel

CHANGE WILL INCLUDE LOSS —GRIEVE WELL

Tears are God's way of bringing inner pain to the outside where it can be healed, grieved and released. —John Ortberg

We need to learn how to practice the God given grace of lamenting and grieving as a means to process what is lost through change. All change is an experience of loss. Every life-giving leader will grieve well and know how to help others grieve.

It seems to me that we do not need to be taught how to lament since we have so many models in Scripture. What we need is simply the assurance that it's okay to lament. . . . We all carry deep within ourselves a pressurized reservoir of tears. It takes only the right key at the right time to unlock them. In God's perfect time, these tears can be released to form a healing flood. That's the beauty and the mystery of the prayer of lament.[6]

Change is always experienced as loss. All losses must be grieved. We must teach and model how to mourn, lament and grieve.

Changes that we do not initiate or influence often call us into deeper levels of loss and grief.

What is grieving?

A dictionary definition may help us clarify this means of grace:

Grief – intense emotional suffering caused by loss, misfortune, injury, or evils of any kind; sorrow; regret; as we experience grief when we lose a friend

Grieve – 2. To lament. [Rare.]

Grieve – to feel deep, acute sorrow or distress; to sorrow; to mourn.

Lament – to mourn; to grieve; to weep or wail; to express or feel deep sorrow. Jeremiah lamented for Josiah. (2 Chr 35:25)

Mourn – to feel or express grief or sorrow; to grieve; to be sorrowful.[7]

Grieving, lamenting and mourning revolve around three ideas:
1. They are the response to suffering
2. They are emotional; coming from deep places in our heart
3. They are triggered by losses

Though there may be some shades of difference I will use the words interchangeably since they overlap so closely in meaning.

Biblical Principles of Grieving, Mourning and Lamenting

In Genesis, after Adam and Eve's rebellion, God removes them from the garden and blocks the way to the tree of life. With sin came death, and separation from eternal life. God, in his original blueprint, designed us to be his family <u>forever.</u> Read from the book of Revelation below and let your heart cry out, "Yes, bring it on; this is the way I was created to live." But, because of the rebellion, there must now be redemption, in order to restore us to the life—eternal life—we were made to live in.

Then I saw a new heaven and a new earth, for the first heaven and the first earth had passed away, and the sea was no more. And I saw the holy city, New Jerusalem, coming down out of heaven from God, prepared as a bride adorned for her husband. And I heard a loud voice from the throne saying, 'Behold, the dwelling place of God is with man. He will dwell with them, and they will be his people, and God himself will be with them as their God.

He will wipe away every tear from their eyes, and death shall be no more, neither shall there be mourning, nor crying, nor pain anymore, for the former things have passed away.' And he who was seated on the throne said, 'Behold, I am making all things new.' Also he said, 'Write this down, for these words are trustworthy and true.'

And he said to me, 'It is done! I am the Alpha and the Omega, the beginning and the end. To the thirsty I will give from the spring of the water of life without payment. The one who conquers will have this heritage, and I will be his God and he will be my son.[8]

Then the angel showed me the river of the water of life, bright as crystal, flowing from the throne of God and of the Lamb through the middle of the street of the city; also, on either side of the river, the tree of life with its twelve kinds of fruit, yielding its fruit each month. The leaves of the tree were for the healing of the nations. No longer will there be anything accursed, but the throne of God and of the Lamb will be in it, and his servants will worship him. They will see his face, and his name will be on their foreheads. And night will be no more. They will need no light of lamp or sun, for the Lord God will be their light, and they will reign forever and ever.[9]

The path God navigated to bring his dead children back to life went from the Genesis garden to the Mount of Olive garden on his way to the King's Revelation garden in the new city. Christ would grieve, mourn and lament, and yet, he would submit, in love, to the Father and for us to the cross. It took the cross to restore the loss of life.

Go back to the scene of Christ's sufferings. Could the sun in the heavens look down unmoved on such a scene? O no, he could not even behold it — but veiled his face from the sight! All nature seemed to put on her robes of deepest mourning. . . he did not pay too much for the soul's redemption — not a pang more than the interests of God's government demanded and the worth of the soul would justify.[10]

God's grace contains much help to his people who live between the gardens. You see, where we live, there are tears that need to be wiped away and death still surrounds and touches us. God gave his people grieving as a means of grace to handle the losses and deaths in this broken world. **Grieving is one of God's gifts to people who must face losses we were not designed to endure. We grieve losses as a God designed process leading to comfort, healing, wisdom and hope.**

Grieving, unlike worship, is not an action by God's people that we will practice forever. Revelation 21:5 clearly describes the end of mourning. Grieving is a "means of grace" to sustain and comfort God's people until he brings us home. And as we grieve our losses, Christians, holding the gift of grace with the wrapping paper of the gospel at our feet, we mourn— yet, we mourn with hope.

But we do not want you to be uninformed, brothers, about those who are asleep, that you may not grieve as others do who have no hope. For since we believe that Jesus died and rose again, even so, through Jesus, God will bring with him those who have fallen asleep. . . . But since we belong to the day, let us be sober, having put on the breastplate of faith and love, and for a helmet the hope of salvation. For God has not destined us for wrath, but to obtain salvation through our Lord Jesus Christ, who died for us so that whether we are awake or asleep we might live with him. Therefore encourage one another and build one another up, just as you are doing.[11]

This path of biblical grieving is a great gift we can give both to ourselves and to others. . . . As I've said earlier, doing the work of grieving is counter to our culture . . . and very different from the way most of us have lived our lives in God.[12]

If you were to script most of our lives in terms of the level of intensity over time, it would follow what I have read in military biographies as training, waiting, and then the battle, repeated over and over. And while intense, the battles are blinks of the eye compared to the amount of hours spent in training or trying not to go crazy in boredom while waiting for the fighting to begin.

I would script our lives as warriors in God's kingdom in a similar way. Most of our life is divided into:

> *   *Long seasons of "waiting"* for God to complete promises and answer prayers. This is where God grows our faith.
> *   *Intense but usually short periods of depleting warfare* where we learn endurance.
> *   *Grieving the losses we sustain* where we learn sacrificial love.
> *   *Glorious "tastes" of victory where we celebrate* in part what will one day be complete, total and final.

One could write books on each of these four seasons of life and some good ones have been written. Much of the Old Testament helps us understand how God's people wait. The Gospels and Acts are great examples of glorious battles that rival anything in the Lord of the Rings. The end of the Gospels, sections in the prophets, poetry and letters to the churches highlight those thrilling tastes of victory when we catch glimpses of the power and victory of God often in and through frail lives. Where is the grieving? The poetry is rich with examples and teaching on mourning, and in the prophets are sermons that are actually pictures of God mourning for the loss of love and obedience of his people.

⏱ PAUSE — TRY IT OUT!

Biblical examples of grief

Read these passages and list WHO is grieving and WHAT is the loss that is being felt?

1. Genesis 6:6 (first occurrence of grieving in the Bible)
2. Isaiah 53:3
3. Isaiah 63:9
4. Luke 19:41
5. John 11:33,35
6. Hebrews 5:7
7. Ephesians 4:30
8. Romans 8: 18-30
9. 2 Corinthians 5:1-10

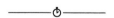

Did your answers surprise you? God is the first to mourn in the Bible. John 11 shows Jesus entering into mourning with his friends. The Spirit can be grieved by the actions of God's children. All creation groans for release from the curse of sin and every Christian joins this groaning as we long to be in the kingdom garden of the city of God. The Spirit even helps us communicate the losses that are too deep for words to bring out.

Read these examples and commands to mourn and lament. What losses are being grieved?

1. 1 Samuel 30:1-6
2. 2 Corinthians 7:9-11
3. James 4:9

As a matter of fact, God and people process loss, often with tears, all through the Bible. Mourning over the losses that come from sin is a dimension of repentance. Sadness is one motivation for godliness.

The greater the loss, the deeper the pain. The deeper the pain, the longer it takes to resolve. Resolution comes when we understand what we have lost and let it go. Healing begins when we say, "good-bye".

We accumulate unresolved losses. The stress and emotional load causes us to become like a juggler where people in the crowd keep throwing one more ball to juggle. At some point they all drop.

To avoid grieving we attempt to use:

➤ Denial
➤ Minimizing
➤ Blaming others or God
➤ Rationalizing
➤ Intellectualizing
➤ Distracting
➤ Hostility
➤ Medicating (unhealthy addictions and attachments numb the pain)

⏱ PAUSE — TRY IT OUT!

Taking time to grieve

Maybe you need to put the book down right now and do some grieving. May I suggest you start with reviewing the losses you sense in your life right now and tell them to God. Then read Psalm 42, 43, 77 and 88, and write your own Psalm of Lament over your losses.

———— ⏱ ————

Following are several practical principles I have learned in my journey to grieve. My family and my culture do not grieve well. Once I became a Jesus-follower, I was never taught what the Bible offers on grieving. I ended up in depression twice, and God used two godly counselors to move me along the healing path of lament. These principles mostly come from journal entries made during those times.

Accepting Sadness is a Godly Response to Loss

We accept seasons of sadness as God's gift to help us respond to the losses we encounter in a sin damaged world.

Make sadness your ally instead of your enemy. God's solution for resolving your loss of relationships, dreams, ideals, and opportunities is sadness. Rather than something to be avoided, sadness, or grief, allows you to let go of what you *cannot* have in order to make room in your heart for what you *can* have. Those who don't feel safe enough to grieve find themselves holding on to lost hopes and relationships. Then it is difficult for them to seek new attachments, since the ghosts of the past still occupy their emotional life.

Solomon understood the value of grieving. *"The mind of the wise is in the house of mourning, while the mind of fools is in the house of pleasure."* [13] While it can be good to be sad, we must not confuse sadness with depression. *Depression is the inability to process loss or rage.* It's a heavy paralysis of the soul that won't allow it to finish resolving a problem. Sadness is actually the antidote to depression. Depression is static and unmoving, but sadness moves toward resolving loss. That's why David declared, *"Weeping may last for a night, but a shout of joy comes in the morning."* [14]

The bottom line is that we are all born into a world we were not really made to inhabit. We were created for God, designed to flourish in the comfort of the presence of our Father, within the warm context of his undeniable loving kindness. In this fallen world, we are cut off from that presence. Only the loving sovereignty of an all-wise God could redeem such a hopeless situation. His solution? To use suffering to save us. To redeem our suffering by going to the cross to pay the price for our sin. In order to turn around and move once more in the direction of God, we must find this path he has carved out. We must call out to him in the language he has provided. We must regain the tearful trail. We must relearn lament. Lamentation is one of the direct paths to the true praise we have lost. In fact, lamenting is not a path *to* worship, but the path *of* worship. But there exists within American Christianity a numb denial of our need to lament.[15]

All Changes Involve Some Level of Mourning

There are a variety of losses that are legitimate to grieve. All changes include some losses. Part of our resistance to change comes from knowing that if we flow with the change some things will be left behind. Of course time and change cannot be stopped, except by God, so grieving change induced losses is not an option we can pass on. For those in leadership, who are often initiating change, I would say don't give up on leading into change but do factor in the emotional losses to the followers and create healthy ways to grieve. Please don't get defensive when people tear up or react in anger in the storm of change.

Can you think of an example where leaders seemed surprised or defensive that people experienced painful losses as they navigated the change? If a person's spouse died you would not show up the next day and say, "Hey, get over it. Look for the opportunities this creates! You must move on." We would react to that counsel as cruel and disrespectful. When people go through change, it often feels closer to the numbing shock of deep loss than leaders are willing to admit. Grace creates space to grieve loss.

All losses need to be grieved for the sake of our emotional and spiritual health

Gerald Sittser's wife, daughter and mother died at the scene of a terrible accident when they were stuck by a drunk driver. Three years later he writes,

I learned that, though entirely unique (as all losses are), it is a manifestation of a universal experience. Sooner or later all people suffer loss, in little doses or big ones, suddenly or over time, privately or in public settings. Loss is as much a part of normal life as birth, for as surely as we are born into this world we suffer loss before we leave it.

It is not the experience of loss that becomes the defining moment of our lives, for that is as inevitable as death, which the loss is awaiting us all. It is how we respond to loss that matters. That response will largely determine the quality, the direction, and the impact of our lives.[16]

All people suffer loss. Being alive means suffering loss. Sometimes the loss is natural, predictable, and even reversible. It occurs at regular intervals, like the seasons. We recover and resume life as usual, the life we wanted and expected. Living means changing, and changing requires that we lose one thing before we gain something else. But there is a different kind of loss that occurs in all of our lives, though less frequently and with less predictability. This kind of loss has more devastating results, and is irreversible. Such losses include terminal illness, disability, divorce, rape, emotional abuse, physical and sexual abuse, chronic unemployment, crushing disappointment, mental illness, and ultimately death.[17]

Grieving is an Aspect of Our Witness to the Good News from God

I love these words of comfort.

But we do not want you to be uninformed, brothers, about those who are asleep, ***that you may not grieve as others do who have no hope****. For since we believe that Jesus died and rose again, even so, through Jesus, God will bring with him those who have fallen asleep. For this we declare to you by a word from the Lord, that we who are alive, who are left until the coming of the Lord, will not precede those who have fallen asleep. For the Lord himself will descend from heaven with a cry of command, with the voice of an archangel, and with the sound of the trumpet of God. And the dead in Christ will rise first. Then we who are alive, who are left, will be caught up together with them in the clouds to meet the Lord in the air, and so we will always be with the Lord. Therefore encourage one another with these words.*

There is life and peace in grieving colored with godly hope. Hope does not deny losses or suppress grieving them but it does mean there is a bottom to our mourning. Our mourning stands on the solid foundation of our confident hope in Christ's ultimate victory over all that brings loss to God's children.

So, learning the language of lament is not only necessary to restore Christian dignity to suffering and repentance and death, it is necessary to provide a Christian witness to a world that has no language for and is therefore oblivious to the glories of wilderness and cross. A doubly necessary book.[18]

Jesus understood that lament was the only true response of faith to the brokenness and fallenness of the world. It provides the only trustworthy bridge to God across the seismic quaking of our lives. His life reveals that those who are truly intimate with the Father know they can pour out any hurt, disappointment, temptation, or even anger with which they struggle.[19]

Grieving is Our Place to Wrestle with God — To Settle Our Faith

In lament we bring out our challenges and our doubts concerning the God we want to find trustworthy and safe.

As we make our way along the shadowy twists and turns of the way of lament, two questions confront us again and again. . . . If you dig deeply enough you will discover that one or both of them lie at the heart of every lament, from Job's to Jesus'. The two fundamental questions of complaint: God, where are you? (Presence); God if you love me, they why? (Lovingkindness) [20]

Is God there?

Does God care?

Is he good but weak and cannot stop this suffering?

Is he powerful and able to stop it but cruel and not to be trusted?

⏻ PAUSE – TRY IT OUT!

Our emotions and grieving

Read Psalm 55 where the singer mourns a betrayal by a friend. What do you learn here about mourning?

Read Psalm 88. It is the only Psalm that does not bring the questions and accusations aimed at God to a resolution. What does this teach you about your mourning?

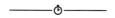

God can handle his children pounding their fists on his chest. He continues to hold us as we lament our loss and he absorbs the blame. He does not answer all of our questions but he can resolve our challenges to his character. Over and over in the Bible, men and women came to trust that

God is with them in their suffering and loss and he cares. Like a parent who cannot explain the timing or answer all of the "why?" questions of a young child, he does what we can receive; his being with us in love.

My God, by Whose loving Providence, sorrows, difficulties, trial, dangers, become means of grace, lessons of patience, channels of hope, grant us good will to use and not abuse those privileges; and, of Thy great goodness, keep us alive through this dying life, that our death Thou mayest raise up to immortality. For his sake who is the Life, Jesus Christ our Lord — Amen. —Christina Rossetti [21]

As we will highlight below, God makes people unique and that includes their emotional response to loss. I do not present this next list so much as stages but as common themes that come up, often more than once, as a person goes through a mourning season. Grief, though it will vary in depth and duration, is an appropriate God designed response to any loss. Grief is essential because it is how we let go of what we can no longer have so that God can give us what we can have.

What have I lost?

When we grieve we are bringing in to focus what is gone. To fully grieve, we must clearly understand what has been lost. Gerald Sittser goes on to write:

Later my sister, Diane, told me that the quickest way for anyone to reach the sun and the light of day is not to run west, chasing after the setting sun, but to head east, plunging into the darkness until one comes to the sunrise.

I discovered in that moment that I had the power to choose the direction my life would head, even if the only choice open to me, at least initially, was either to run from the loss or to face it as best I could. [22]

Healthy people grieve all losses and they identify specifically what they have lost. When a family experiences a loss of their passport culture, they are very likely all grieving different losses within that larger loss. One grieves the loss primarily of relationships, and another feels loss in lost opportunities (certain schools or work). One grieves the loss in terms of personal loss, while another grieves how the losses will impact and change the immediate and extended family as a whole.

The power of specifically "naming" your losses.

Examples of losses faced by cross-cultural workers might include:

1. Relationships left behind.

2. Grieving the distance and sense of being "out of touch" or not "up to date" on one's passport culture as part of the process of embracing the host culture.

3. Receiving a "Dear John" letter from a relationship that you thought might move to marriage.

There are many types of losses, and within a major loss, there are many smaller losses. Archibald Hart described grieving as working with a funnel filled with marbles. One marble is larger than the rest and has the funnel clogged so the rest of the marbles cannot pass through. Those marbles represent all of the losses that are part of a major loss. As we mourn, we say "good-bye" to each marble falling through the funnel. The large marble represents the unique major loss within the event. We need to identify what the large marble is for us. As we grieve that specific loss, the others will then pass through as well.

Is the big marble more "concrete" or "abstract"? Both are legitimate types of losses to grieve. In 2007, my son was married. This was a good and "necessary" loss. I regained money for our food budget and a decrease in our hot water bill. But we had been very close. We backpacked, played racquetball, and processed books and music together. He was my day off companion for guy stuff. I have had to grieve that loss of companionship. Marriage is good! Our daughter-in-law is a wonderful partner for him. A new family following hard after Christ is a lifelong answer to prayer. But was I grieving? Yes.

I received my first speeding ticket in over twenty years a few months ago. That was an "unnecessary" loss, but it still needed to be grieved. The big marble in that loss was not the fine, but the fact that it came about because I was in a hurry to get to a meeting. The loss in the speeding violation was the realization that I had failed to handle my busy day well.

A few years ago I was out of state speaking at a church when my doctor called. My doctor had never called me. Now he had tracked me down to tell me I had a very bad test result and to be in his office Monday morning to repeat the test. It was Saturday. I had several hours of driving by myself where I could grieve a "created" and possible "threatened" loss. But all losses need to be grieved. It turned out to be an inaccurate result and everything was fine. But that time of reflection helped me re-examine my priorities and how I was relating to my children — what did I want to leave behind?

Being sinned against is a loss. To forgive I must grieve as part of releasing the debt incurred. To forgive will involve grieving and focusing on what specifically has been lost by the sinful act.

I do not believe it is possible to truly forgive another person from the heart until we allow ourselves to feel the pain of what was lost. People who say it is simply an act of the will do not understand grieving.[23]

○ PAUSE — TRY IT OUT!

Reflecting on losses

Use the chart on the following page to review what you just read of the examples on losses to be grieved.

What is a major loss in your life that you sense you are still grieving? What is the big marble? Make a list of all of the losses connected to this situation to help you reflect and begin to see what the major losses are for you.

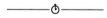

To grieve is to embrace sadness

It is normal and helpful to grieve and feel the sadness. The Bible is filled with men and women using words to move pain from inside to outside where it can be healed. A good safe listening friend helps. Tears are another gift. *Tears are God's gift to take "inside" pain and bring it to the outside where it can be healed and produce fruit.*

Gerald describes caring for his children that survived the accident but living in the sadness that numbed his soul for a long time.

I remember sinking into my favorite chair night after night, feeling so

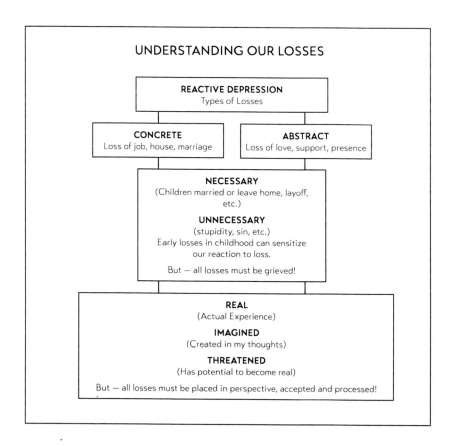

UNDERSTANDING OUR LOSSES

REACTIVE DEPRESSION
Types of Losses

CONCRETE
Loss of job, house, marriage

ABSTRACT
Loss of love, support, presence

NECESSARY
(Children married or leave home, layoff, etc.)

UNNECESSARY
(stupidity, sin, etc.)
Early losses in childhood can sensitize our reaction to loss.

But — all losses must be grieved!

REAL
(Actual Experience)

IMAGINED
(Created in my thoughts)

THREATENED
(Has potential to become real)

But — all losses must be placed in perspective, accepted and processed!

exhausted and anguished that I wondered whether I could survive another day, whether I wanted to survive another day. I felt punished by simply being alive and thought death would bring welcome relief.

I remember counting the consecutive days in which I cried. Tears came for forty days, and then they stopped, at least for a few days. . . . After those forty days that my mourning became too deep for tears. . . . In the months that followed I actually longed for the time when sorrow had been fresh and tears came easily. The emotional release would have lifted the burden, if only for a while.[24]

Let me offer a word for friends seeking to comfort. In times of deep sadness, being reminded of things we know to be true — including many Bible passages about heaven — is not comforting. Just listening and offering an attentive presence is very good. And sharing a memory of a funny or special moment about the person who has died will often help. A grieving husband shared with me, "You have added to my mental scrap book. I did not know she said that, but I can see it happening now. Thank you."

It is normal to be negative about the present, the past and the future as you are in mourning. This negativity should not be seen as a spiritual failure; it is instead how sadness tends to color the pages of our life with dark hues like walking under a cold gray dark sky. It will pass. The sun is still in its place. It is only covered by the clouds for this time. And God is more faithful than the sun.

Be prepared that not all will grieve in the same manner or at the same time. Mourning losses, like praying, studying the Bible, praising and fasting, are all shaped by our uniqueness designed by God. Depending on the age and maturity of the persons in your family, they may not all be able to fully understand or express what they are feeling. Be patient. Let them tell stories. Let them ask questions. Let them draw pictures. Certain music may become a dominant style that somehow connects to the sadness.

When Jesus was in the garden in deep agony before the many losses to come in his arrest and death, he wanted friends close by, and yet he also needed to draw a curtain and be alone. It is OK to go between safe presence and solitude when mourning. Some will write and some will wail. Some will sob quietly and some will want to talk But in a deep loss it is very common for us to experience a season of embracing the loss alone.

Grieving does have a goal

Just like all other spiritual disciplines, grieving is the means to an end. For example, Bible study is not the goal, it is the means to the goal of the truth of God working in and through us. The goal of grieving is to say, "good- bye" to what is gone and to kneel before God with empty hands. We echo with Job, "The Lord gives and the Lord takes away, but blessed be the name of the Lord." We can begin a journey from death to life, as we find hope for new life in the midst of our grief. We hold to the belief that from every grave God can give new life. The God who loves us places new life in the empty hands that we tearfully hold up to him.

Remember that it takes time for our heart to come to this place. Major grief will take longer than the time required to read a Psalm where we see the psalmist move from deep grief to confident renewed faith in God.

Grieving gently guides our heart to a place where we are "remembering" and "anticipating"— seeing what God has done and hoping for what he will do. God does redeem loss. God's life that comes out of death does not seek to replace what has been lost but does bring good from it.

⏱ PAUSE — TRY IT OUT!

Jesus' teaching on grieving

Read John 16:20-24 and summarize how Jesus describes the movement of the grieving heart.

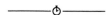

God can be trusted to bring life out of losses

It was a surprise for Simon. He was from North Africa, and to be in Jerusalem for the Passover was a dream come true. But a surprising thing happened. Jesus stumbled under the weight of the cross, right in front of him. Roman soldiers could draft anyone into their service with the touch of a spear blade. Simon was the closest person, so he was forced to pick up the cross and carry it, a humiliating task.

Mark recounts the same story but adds another detail — Simon was the father of Alexander and Rufus. It's unusual for a father to be identified by his children, unless the children are quite famous. By the time Mark's Gospel was circulated, two of the most famous Christians in all of the empire must have been Alexander and Rufus.

In Romans 16:13, Rufus is described as the son of a woman whom the apostle Paul considered his surrogate mother. Put the pieces together and it's obvious that when Simon returned home, he told his wife about Christ and the crucifixion. She became a godly woman and an influence to Paul. Simon told his sons what he had witnessed, and they became two of the greatest believers in the first-century church. The surprising embarrassment Simon endured that day turned out to be a great good for Simon and his family.[25]

Do not push yourself or others to get past identifying the loss, feeling the sadness and saying, "good-bye" to get to this place of expecting new life to be given to you. But God will be faithful. As I look back over some tragic losses and some losses that are simply the result of growing older, God is always faithful to pour the grace of his gifts into my hands wet with tears.

Archibald Hart, among other counselors, believes that one of the leading root causes or triggers to depression is a failure in properly grieving a loss. Losses not grieved accumulate and lead to many of the tragedies we see in leadership failures. Many leadership sinful failures were attempts to get away from pain and losses that had not been properly mourned. When this happens, the losses fester and move our heart away from trusting God in our pain to us taking responsibility to escape or dull our senses.

SUMMARY

Expect change to generate the heat of conflict. Minimize heat with clarity, trust and consistent assessment and evaluation. To love well in conflict moments requires one to listen well. Listen for how the change is a perceived threat or challenge to a person's definitions, expectations, motivations or values. Address those wounds with grace and truth. Do not seek to eliminate conflict with simply more communication.

People play various roles as they react to change and they process change at different rates. God knows that about us. Don't deny how people are responding but also place it under the rule of the King.

All change will cause loss. Learn to grieve well and teach others to grieve well. How we grieve is one of our best means of witness to the truth about Jesus.

THINKING IT THROUGH

1. How can your leadership demonstrate being a good comforter?
2. How people grieve is one deeply emotional part of life and death that is defined by culture and family. Do you know the cultural expectations for how to grieve in the cross-cultural or multi-cultural setting where you lead?
3. How can we effectively care for one another?
4. How do we create safe places to mourn?
5. How do we detect when someone is refusing to grieve?
6. How do we help them?

PART FIVE

THE OBJECTIVE OF LIFE-GIVING LEADERSHIP

No one can hold life. We either waste it, give it away, or pour it out for a cause worth dying for. —Gary Thomas

If you want your leadership to count, lead in things that matter to God. —Gary Hagen

GOD'S LIVING CREATION is incredibly complex and diverse but not lacking in direction. The Bible stands as an example that history from creation to the finale of the eternal redeemed kingdom has a current like a stream moving to the ocean.

Life-giving leaders never lead for their own survival or to perpetuate the life of the organization.

Life-giving leaders always place consistent, vibrant, and effective pursuit of God's objective as their life aim.

We find our life by losing it in his life-giving cause.

CHAPTER FOURTEEN

GOD'S LIFE-GIVING MISSION

ALMOST ANY LEADER will tell you that the greatest threat to effective leadership is failing to stay focused on the primary objectives of the enterprise. This failure can come from:

- ➤ Distraction,
- ➤ Loss of focus,
- ➤ Urgent cries crowding out intentional priority investments,
- ➤ Seeking to get a clean desk or a clear calendar before we act on the "big" things,
- ➤ "I will have more time next week, next month, next year — so just get the demanding piles screaming for attention go down for now."

These are all different ways to express failing to press our influence into what is most important. This kind of lifestyle drains the vitality in leaders. The seeds of fatigue and depression are sown when we are surviving the day rather than investing the day in what we know will count.

Remember our definition of life-giving leadership used throughout this book: *Effective (fruitful) and Vibrant (joyful, contented, and peaceful) loving leadership best describes God's life in his people.*

SO — what is the point of God's leadership?

What is his objective?

What should be the point of our self-leadership of ourselves?

What are the goals of the mission assigned to those led by God?

The objective of life-giving leadership is to be consistently aligned with Christ's work of revealing the kingdom by the power of the Holy Spirit. Our lives are fruitful from God's perspective as we invest in God's good news being present among all people. It can be summarized in these two statements:

1. The gospel of the kingdom is being lived out and offered in Christ-like love as the source of life among all people.
2. Those who become Jesus-followers will be gathered as the people of God, i.e., churches multiplying among every people group on earth.

Peter, the former fisherman, who has spent his life in fishing for men, writes, "But you are a chosen race, a royal priesthood, a holy nation, a people for his own possession, *that* you may proclaim the excellencies of him who called you out of darkness into his marvelous light." [1] Notice the purpose clause in the second half of the sentence. "You are" speaks of our identity as Jesus-followers, "that," for the purpose of proclaiming our great God who has brought us to life. God has given every follower of Jesus the same basic purpose.

God goes to great lengths to communicate with the people he created in order to restore a relationship; the relationship being the key to us being brought from death to life. For God to be redemptive, he came where we were. The incarnation is the holy God among us, seeking us out, serving us, and accomplishing what we could never do for ourselves. Is there a pattern, a guide for the church to follow in living as the body of Christ? Is the good news today seeing and hearing the presence and power of the King and introducing the kingdom of life into the domain of death?

Jesus had a practice of redeeming common stuff and infusing it with truth about the kingdom life. Bread, wine, sheep, branches, plows, seeds, and fish were all every day, known in our world stuff. They were the "pop-culture" of the first century. They were the objects of daily conversations. "Wow! Look at that catch of fish!" "Best wine we have had at a wedding!" "You know I saw this very loyal and caring shepherd. What a guy." "Look at the harvest this year!" As Jesus walked with the people, this common stuff became pointers to the kingdom.

How can the church show the redemptive pointers in our culture? "Wow, this child is learning to read!" "Isn't clean water good?" "This medicine makes daily life activity possible again!" "Did you hear Amena Brown's spoken word poetry — what a story of life?"

"And this Gospel of the kingdom will be proclaimed throughout the whole world as a testimony to the all nations, and then the end will come." [2]

WHAT IS THE GOSPEL OF THE KINGDOM?

Psalm 107 could be called the "salvation Psalm". The Psalm begins with giving thanks for who God is; "he is good and his steadfast love endures forever." The thanks are being declared by the redeemed who have been gathered from all points on the globe. (Psalm 107:1-3) The psalmist then presents four different journeys of the redeemed. For each type of person, he includes the same chorus, "Let them thank the Lord for his steadfast love, for his wondrous works to the children of man!" (Psalm 107: 8, 15, 21, and 31).

Describe the unique lostness of each group and the specific way God redeems.

1. Psalm 107:4-9
2. Psalm 107:10-16
3. Psalm 107:17-22
4. Psalm 107:23-32

Are there people with a similar journey among the people you are seeking to share the gospel? Are some of these people more challenging for you to respond to with God's love?

Here were some of my thoughts:

1. Psalm 107:4-9 — homeless, wandering, many needs, lifeless
2. Psalm 107:10-16 — bondage as a result of rebellion, addictions, captured and imprisoned in darkness
3. Psalm 107:17-22 — foolish losses as a result of sin, near death, sounds like eating disorder "loathed any kind of food"
4. Psalm 107:23-32 — They have access to the city elders, strong people, out to see and conquer the world but their courage melts away as they encounter a world they cannot control, and now are at their wit's end. They are the "up-and-outers" in our world.

Yet the Psalmist declares one consistency; the love of God. He is adequate to respond to their cry. His attention to their need and powerful deliverance turns wholehearted cries to the Lord to wholehearted thanks for his salvation.

Notice also that salvation is holistic. Our life-giving God births his life in his people: physically, mentally, emotionally, socially and certainly spiritually. Horizontal and vertical relationships are impacted. God's people are set free to love God and one another. Eternal life is an eternal spring of joyful, sacrificial love that flows from God to the redeemed heart. The kingdom lifestyle is not a surface political correctness or an inauthentic veneer of a mask. God's salvation is the revelation of the kingdom of light and we are being made alive to love as our King loves us.

From the Psalms we move to the prophets.

The Spirit of the Lord God is upon me, because the LORD has anointed me to bring good news to the poor; he has sent me to bind up the brokenhearted, to proclaim liberty to the captives, and the opening of the prison to those who are bound; to proclaim the year of the LORD's favor, and the day of vengeance of our God; to comfort all who mourn. [3]

The New Testament continues the theme of the Old Testament redeemer in the good news from God. Jesus presented the objective of his life as fulfilling the Isaiah passage in Luke 4:18-19. Robert Coleman explains:

He saw himself as an evangelist announcing the coming of the kingdom of God. There was joy in his life and work because he knew that in God's will he was bringing salvation to all men. The offering of Himself at Calvary was seen as the fulfillment and confirmation of the gospel he proclaimed. What he did and what he said were never intended to be separated in evangelism.

At this point, there is often confusion among churchmen. Some contend that evangelism consists largely in establishing a caring presence with people, passively identifying with their sufferings and difficulties. Others with an activist bent insist upon rectifying social and political injustices, virtually equaling evangelism and human endeavors to change the secular order.

That Christians should be involved in worthy humanitarian concerns cannot be ignored. In fact, genuine works of compassion in the world are a necessary precondition for effective communication of the gospel. But that alone does not make the gospel known. If Jesus had only listened to the heartbreak of the people and had performed deeds of kindness among them, we may admire his noble character, perhaps even recognize his deity; but still may wonder why he came. But because he told us God's saving Word we can understand the purpose of his mission.

So it is with all who follow in his steps. Good new demands that it be told — the more so when it is the difference between life and death. The world simply must heart the gospel, otherwise there is no hope. [4]

Every time a follower of Jesus spreads the salt and light of the gospel, he or she is joining what the angels started with some shepherds. [5]

The Gospel Is...

Good News — Luke begins with angels worshiping the savior and ends with the disciples worshiping as Christ ascends. Just like the redeemed in Psalm 107; gratefulness and praise flow freely.

Of Great Joy — We are lost and God sends a search party. It is like being a child who realizes they are lost in the deep woods and yet confident that help is coming because of their parents love for them. The joy is the certainty of the salvation. I have made the mistake of seeing "joy" as an optional emotion that you have in very special moments. Now I see joy as a daily expression and part of God's will for his children.

Truly, truly, I say to you, you will weep and lament, but the world will rejoice. You will be sorrowful, but your sorrow will turn into joy. When a woman is giving birth, she has sorrow because her hour has come, but when she has delivered the baby, she no longer remembers the anguish, for joy that a human being has been born into the world. So also you have sorrow now, but I will see you again, and **your hearts will rejoice, and no one will take your joy from you**. *In that day you will ask nothing of me. Truly, truly, I say to you, whatever you ask of the Father in my name, he will give it to you. Until now you have asked nothing in my name. Ask, and you will receive,* **that your joy may be full**. [6]

For All the People — Once again God's heart for all people is revealed. Like those described in Psalm 107, being lost creates an endless variety of stories. But none are beyond the reach of the God's love and his desire to redeem those lost from despair to joy.

God is making the universe again, and he is making it again in Jesus Christ. Being missional is having a delegated mission within God's universal mission. The purpose of God is to cross every culture until the good news of his kingdom reaches the ends of the earth. God loves to touch all aspects of the world.[7]

As seen in the four examples of the redeemed in Psalm 107, good news includes facing the failure of attempting to find life while being in opposition to God. As we trace the spread of the gospel through Acts, we also see people recognizing that the gospel is worth the loss of their idols. Idols are dead ends; they are only life substitutes. Idols must be abandoned to embrace the true source of life.

For not only has the word of the Lord sounded forth from you in Macedonia and Achaia, but your faith in God has gone forth everywhere, so that we need not say anything. For they themselves report concerning us the kind of reception we had among you, and how **you turned to God from idols** *to serve the living and true God, and to wait for his Son from heaven, whom he raised from the* *dead, Jesus who delivers us from the wrath to come.* [8]

True mission implies living under the Lordship of Christ and also implies exposing idols. Missionaries are not true missionaries unless they live and announce the gospel in such a way that makes it clear that they do not worship Mammon or Caesar. [9]

Summary

The gospel is good news because:

1. It is the demonstration of God's steadfast love
2. It is the encounter with God's redeeming power
3. It is the source of joy for all people
4. It confronts and replaces idols who rob their followers of life

PRACTICAL APPROACHES TO SPREADING THE GOOD NEWS

Solitude is a good school, but the world is the best theatre; the institution is best there, but the practice here; the wilderness hath the advantage of discipline, and society opportunities of perfection. —*Jeremy Taylor*

Life's most urgent question is: what are you doing for others? —*Martin Luther King, Jr.*

Perhaps one of the greatest weakness in much of Christian leadership is we spend too much time talking about the good news to one another and not enough time being the good news to the world. The great commission is to teach them to "OBEY" (Matthew 28:19), not teach them to simply understand. We operate under a faulty premise: "*If I make truth clear people will live it out.*" In reality, clarity is simply a first step toward the actions of life. Doing kingdom life together *in* the world is the calling of Jesus.

Being consistently passionate and motivated to spread the gospel

To make this personal, how do you stay passionate and intentional in declaring the gospel? Perhaps what sparks motivation in parents with young children is concern for their salvation? I have had the opportunity to sit in small groups with Russian schoolteachers. They shared with me that they have been passed over in an offer for new life. They believe it is too late for them. But, they are living for the next generation; they were teaching, even at times without receiving pay, in order to see their hope bear fruit in their children.

Motivation to share the gospel may start with concern for a seriously sick co-worker, or perhaps it is a fresh vision of the eternal lostness of humanity without Christ. But one way God turns my heart outward to share his good news is for me to relive my own coming to Him.

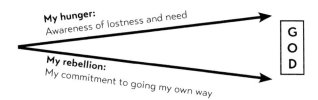

In remembering my own journey, my vision of God gets bigger and my sense of my need for God also grows. That is why a mature believer may genuinely shout with Paul, "I am the chief of sinners." But as I review walking toward the true God, I also sense the corresponding greatness of his grace. And I agree with Paul in Romans, that as "sin abounds grace exceeds it in abounding". I am not sure we can have a close intimate relationship with the Holy One and not have a corresponding sense of need and God's more than adequate provision of grace.

It helps those seeking to witness to prodigals and judgmental elder sons (like those in the Luke 15 parable) to remember their own heart's wandering and judging tendencies and recall the emotions of their journey of responding to the Father's love.

But it certainly seems easy to lose sight on why the gospel really is good news. I seem to be very creative at growing thorns, which choke out the fruitfulness of the seed. But I do not think I am alone. Do you have any thorn bushes?

*And others are the ones sown among thorns. They are those who hear the word, but the cares of the world and the deceitfulness of riches and the desires for other things **enter in and choke** the word, and **it proves unfruitful**.* [10]

God is very committed to seeing us enjoying his life. Fruitfulness equals life. Being choked-out equals loss of fruitful life.

⏱ PAUSE — TRY IT OUT!

Evaluating your lifestyle

Use these questions to pull some of the seven "thorns" choking out the fruitfulness of God's life in you.

1. **Do you find yourself caught up in ministry administrative machinery and out of the witness loop?**

Many Christian workers have shared with me of the dangerous third promotion that we practice in ministry. We take a growing volunteer who is shining in witness and we give them a step up to walking with and training others. (That is the first step) Then as they excel, we have them quit their job, go to school and promote them into full-time ministry. Even after this second promotion, they may have consistent opportunity for witness as a youth pastor or university campus minister. Then comes the deadly third promotion. We take those who have made an impact and we move them into an office and give them responsibility for the process and function of a "system" of ministry. Now the front lines of gospel witness can seem a long way off.

What happens to Christian leaders who are no longer consistent in witness?

How does the leader "break out" of the expectations of the role, and the numbing and overwhelming commitments which compete with being salt and light?

2. **What "good ministry stuff" gives you a convenient excuse for not taking the time to share the gospel?** Being a New Testament witness is not a vocation or profession. Yes, the spiritually gifted evangelist may consistently be involved in more new births, but witness of God's good news in Jesus is the Spirit powered calling of every Christian (Acts 1:8). An IMB missionary in Taiwan shared his inner conflict with me over lunch in Taipei. He was struggling with new priorities assigned to missionaries. He was very comfortable in supporting the Taiwan Baptist church with

administrative and technology resources. Yet now he was being assigned to focus on people groups on the island with very limited access to the gospel. These groups were also largely ignored by the national church.

For the past ten years he had basically had the same schedule and responsibilities of someone working in the administration of a business or school in the States. Now he was being told that this was not in alignment with being an apostolic cross-cultural worker. In short, he was not being paid to live cross-culturally insulated among national Christians. I suggested it seemed he had three options: return to the States and engage in administrative work, leave IMB and be hired by the Taiwan Baptist convention to support their churches, or shift his time investment to doing the missionary work of spreading the good news and planting churches among those beyond the reach of the gospel.

How can you use your strengths and competency in certain types of work to fill up any space devoted to witness?

Are you using the excuse that your contribution is to be "behind the scenes" and evangelism in not specifically your role?

3. Are you uncomfortable building new circles of relationship and influence? It is a constant challenge for me to pray and then intentionally move in to circles of relationship that our outside my normal orbit. I often reread John 4 and ask, *how do I find the well in the middle of the day and intersect those who need the love, hope and living water Jesus offers?* For me, those circles are people working in convenience stores or sitting in laundromats. Creating new webs of relationships is exhausting and takes me out of my comfort zone.

Where do the least reached people gather to be in community with one another in your host country?

Who can partner with you to penetrate these settings with the love and truth of Christ?

4. Are you keeping a sin buried in the darkness instead of bringing it into the light of confession?

In Philippians 4:6-7, Paul encourages us not to be in bondage to anxiety, but to bring everything to God in prayer with thanksgiving, and be guarded by the peace of God. We can exchange worry for peace through thankful prayer. How do you define "everything"? Could temptation and hidden sin be on the "everything" list? Sin easily becomes a living growing taproot in our heart like the thorns that grow up among my flowering hedges. No matter how many times I cut them off, in just a few weeks the thorns are spreading and are taller than my Azaleas. The only way to get rid of them is wait until the ground has loosed its grip after a hard rain then put on heavy gloves, grip the thorn, and pull it up by the roots.

What is being allowed to grow in your heart that you worry may be uncovered?

Who can you go to and bring the struggle to light and gain a prayer partner and the peace of God?

5. Have you stopped praying for opportunities to share the gospel? What I pray for consistently and passionately is my priority. Prayer is the primary way that needed realignment occurs. What we pray about becomes what we do.

Read these passages, and then pray, inspired by their examples: Acts 4:23-31, Colossians 4:2-6

6. Do you not know the language well enough? Let's play a game! Assume you have the disability of being deaf and dumb. Now how would you be a faithful witness? Would your physical handicap give you a good excuse for disobedience?

Your witness in your host culture may look very different from how you would share God's good news in your passport culture. In your host culture, you are the minority and you will often have weaknesses in communicating.

How can God use you, with your weaknesses and limits, in spreading his good news?

When you are on a mission to go from "zero to one" how can you use your "outsider" status to ask for help? Reciprocating hospitality may be one way to share the greatest treasure you have received.

In 2 Corinthians 12 Paul learned to let God fill weakness with his strength. What would that look like in your ministry context?

7. Have you created a "sacred" and "secular" separation that limits the spread of the good news of the kingdom?

My prophetic friend Reggie McNeal is wildly optimistic about God's kingdom work in the world but saddened by the creation of a "church world" where Jesus-followers are encouraged to live apart from the invasion God is pulling off. He says:

Jesus wants us to pray for, deeply desire, and dedicate ourselves to seeing the kingdom as it operates in heaven made visible and active in our daily experience here on earth. . . . The kingdom champions the life God intends for all of us to experience on this planet, in this lifetime.

God's perfect plan will not be fully realized until Jesus returns, but in the meantime, he wants us to pray that the kingdom will break in to our hearts, bringing transformation to our lives, and break out into the world, bringing hope amid hurt and fostering a better world in the face of immense problems, as we refuse to allow evil and suffering to have the final word in our lives.

My urgency is rooted in the desire that we not miss out on being a part of what God is already doing in the world.

The purpose, goal and result of the kingdom is life, not church-centered metrics and outcomes. Jesus said, 'I have come to give you abundant life,' not abundant church. Moreover, the church is not forever; the kingdom is. . . . Being church is more than just a catchy way of saying it. It means finding organic ways to express our covenantal relationship with God. Church is incarnated in every aspect of our lives, not just as part of our 'church experience' in a local congregation. It means that we see all of life as a mission trip. [11]

God uses full-time Christian workers

God uses bi-vocational Christian workers

God uses volunteers working in a limitless variety of arenas

God uses non-Christians he has allowed into places of leadership

Never let your vision become limited to roles of church or mission worker created over the last 200 years by protestant organizations. God's kingdom will not fit in any of our church or mission boxes. There is no place God is not working! He is calling his kingdom kids to come join him.

Summary

God uses many different internal and external motivations to stir up wholehearted devotion to sharing the good news. Our hearts do tend to continually grow weeds. It is very easy to kill the fruit-bearing plants and requires no effort to grow weeds. There were seven different thorns described that can choke out fruit.

> You may be transferred, enlisted, commissioned, reassigned, or hospitalized—but brand this on your heart—you can never go where God is not. —Max Lucado

⏱ PAUSE — TRY IT OUT!

Letting God's heart become my heart

Prayer and the Bible are two tools in every life-giving leader's tool box. Let's use them today. Below you will find a list of passages. Read them slowly and pray them in your own words back to the Father.

Numbers 14:21	1 Kings 8:60	1 Chronicles 16:24-29
Psalm 2:8	Psalm 22:7,27	Psalm 57:9-11
Psalm 67:4	Psalm 72:13	Psalm 72:18-19
Psalm 86:9	Psalm 96:3	Psalm 105:1
Psalm 108:3	Isaiah 2:2	Isaiah 25:6-8
Isaiah 49:6	Isaiah 52:7,10	Isaiah 60:2-3
Isaiah 66:18	Daniel 7:14	Daniel 12:3
Habakkuk 2:14	Malachi 1:11	Matthew 22:9
Matthew 24:14	Matthew 28:18-20	Mark 13:10
Mark 16:15	Luke 24:46-47	John 4:35
John 17:21	Acts 11:18	Acts 17:30-31
Romans 1:5	Romans 10:14-15	Revelation 5:9
Revelation 7:9-10	Revelation 14:6	

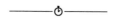

LIFE-GIVING LEADERS FEED THE PASSION TO SPREAD THE GOOD NEWS

The proverb that shapes my life and leadership investments is, **"Every day do something to advance the mission. Never stop being a builder in order to manage."** Leaders can easily become entangled and consumed in maintaining the systems, programs, events and services that we create to support a gathering of Christ-followers. When the leadership energy is going primarily inward, those in the orbit and influence of those leaders are pulled into the swirl—it is the action you see when you flush a toilet.

When leaders are outward kingdom focused, that too directs the energy of the group. This looks like a watering hose turned on full blast through a focused high pressure nozzle. The spray goes outward with force and distance. It makes an impact.

God matures hearts of faith in a community of disciples who are engaging in the spiritual disciplines of giving, prayer and evangelism. Attending meetings, on its own, does little to grow faith. It is like the difference between going to the gym or the doughnut shop.

As I write, I am having to push aside my concerns and prayers for a family our church is seeking to welcome into kingdom life. The Mom speaks little English, has seven children ranging in age from 9 to 18, and her husband was suddenly deported eight months ago. They have all kinds of needs including no transportation in a city where there is very little public transportation.

Several in the family are showing interest in Jesus and are asking good questions. They are willing to meet in groups of two and three with church members to discuss the Bible. We paid a plumber to open drains that had shut down their kitchen sink and washing machine for months, and we are helping with transportation.

The father calls often and is seeking to run the family from afar. We want to assist the family, but do not want to undermine or disrespect his leadership. They have asked the church for nothing, yet there are challenges and needs everywhere our church looks.

I love sitting with the oldest son after school and engaging his spiritual hunger and desire to follow Jesus. My first impulse is to open the pockets of our church and give to every one of the dozen needs we see. But I know that sincere helping can often hurt more than help. I know the truth of "teaching to fish rather than just giving fish." I just do not know what to do next.

These dear people are deepening the passion of my prayers. I have no lack of motivation to give as the Spirit shows us how to give under his leading. My dependence on God is being ratcheted up because I feel like the one of the Twelve facing a large crowd and being told by Jesus to feed them! Every person in our church is being stretched, and when the leadership team meets, we have more questions than answers.

That is a great place to be. That is the place where we grow.

The church is healthier and grows more when the people of God are touching lives the way Jesus did when he was here on earth. I first read Robert Coleman's book *The Master Plan of Evangelism* in 1973, during my college days at East Tennessee State University. I was involved in CRU (formerly Campus Crusade for Christ). I wrote the summary found in the exercise section after studying through the book with some dear Christian brothers in a small group. It stayed in my journal and has been a North Star to orient me throughout my 40 years in parachurch and congregational service. His book is still in print. And a version with a small group study guide in the back is also available.

Around 1980 when I was in seminary, Dr. Coleman came to speak on campus and I asked for an appointment. This gentle man listened to my story from becoming a Jesus-follower in 1972 to my present work as a student and staff member at the school. At the end of my sharing he looked me straight in the eye and asked, "So, where are your men?" I realized I had abandoned the strategy I had just thanked him for writing. His encouragement to pray and invite some men to walk with me contained no harsh judgment. He poured out confidence that the Spirit would show me how to fit some intentional discipling relationships into my busy married, student, working full-time life.

I still can picture that conversation in my mind. Over the next three months God provided three men, and I have kept men and some women (with my wife's full knowledge and support and with appropriate boundaries) in a relational circle of making disciples who then make disciples. I have been Department Head, Assistant Director, Pastor of Mission, Pastor, Alumni Director, and now Professor, but I always have it on my personal prayer list. "Father, who are the people you want me to invest in right now?" He always answers.

⏱ PAUSE — TRY IT OUT!

Building and sending people to the world

Read through this summary of Coleman's book and then begin your own prayer for the people through whom you are called to multiply the life of Christ.

1. SELECTION

Luke 6:13 — People were Christ's method.

No evidence of haste, just determination.

No big impact at this time, just investing in people willing to learn.

Jesus does not neglect the masses, but realizes that victory will never be won by the multitudes.

2. ASSOCIATION

Matthew 28:20 — He was with his disciples.

He let them follow him, and this was his initial requirement.

Luke 8:10 — Knowledge was gained by association before being understood by explanation.

IT TAKES TIME.

Discipleship involves the sacrifice of personal indulgence.

3. CONSECRATION

Matthew 11:29 — He required obedience.

Luke16:13 — The surrender of one's whole life to the master in absolute submission to his sovereignty was required.

Matthew 27:3-10; Acts 1:18, 19 — Few would pay the price.

Obedience to Christ was the means by which those in his company learned more truth.

John 5:30, 6:38 — Obedience was modeled by Jesus as he lived in absolute obedience to the Father's will.

4. IMPARTATION

John 20:22 — He gave himself away.

John16:33, Matthew11:28 — He gave his peace.

John 15:11, 17:13 — He gave his joy.

Matthew 6:19, Luke 12:32 — He gave the keys to the kingdom which the power of hell could not prevail against.

John17:22, 24 — He gave them his own glory so he could be as one with the Father.

John 17:18, 19 — He gave them a compulsion for evangelism. As the context reveals, his sanctification was in an area of commitment to the task for which he had been sent into the world, and in dedication to that purpose of evangelism, He continually gave his life "for their sakes". "The ministry of the Holy Spirit is God in operation in men's lives." [12]

5. DEMONSTRATION

John 13:15 — He showed them how to live.

The practice of prayer — Luke 11:1; Matthew 6:9-13.

The use of Scripture/Abide in his word — John 15:7.

Training to evangelism — No fancy classes or tools, only a teacher who practiced with them what he expected them to learn.

6. DELEGATION

Matthew 4:19 — He assigned them work. He provided them with a vital experience with God and showed them how he worked, before telling them they had to do it.

Their briefing instructions: Luke 9, Matthew 10, Mark 6

Go where the most receptive audience is — Matthew 10:5,6

Move with the movers — Matthew 10:11; Mark 6:10; Luke 9:41

Expect Hardship.

Remember — They are one with Christ — Matthew 10:40-42; John 13:20 "Think of this identity! The disciples were to be the actual representatives of Christ as they went forth. So clear was this association that if someone gave a child a cup of cold water in the name of a disciple that act of mercy would be rewarded."

They were sent out two by two. Evangelism set up Christ for his ministry — Luke 10:1

"Christian disciples are sent men—sent out in the same work of world evangelism to which our Lord was sent, and for which he gave His life. Evangelism is not an optional accessory to our life. It is the heartbeat of all that we are called to be and do."

7. SUPERVISION

Mark 8:17 — He kept check on them

He gave instruction, assignments and then regrouping to iron out problems.

Jesus used mistakes and failures for learning — Mark 9:17-29; Mark 6:30-44; Mark 8:10-19.

Plan of teaching:

1. Example
2. Assignment
3. Constant check-up

8. REPRODUCTION

John 15:16 — He expected them to reproduce — John 17:20, 21, 23

"His whole evangelistic strategy, indeed, the fulfillment of his very purpose in coming into the world, dying on the cross, and rising from the grave depended upon the faithfulness of his chosen disciples to this task."

A barren Christian is a contradiction. A tree is known by its fruit.

"The only hope for the world is for men to go to them with the gospel of salvation, and having won them to the Savior, not to leave them, but to work with them faithfully, patiently, painstakingly, until they become fruitful Christians savoring the world about them with the Redeemer's love."

"The criteria upon which a Church should measure its success is not how much the budget is increased, or how many names are added to the roll, but rather how many Christians are actively winning souls and training them to win the multitudes." [13]

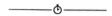

Conclusion: The Steps Summarized

1. Begin with a few
2. Stay together
3. Give them time
4. Group meetings
5. Expect something from them
6. Keep them going
7. Help them carry their burdens
8. Let them carry on
9. Their personal spiritual relationship with Jesus is priority
10. The price of victory comes high. [14]

LIFE-GIVING LEADERS EMPOWER JESUS FOLLOWERS

How do we effectively give witness to the gospel of the kingdom and mobilize others with us in spreading it? Most people learn only what they are motivated to learn by need or interest. If the adult learner cannot connect the learning opportunity to a need they have or a goal they desire, they will vote with their feet and leave. If the learning opportunity is perceived as being of high value, they engage. Otherwise there is simply too much distraction flashing before them and they will walk right on by. It is almost impossible to teach anyone anything unless internal motivation is present. What can teachers do to arouse this interest? Can we really teach anyone much of anything if they have not asked for help?

Adults learn by connecting new knowledge to past learning and experience. So how can we connect these principles of adult learning to Christians becoming or recovering an effective witness?

⏱ PAUSE — TRY IT OUT!

Sharpening our witness

As you read this example of a small group experience think through how you can adapt it to your context.

STEP 1

Start with a small group of Jesus-followers and give each person a blank sheet of paper. Show them an example of a basic life timeline.

Chapter One: Childhood	Chapter Two: Teens	Chapter Three: College & Marriage	Chapter Four: Firsts
Parents die	Influence of scout leader	Christian challenged me to read Bible	First real job
Grandmother prayed for me	Caring teacher	Met people I respected who were followers of Christ	First home
Moved several times	Met Christians at coffee house	Commitment at retreat	First child
		Met wife	First visit to church as family
			Dick & Wilma older caring couple

Explain how the segments on the time line are similar to chapters in a book about their life. The chapters can be based on where a person lived, key events that shaped one's life, or more general stages of development. This is a specific timeline, not of their entire life, but of their journey to becoming a Christ-follower. Being a Christ-follower may look like a story reaching a climax at a very specific point in time, or it may be more of a long journey where a person slowly moved from outside to inside the family of God.

In the columns on the time line, list people, events, and circumstances (P, E, C) that contributed to their conversion during that chapter. Many times we only become aware of the people and situations God used to bring us to himself as we look back. In the example above, the person may not have become aware that their Grandmother was praying for them until after they become a Christian. The time line is an exercise in seeing at least some of how the Sovereign God wove a net that caught this "fish".

Have each person tell their story encouraging them to share specifically what other *people* did, how *events* influenced their movement toward Christ and the circumstances that impacted their progress. Ask those listening to jot down general principles and patterns they hear in the story.

STEP 2

After all have shared, create a list of repeated or strong influences that God used in bringing the people in the room to faith.

What do you think are some items that often show up?

Here are some that I have heard:

> I found out later that a family member or friend was praying for me.

> A person really cared about me and the concerns in my life.

> A person invited me to a service, camp, etc., where the gospel was clearly presented.

> . I observed how a person was handling life's problems difficulty or noticed a quality of life that I wanted to be true of me.

> I slowly realized that my definition of being a Christian was wrong. I thought I was a Christian because I was not Jewish or Muslim.

> I began to see God as personal; loving, forgiving, and caring for **me**.

> There was a journey with several small steps of increased understanding and commitment that led to a settled new relationship.

What are the common elements that show up in the journeys on your team or in your cultural setting?

I had the opportunity to do this exercise in China with some new believers. By the time they each finished sharing, we had an amazing list of how God used people, events, and circumstances, often over at least a two year period, before they "crossed over". Their journey from atheism to salvation included very similar hurdles and blessings. Here are few they shared:

> Had to hear of other world views and begin to doubt the credibility of some of what I had been taught.

> Even before I believed, I prayed, and God answered dramatically in healing or some other miraculous way that led me to believe that the spiritual realm existed.

> I had to observe the joy, peace and generosity of Christians, and test it with anger or debate to prove it was real.

> I had to accept that there might be life after death.

From these common steps to faith, these Chinese believers and guest workers among them developed an intentional plan for being witnesses and training other Christians, including those coming from outside their culture, in understanding the Chinese journey.

STEP 3

The "journey" experiences should include the **specific knowledge** of the Bible that is important.

See the appendix for a helpful article by Robertson McQuilkin on the need for the gospel to be spread as the only means of salvation presented in the Bible.

Here are two sample questions to use to evaluate what biblical content needs to be part of an effective witness.

1. As you look back what was critical that you came to understand?
2. What questions, objections or concerns needed to be addressed?

The specific journey includes *what needs to occur as steps* in the journey and *what needs to be understood* for a faith response to the good news.

STEP 4

Making the learning personal and life changing. Discuss each of these following ideas for several minutes with the group.

1. Think about the people God brought into your life to be part

of your grace story and share how you could be used by God to contribute to someone's journey to Christ.

2. Consider the people within your circle of influence (your children, young people/students, co-workers, neighbors, those in need, widows or orphans, and enemies, etc.) What contribution could you make to their spiritual journey?

3. What do you need to learn, or intentionally choose to do, to make this contribution to their journey?

4. What barriers could hinder you from making your contribution?

Each person in the group should also summarize what they are learning:

1. Understanding WHO God wants me to become

2. WHAT I need to learn so I can be a better kingdom representative

3. WHAT I NEED TO DO and who are my partners in the kingdom

Use the findings to create an evangelism message tailored to the cultural group that includes: biblical passages to memorize, questions to be answered, and ways to serve and care for those in the community.

One common theme that runs through many of the salvation experiences across cultures is how another person interacted or responded to them. When Christ-followers treat everyone around them as bearing the image of God, as being his unique creations who are treasured and loved by Him, the Spirit bears witness with our witness. **What specific actions treasure people the way God does?**

1. Asks good questions and really listens

2. Gives the gift of presence by being in the messy life of the lost whom God is seeking

3. Are transparent about their own questions and struggles but also overwhelmed by the gift of grace

4. What else would you add to the list?

In most journeys there are multiple people, events and circumstances that contributed to the spiritual movement. The act of conversion was supported by team effort, not just one individual. A worker in China for over 17 years shared with me how she had been convicted of complaining to God. She would invest months and even years in cultivating relationships with Chinese outside of God's family. Then a guest worker would show up for a few weeks and report being with one of her friends when they crossed over to personal faith. The long-term worker shared, "When I got alone with God, I was trying to be thankful for the new Christ-follower, but I had to admit that I was also complaining that it didn't seem fair for someone else to be in the room when they responded. God showed me a great deal of pride in my heart, evidenced by my subtle complaining and demanding that I be able to experience the new birth moment and not just the discomfort and sacrifice of the 'pregnancy'."

STEP 5

The final step, (or is it really the first step)? What are some **practical ways** we can train ourselves to see, and then act, in alignment with Jesus' kingdom life?

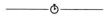

Look and Listen — see where God is working around you.

What do you do as you navigate through your day? Can we train ourselves to turn down the noise and reflect in gratitude on the moment we just had with someone. Can we anticipate that the Spirit may have a question for us to ask, a face to focus our attention on, or an encouraging word to offer? Can we pray and offer up our plan for the day up to the Lord and invite the Spirit to bring a phone call or other "interruption" into our path as an opportunity to model the kingdom?

Do some reverse engineering to calculate the next step in getting from where you would like to be to where you are now.

Often I help create crisis because I fail to count the cost to accomplish a goal. The project may be fine, but my failure to plan for the steps to get from here to there will lead me into pushing over and past people around me. A kingdom life is focused and intentional but also compassionate.

Did the Samaritan on the road who cared for the hurting Jewish man have margins in his life to allow him to see and stop?

Sow seeds consistently over time to reap a harvest.

We have been trained in our culture to look for an instant reaction to any action we take. Yet valuable harvest often comes after many days of the small actions of weeding, watering and caring with no immediate reward. Does kingdom living training involve a required course in patience and endurance in doing the right things consistently just because they are Christ-like?

Not every seed will bear fruit, but just as in Jesus' parable, the unfruitful seed may contain valuable insight. We need to stress that the life of God, based on his grace, changes our view about what we might label "failure". "Failure is not an option it is an essential." [15] We are exploring new space when we talk about spreading the gospel. We are walking off the part of the map where the good news is accessible and going into the "not-known" (similar to the unknown!) All explorers take dead ends and have to turn around. Many times explorers learn much about which paths do not lead to the destination before they discover the right one.

See every Christ-follower as a Kingdom Partner and Disciple Maker

Just a dream — What if every church of 100 adults adopted a mindset of dividing into groups of 10 to 12 and planting a new church? There is something about a shared responsibility for the mission that is not experienced by our consumer oriented congregations.

I have been in some Communist state-owned farms, villages, and businesses in my travels and have made an interesting observation. When the state "owns" it, no one owns responsibility for it. It shows in the care and quality of the work. Have we created churches where 80% or more of the congregation do not own it? Is that kingdom? I heard Dallas Willard say in class, "The kingdom runs on personal responsibility." Is that true? Does God's life-giving culture run on a freedom to choose and a responsibility for choices? Is our acceptance of being in a circle of freedom and responsibility essential to experiencing LIFE as God intended?

See those who need the gospel — see them geographically or ethnically as a "People Group".

Are my circles of contacts in my normal flow of life saturated or primarily made up of people who have access to the good news? Yet almost one half of the global population has very little or no access to the good news. It will require intentional action to look beyond my own "fence" and see those who need the message of the kingdom. We see this in the book of Acts. God prompted, burdened, and invited Jewish Christians to take the Jesus news to the world. Are we listening and ready for God to use us to extend the kingdom? It might be a people group in our city, an inner city or under served population, or it may be a in coffee shop in Northern China or Moldova.

An ongoing effective kingdom lifestyle will call for investing relational resources.

Ministry flows through relational pipelines. We form personal, relational partnerships at local, regional and global levels. I have a pastor friend who keeps notes on the places he eats. At each restaurant, he makes notes on servers' names and other things he learns about the owner or manager of the business. When preparing to return to that eating establishment, he reviews his notes, prays and seeks to build on his prior contacts. The life-giving God knows that life flows from one person to another through relationship. There is nothing wrong with making an online gift or attending a fund raising banquet for a worthy mission or project, but are we relationally open to God expanding our network of partners?

Be careful of seeing a kingdom network as directed one-way — your giving to others. Kingdom partnerships are also critical for your own learning and growth. God often delights in surprising us as we spend time exploring what we can learn from others. These informal coaches and mentors enrich us and are part of God's kingdom curriculum for our life.

Listen to a summary of a cross-cultural worker's exploring. He shared how they had attempted and failed in using media effectively. A conversation with a worker from another region reshaped the entire strategy from seeking decision to creating dialogue and opportunities for relationships.

Recently in a partnership with others we aired Mel Gibson's 'Passion of the Christ' on national television in a Muslim-majority country. From that showing, we had 65,000 people respond using a text message to request a video called 'The Secret Life'. We chose to use text messaging as a response system because radicals monitor other response systems such as the Internet or local mail.

In the video were testimonies of people who explained how God had changed them. If the respondent wanted more information, he could send us a text message to receive a discussion guide. In this guide they could send a request for an Injil (Muslim term for the New Testament). Of the 6,500 who asked for a New Testament, we know of 85 who made professions of faith. Interestingly, of the 85, 25 were not individuals asking for one Bible but small groups scattered across five states. [16]

If a witness to the gospel lives like Christ lived, loves like God loves, shows up where God shows up, offers God's grace and God's truth by faith in God's power (as this long run-on sentence attempts to stress), God must supply us with what is needed for that mission. And he has provided.

*His divine power has granted to us **all things** that pertain to life and godliness, through the knowledge of him who called us to his own glory and excellence, by which he has granted to us **his precious and very great promises**, so that through them you may become **partakers of the divine nature**, having escaped from the corruption that is in the world because of sinful desire.* [17]

A major barrier to being consistent witnesses is a wrong perspective. A scarcity mentality will blind us to what God has brought to us. When the church is correctly focused, it becomes a resounding witness alongside the angels declaring, "God has good news, of great joy, for all people!"

I heard Pastor Craig Groeschel say words close to these, "I tried to be like Rick Warren but I came to realize I'm not "purpose driven" I am "accident driven". Do your attempts at spreading the gospel feel like a series of mishaps? You are in good company!

What are the failures teaching you about a more fruitful approach?

SUMMARY

Evangelism is the spreading of the good news of Jesus as Savior and King. It must be done *in* the world.

The best demonstrations of the power of Jesus to bring life to dead hearts are the love we practice with one another (think the one-another commands) and a sacrificial, compassion-filled life of good works living out God's grace and truth in what Jesus called "salt" and "light".

Evangelism does include words and those words have deeper impact when they are mined out of our own journeys and spoken from the heart, covered in prayer, and supported by other Jesus-followers.

Jesus faced the cross but his vision was filled with the faces of the people covering the whole earth.

*And truly, I say to you, wherever **the gospel is proclaimed in the whole world**, what she has done will be told in memory of her.* [18]

To share his life-giving heart we will also see the whole world, not just family or friends who are far from God's life.

THINKING IT THROUGH

1. Are we taking the gospel to the dark places where those who have least access to it and are least valued by others?
2. Are we, as a community, longing in prayer for salvation to occur?
3. What is our strategy to sow the seeds of opportunities to love our neighbor?
4. Are we sharing the good news in the power of the Holy Spirit and leaving the results up to God?
5. Do we, as leaders, study where the Jesus-followers gathered around us in church spend the bulk of their waking hours? Are we equipping and walking beside them so they can be effective in their world? Are we providing a support system of prayer and other resources supporting the kingdom work they do where they live the majority of their hours?

Thinking about what it means to be a "Kingdom Player-Coach" style of leader and how that differs from a "Tell and Send" style leader from the sideline will be a focus in our next chapter.

CHAPTER FIFTEEN

MULTIPLYING CLUSTERS OF CHRIST-FOLLOWERS

Jesus taught that the kingdom would have small beginnings but that it would grow exponentially — even becoming global in its influence.

How does the kingdom grow in size and influence?

Again God is our model leader. Jesus used a "multiplication" strategy. To use today's leadership language, he was "mentoring" and "coaching" the next wave of leaders. A great danger in leadership is to be so focused on one's own contribution and focus that we fail to invest in developing leaders. Remember the pyramid. The base must expand to support the growth.

How does Jesus' leadership reflect the continuing existence and expansion of the kingdom? Jesus has not changed his priority since he walked on this earth. During his ministry, the people often wanted him to stay. Instead, he went on to other villages. He sent out the twelve. He sent out the seventy. He has not changed his strategy. He is a SENDING leader. In his daily devotional, Robert Morgan reminds us of the assignment we have received.

Luke was not only summarizing his first book but previewing his second. He was saying, in effect: 'My first book, the Gospel of Luke, is the story of all Jesus began to do and to teach while on earth in the flesh. My second book, the Acts of the Apostles, is the account of all that Jesus continued to do and to teach by his Spirit through his church.' That statement applies to subsequent Christian history and to us today. It's not our work, nor is it a matter of working for Him. It's his work, and it's a matter of his working through us. Jesus is continuing to do his work and teach his truths just as surely as he did in the Gospels. It's by his Spirit and through his people like you and me.[1]

Life-Giving Leaders focus on people and not stuff

There is a tension that exists in leadership over investing in structure or people. The reality is that a group of people requires a certain amount of structure and systems to be able to walk together.

Families can have a schedule of meal times together, or evening prayers together, or family council times to plan or solve problems together.

Churches adopt a calendar to prioritize time of being together and a budget to guide in using funds pooled together.

But, we all know the danger of structure becoming an end instead of the means to the end.

What does a maturing Christian look like? Answer: A walk of faith in the power of the Holy Spirit. Tozer says, "What I am anxious to see in Christian believers is a beautiful paradox. I want to see in them the joy of finding God while at the same time they are blessedly pursuing Him. I want to see in them the great joy of having God yet always wanting Him."

Life-Giving Leaders present truth in a way that make it easily transferred

Just look at the layout of the Bible.

"Neither plants nor talented people can be instructed or commanded to grow," says Keith Reinhard. I like the way Larry Crabb uses the word "enticing" in many of his descriptions of God's grace luring us and drawing us toward himself. Jesus never forced anyone to follow him but he made it an attractive option even with its high cost.

Life-Giving Leaders Expect Generational Transfer

Again I draw on Robert Coleman's wise reflection on how the impact of Jesus on the first generation of his followers carried over into what we find in the book of Acts and the letters written to those churches:

In the company of Jesus, the disciples had a demonstration of his mission: his life was the object lesson of his doctrine. He practiced before his men what he wanted them to learn, thereby proving both its workability and its relevance. Take, for example his habit of prayer. Surely it was no accident that Jesus often let his disciples see him conversing with the Father. Though they may not have understood its full significance, they could not help but notice, the time came when they said to Him, 'Lord, teach us to pray' (Luke 11:1).

Having awakened their desire to learn, Jesus proceeded to explain some elemental truths and then led them in reciting the model prayer. Thereafter, he opened the subject of prayer again and again, continually enlarging upon its meaning and as he saw their spiritual comprehension deepening.

In the same manner, Jesus taught his disciples the importance and use of Scripture, worship, stewardship of talents, civil and social responsibility, and every other aspect of his life. All the while, He was showing them how to minister to the total need of people. In all kinds of situations among all strata of society, the disciples watched their Teacher at work; evangelism was seen as a way of life. This was the genius of his approach. Practical lessons just seem to grow out of life situations. Nothing seems forced. It is all so natural that at first we may not even be aware that he is teaching.[2]

Life-Giving Leaders Intend for every Jesus-follower to be Trained to a "Teaching to Obey" Level

What is John 15 "fruit"? Answer: Obedience that brings me into a lifestyle aligned with how Jesus lives.

Obedience for a Jesus-follower often begins when they are given opportunity.

Jesus found ways to use everybody, depending upon each person's gift and ability. At first, about all they could do was contribute to the group's solidarity by their attendance. However, since Jesus had no home of his own, some could offer him hospitality. In these small, ordinary, domestic duties, they were rendering a real service. As far as I can find, our Lord never turned down an invitation to dinner. What a beautiful way to let one exercise a talent!

After a while, Jesus allowed the disciples to baptize people that were converted under his preaching (John 4:2). Later, he sent out the twelve two by two to practice what they had learned (Matthew 10:1; Mark 6:7; Luke 9:1-2). Before they left, he commissioned them to preach and to heal, spelling out more completely their authority. He also gave them specific instructions on where to begin, what to take, and how to act (Matthew 10:5-42). Apparently they met with some success, for not long after this, "seventy others" were dispatched, which probably included the original twelve (Luke 10:1-16).[3]

The other day a 12 year-old boy was visiting our small group during a supper meal at Chick-fil-A. I watched as my son asked him to pray a prayer of thanks for our food. The youngster, very new to being around Christians, confessed he did not know how to pray. Mark, gave him two or three simple instructions and encouraged him. Afterwards he got back slaps from us "big adults" in the group. He was grinning ear to ear. He was learning to step out in faith and obey with the Spirit's help, just as Mark had told him.

We need to see every step of obedience as a win for the life of God coming into bloom in someone's life. We can then intentionally build on that action by offering them other opportunities which fit the person we see them becoming.

Life-Giving Leaders design for necessary interdependence

No one stands alone! Seldom does one leader have all of the leadership skills or capacity that a group of disciples need.

NO ONE SERVES ALONE... ECCLESIASTES 4:9-12

Leaders enjoy contributing their gifts to the work of God in human hearts. But an even greater joy is seeing people around them beginning to contribute what God has entrusted to them. Leading requires being "player-coaches". The leaders may run, block or tackle, but the effective player/coaches know the most strategic part of their work is when they are assisting others on the team in being effective.

Does it often take more time to do something "through" or "with" someone else for the sake of their development versus doing it myself? Yes! But as we can observe in both God's creation and redemptive dramas, he does not place priority on efficiency like some cultures do. God is surely effective, but he is often extravagant, or patient, or willing to go to the extreme to connect with us and involve us in his work.

Those engaged in cross-cultural work know the value of seeking and learning from peer coaches. Paul describes this dependence on God and interdependence with other Christians when he recounts the resistance and attacks to his witness and church starting activities.

For we do not want you to be ignorant, brothers, of the affliction we experienced in Asia. For we were so utterly burdened beyond our strength that we despaired of life itself. Indeed, we felt that we had received the sentence of death. But that was to make us rely not on ourselves but on God who raises the dead. He delivered us from such a deadly peril, and he will deliver us. On him we have set our hope that he will deliver us again. <u>You also must help us by prayer</u>, so that many will give thanks on our behalf for the blessing granted us through the prayers of many.[4]

For a Christian to stay on course as a witness, most will need some visits with a "coach". And we also need some other Christians, who are also committed to growing as witnesses, who pray for us, with us, and at times even walk with us in reaching out to others.

What would a peer coaching model focused on spreading the gospel look like in your context?

Are these mistakes to avoid in your setting? Here are some ideas:

1. The missionary arrives as the "expert" and approaches the task with the assumption that others have nothing of value to contribute.

2. Many of our approaches start with the message, yet most people remember their journey as the relationship with the messenger being critical.

3. When it comes to gospel truth, the message becomes most relevant when it is structured as addressing a need, hunger or question in the heart of the seeker. These will vary greatly across cultures. I have seen cross-culture workers gain very significant insight into what parts of the gospel truth to stress by studying the proverbs of the host culture.[5] For additional principles see Robertson McQuilkin's article in the appendix.

4. Training people to go out as isolated individuals as a witness while the biblical model is a witnessing community of Christ-followers. We should not ignore or devalue individual opportunities for proclaiming the gospel but as we noted, even Paul connected his witness to the Corinthians behind the scenes. Does your witness strategy include a support system for this warfare?

⏱ PAUSE – TRY IT OUT!

Organizing a leadership team

God's Spirit supplies the church with a variety of "coaches" to help the team execute effectively. Consider these draft definitions for these leadership roles. Then consider the questions below.

And he gave the apostles, the prophets, the evangelists, the shepherds and teachers, to equip the saints for the work of ministry, for building up the body of Christ.[6]

A – Apostles – pioneer, entrepreneur, ground breakers

P – Prophets – warn of polluting or compromising biblical truth with culture, protectors

E – Evangelists – connect simple gospel with deep heart hunger, network, open doors

P – Pastors – shepherd, counsel, encourage, model mercy, comforters

T – Teachers – clarify biblical truth so it can be relevant and applicable,

wrestle with meaning and application⁻

> ➤ What is your leadership contribution?
> ➤ What are the weaknesses or blind spots each of the APEPT roles may have if not balanced by the others?
> ➤ How can you identify and work as an APEPT team?

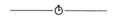

Life-Giving Leaders "Bubble Up" new leaders

There are only two lasting bequests we can hope to give our children. One of these is roots, the other, wings. Roots are a home; a secure safe base to rest on and launch from. Wings are the opportunities, empowerment, and encouragement to risk flying out. The flying for the Jesus-follower is primarily about bringing life to those in decay and darkness. Jesus used the images of salt and light. **What does it mean to live as "salt" and "light" being sent INTO the world but not being OF the world?** Answer: I live daily in a faith filled adventure with God. I show up and expect Jesus to be Jesus.

⏱ PAUSE — TRY IT OUT!

Soldier, athlete, farmer

Read these passages and then picture how each of these personalities would join Jesus in his mission.

1. 2 Timothy 2:3-7
2. 1 Corinthians 9: 7, 10-11, 24-27
3. Hebrews 12:1-3
4. 2 Corinthians 10:3-6
5. Ephesians 6:10-20
6. Timothy 1:18

Solider — Athlete — Farmer

List the characteristics of each role that describe how they would approach a salt and light lifestyle.

THINKING IT THROUGH

1. Review the chapter.. How could you adapt some of these principles to yourself and others around you?
2. List three specific prayer requests related to your life being invested in developing leaders to serve clusters of Jesus-followers.
3. How can you help others shift from a consuming to a contributing lifestyle?

RESOURCES FOR LIFE LONG LEARNING

1. Craig Groeschel. *It: How Church Leaders can Get IT and Keep IT.* Grand Rapids: Zondervan, 2008. (A passionate and creative perspective on the work of the Holy Spirit in growing Christ's Church)
2. Gary Haugen. *Just Courage: God's Great Expedition for the Restless Christian.* Downers Grove: IVP, 2008. (A highly motivated challenge to see injustice as God sees it)
3. Google, "Malcolm Knowles" who died in 1997. His many books and articles made him the father of Adult Education known as (andragogy) in contrast to educating children (pedagogy).

CONCLUSION

BE A LIFE-GIVING LEADER

IMAGINE AN OLD wooden school desk. It has been sitting in a classroom for years in rows with thirty other ones. You sit down and run your hand across the underside of the wooden desktop. What would you find? You would probably rub across dried old ABC (already been chewed) gum stuck there (now go wash your hands!). The really big stuff that God says is important, should be on top of the desk or should BE the desk, but too many congregations and ministry structures make God's kingdom priorities the bubble gum on the bottom of the desk.

Missions isn't bubble gum.

Prayer isn't bubble gum.

Evangelism and making disciples isn't bubble gum.

You have read the book. You add some more.

Life-Giving Leaders Stay Focused on what the Bible says is important to God.

Invest in what God says is important: PEOPLE. Be careful how much of yourself you pour into buildings, programs, etc. — they don't last. Here's a challenge: If you raise two million dollars to build a building, match it with two million for missions.

Don't lead if you can't lead out of prayer.

Be intent on making disciples. Pray daily for God to use you to help others move from darkness to light to growing in Christ. And then anticipate the Spirit showing you how to join him in that kingdom work.

You have to multiply leaders. It is not an option you will address someday when you have time. You have to help those leaders be effective in their circles of influence. Leadership is not an individual sport, it's a team sport.

Always be investing leadership in unity and diversity. I dream for there no longer to be a black church or white church in America. If there is a Chinese, Korean, etc. church with a non-English ministry, they are in deep partnership with a broader ethnic mix of the church, enjoying their own culture, but feeling fully engaged in the body of Christ. If the Apostles didn't go into a city to build a Jewish church and a Gentile church, then we shouldn't either. We lose something from the gospel when believers separate based on race, ethnicity, and socioeconomic lines.

Life-Giving Leaders Invite Others into Their Journey

Anchor yourself to something solid. Vision leaks; it has to be revisited every 30 days.

Know who are your current coaches, mentors, and friends who speak deeply into your life. If you need more time cut back on Facebook and go for Face to Face.

Life-Giving Leaders Live Under the Flow

Picture standing under a cascading waterfall. God's grace, never exhaustible, God's truth, always cleansing and nourishing. Everything alive lives in a flow of GRACE and TRUTH.

What I receive I give.

How is God speaking to you today?

How is this truth going to affect your life?

Who are you going to share it with?

Our lives, like a sponge, will sour if we are not squeezed out on occasion.

God's Life-Giving Leadership is Always Found by Losing Your Life

Jesus in teaching mode says,

If anyone comes to me and does not hate his own father and mother and wife and children and brothers and sisters, yes, and even his own life, he cannot be my disciple. Whoever does not bear his own cross and come after me cannot be my disciple. For which of you, desiring to build a tower, does not first sit down and count the cost, whether he has enough to complete it? Otherwise, when he has laid a foundation and is not able to finish, all who see it begin to mock him, saying, "This man began to build and was not able to finish." Or what king, going out to encounter another king in war, will not sit down first and deliberate whether he is able with ten thousand to meet him who comes against him with twenty thousand? And if not, while the other is yet a great way off, he sends a delegation and asks for terms of peace. So therefore, any one of you who does not renounce all that he has cannot be my disciple.[1]

Don't miss the parables in the middle about building a tower without enough money, or having to seek peace because you went to war without enough men. ***Help people count the cost.*** There is only one check they need to write to Jesus. Write on the line: *Everything I have, everything I am.* God has full permission to give me to anyone and do whatever he wants with me. The cost of burning up years of physical life not being a Jesus-follower is much higher than the joyous life-giving adventure of one fully surrendered to him.

Life-Giving Leaders are Friends with Jesus

Hear this invitation from Jesus.

*No longer do I call you servants, for the servant does not know what his master is doing; but **I have called you friends,** for all that I have heard from my Father I have made known to you.*[2]

How will you respond to Jesus inviting you to be his friend (and I don't think he meant a Facebook "friend")? We could have started this book on life-giving leadership with this invitation and then stopped. To walk with Jesus every day as a friend is LIFE.

APPENDIX 1

LIST OF EXERCISES

⏱ PAUSE — TRY IT OUT!

PAGE	TITLE	DATE/NOTES
30	Inner meditation in the Psalms	
34	The Lord's Prayer as a template	
36	Questions to evaluate prayer life	
37	Writing out a prayer to God	
47	Applying principles of learning	
55	Evaluating leadership decisions	
57	The truth of God living in you	
71	Reflections on Kingdom citizenship	
84	Resources for Jesus-followers	
85	Inventory of creative styles	
87	Exposing blind spots	
87	Anticipating the Spirit's creativity	
88	Recalling the Spirit's beautiful creations	
89	Partnership of God's Spirit and Church	
97	Ministry of the twelve — pass or fail?	
115	Taking an honest look at your heart	
122	Don't miss seeing the throne room	
134	A prayer for hearing	
148	Checking my pride gauge	
154	Trusting my own performance	
156	God's counsel to those wrestling with pride	
157	Pride polluting my relationships	
158	Reconstruction in the leader's heart	

APPENDIX 2

LOST

By Robertson McQuilkin

Robertson McQuilkin is President Emeritus of Columbia International University.
For 22 years he served as President of Columbia International University and prior
to that was a missionary to Japan for 12 years.

Salvation is found in no one else, for there is no other name under heaven
given to men, by which we must be saved (Acts 4:12).

Have you ever experienced the terror of being lost — in some trackless
mountain wilderness, perhaps, or in the labyrinth of a great, strange city?
Hope of finding your way out fades and fear begins to seep in. You have
likely seen that fear of lostness on the tear-streaked face of a child frantically
screaming or quietly sobbing because he is separated from his parent in a
huge shopping center. Lost. Alone.

Equally terrifying and more common is the feeling of being hopelessly
entangled or trapped in a frustrating personal condition or circumstance:
alcoholism, cancer, divorce. Incredibly alone! Lost.

The Bible uses the word "lost" to describe an even more terrible condition. Those who are away from the Father's house and haven't found the way

back to Him are "lost." Jesus saw the crowds of people surging about Him as sheep without a shepherd, helpless and hopeless, and he was deeply moved.

Worse than being trapped and not knowing the way out is to be lost and not even know it, for then one does not look for salvation, recognize it when it comes, nor accept it when it is offered. That's being lost.

How many are lost in our world? We are told there are 200 million evangelicals. Some of these are no doubt lost, but at least that many people believe Jesus is the only way of salvation and that through faith in Him one is forgiven and made a member of God's family. Surely some who are not evangelical have saving faith. So let us double the number to a hypothetical 400 million. Those who remain number more than four billion people or nine of every ten on earth. These are the lost — longing for salvation but not finding it, or trusting some other way to find meaning and hope.

The tragedy of this century of exploding population is that three of four people have never heard with understanding the way to life in Christ, and even more tragic, half the people of the world cannot hear because there is no one near enough to tell them. As we approach the end of the second millennium A.D., one of every two on planet Earth lives in a tribe or culture or language group that has no evangelizing church at all. If someone does not go in from the outside they have no way of knowing about Jesus.

But are these people in the "dark half of the world" really lost? What of those who have never had a chance, who have never heard — are any of them lost? Are all of them lost?

Throughout Church history there have been those who teach that none will finally be lost. The old universalism taught that all ultimately will be saved because God is good. Not much was heard of this position from the days of Origen in the third century until the nineteenth century when it was revived, especially by the Universalist Church. Simultaneously with the founding of the Universalist Church, which was honest enough to be up front and call itself by that name, this teaching began to spread in many main-line denominations.

There are problems with this position. Philosophically, such a teaching undermines belief in the atoning death of Christ. For if all sin will ultimately be overlooked by a gracious deity, Christ never should have died. It was not only unnecessary, it was surely the greatest error in history, if not actually criminal on the part of God for allowing it to happen. Universalism, therefore, philosophically demands a view of the death of Christ as having some purpose other than as an atonement for sin.

Another problem the Universalists face is that Scripture consistently teaches a division after death between those who are acceptable to God and those who are not. This teaching, and that concerning the atonement, are so strong in the Bible that Universalists did not accept the authority of Scripture. Thus the marriage between the Universalist Church and the Unitarian Church was quite natural.

A New Universalism arose in the twentieth century which took the Bible more seriously. It was Trinitarian. Christ did die for sinners, and *all* will ultimately be saved on the basis of Christ's provision.

Karl Barth and many of his neo-orthodox disciples took such a position. All will be saved because God is all-powerful. His purposes will be accomplished. And he purposes redemption.

There were philosophical and biblical problems with this position also. Philosophically, if all will be saved eventually, for whatever reason, preaching the gospel is not really necessary. Why did Christ make this the primary mission of the church if all will ultimately find acceptance with God with or without the gospel? The more serious problem is biblical: Christ clearly taught of an eternal hell, of a great gulf between the saved and the lost (Luke 16:19-31). In fact, he clearly taught that the majority are on the broad road that leads to destruction (Matt 7:13-14).

Because Universalism cannot be reconciled with biblical data, there were those who promoted what was called a "Wider Hope." Not all will be saved, but many who have not heard of Christ will be saved because God is just and will not condemn the sincere seeker after truth. The problem is that if sincerity saves in religion, it is the only realm in which it saves. For example, it does not save in engineering. The architect who designed the magnificent John Hancock building in Boston was sincere. The builder was sincere. The glass-maker was sincere. The owner, especially, was sincere. But when the giant sheets of glass began to fall on the streets below, sincerity did not atone for error. Neither does sincerity save in chemistry. We do not say, "If you drink arsenic, sincerely believing it to be Coca-Cola, according to your faith be it unto you." Sincerity does not alter reality. We shall consider the question of God's justice later.

The 19th century doctrine of the Wider Hope has been superseded by what I call the "New Wider Hope." According to this teaching, those who live by the light they have may be saved on the merits of Christ's death through general revelation. Or, at least, they will be given a chance at death or after death. This is a more conservative version of the New Universalism. Richard Quebedeaux identifies this position as held by some "younger evangelicals," the New Left. A practical problem is that preaching the gospel seems almost criminal, for it brings with it greater condemnation for those who reject it, whereas they conceivably could have been saved through general revelation had they not heard the gospel. It certainly seems less urgent to proclaim the way of salvation to those who may well be saved without that knowledge. A mutation of this view is the idea that only those who reject the gospel will be lost. This viewpoint is not widespread because it makes bad news of the good news! If people are lost only if they hear and reject, it is far better not to hear and be saved. According to this view, it would be better to destroy the message than to proclaim it!

For one committed to the authority of Scripture, our debate concerning the reasonableness of each position must yield to the authority of Scripture. What does Scripture teach concerning the eternal spiritual condition of those who have not heard the gospel?

For God so loved the world that He gave His one and only Son, that whoever believes in Him shall not perish but have eternal life. For God did not send His Son into the world to condemn the world, but to save the world through Him. Whoever believes in him is not condemned, but whoever does not believe stands condemned already because he has not believed in the name of God's one and only Son.

Whoever believes in the Son has eternal life, but whoever rejects the Son will not see life, for God's wrath remains on him. (John 3:16-18, 36)

Scripture teaches clearly that there are those who perish and those who do not. Notice that it is those who believe *on Christ* — not simply those who, through their encounter with creation and their own innate moral judgment, believe in a righteous Creator — who receive eternal life. God's intent is to "save the world through Him [Christ]" (3:17). The word "through" speaks of agency: it is by means of Jesus Christ that a person gains eternal life.

The passage does not deny other agencies, however. The Japanese proverb assures us that many roads lead up famed Mount Fuji but they all reach the top. This is the Japanese way of expressing the viewpoint that all religions will have a good outcome. But Jesus Christ Himself said, "No one comes to the Father except through me :"(John 14:6). In other words, Jesus Christ is the *only* agency of salvation.

The New Wider Hope would affirm this. Salvation is by Jesus Christ alone. But, it would hold, that does not mean Jesus Christ must be known by a person for that person to be saved.

Jesus assures us that people will be judged because they have not believed on the *name* (John 3:18). Peter is even more explicit in telling us that there is no salvation in any other *name* given among men (Acts 4:12). Surely it is no accident that the name is so prominent in the Bible, especially in teaching on saving faith. Peter did not say, "in no other person." When a person is named, the identity is settled and ambiguity is done away with. Peter does not make room for us to call on the Ground of Being or the great "all." You will be saved, he tells us, if you call on and believe in the name of Jesus of Nazareth, the Messiah. John, Jesus and Peter are not the only ones with this emphasis. Paul also speaks to the issue:

Everyone who calls on the name of the Lord will be saved." How, then, can they call on the one they have not believed in? And how can they believe in the one of whom they have not heard? And how can they hear without someone preaching to them? And how can they preach unless they are sent? As it is written, "How beautiful are the feet of those who bring good news! (Rom 10:13-15).

The ones who call on *the name* are the ones who will be saved. But what of those who have not heard so they cannot call? Paul does not assure us that those who have not heard may simply believe on whatever they have heard. Rather, "faith comes from hearing the message, and the message is heard through the word of Christ" (Rom 10:17).

Scripture is very clear that there are two kinds of people, both in life and in death: the saved and the lost. It is also very clear on the way of salvation. But still, for those who truly care, questions may remain: Is God loving, powerful, fair, and just?

Is God loving? Yes, God is good and that is why men are lost. In love he created a being in His own image, not a robot programmed to respond as the Maker designed. In creating such a being to freely love and be loved, God risked the possibility of such a being rejecting His love in favor of independence or even self-love. Humankind did, in fact, choose this option. Still true to His character, God provided a way back even though the cost was terrible. But the way back must not violate the image of God in man and must not force an obedient response. Rather, the God of love chooses to wait lovingly for the response of love. Those who wish to reject Him may do so.

But is it fair and just for God to condemn those who have not had an opportunity to respond to His offer of grace? The Bible does not teach that God will judge a person for rejecting Christ if he has not heard of Christ. In fact, the Bible teaches clearly that God's judgment is based on a person's response to the truth he has received.

"That servant who knows his master's will and does not get ready or does not do what his master wants will be beaten with many blows. But the one who does not know and does things deserving punishment will be beaten with few blows. From everyone who has been given much, much will be demanded; and from the one who has been entrusted with much, much more will be asked" (Luke 12:47-48).

"When you enter a town and are welcomed, eat what is set before you. Heal the sick who are there and tell them, "The kingdom of God is near you." But when you enter a town and are not welcomed, go into its streets and say, "Even the dust of your town that sticks to our feet we wipe off against you. Yet be sure of this: The kingdom of God is near." I tell you, it will be more bearable on that

day for Sodom than for that town. Woe to you, Korazin! Woe to you, Bethsaida! For if the miracles that were performed in you had been performed in Tyre and Sidon, they would have repented long ago, sitting in sackcloth and ashes. But it will be more bearable for Tyre and Sidon at the judgment than for you. And you, Capernaum, will you be lifted up to the skies? No, you will go down to the depths. He who listens to you listens to me; he who rejects you rejects me; but he who rejects me rejects him who sent me" (Luke 10:8-16).

Judgment is against a person in proportion to his rejection of moral light. All have sinned; no one is innocent. Therefore, all stand condemned. But not all have the same measure of condemnation, for not all have sinned against equal amounts of light. God does not condemn a person who has not heard of Christ for rejecting Him, but rather for rejecting the light he does have.

Not all respond to the light they have by seeking to follow that light. But God's response to those who seek to obey the truth they have is the provision of more truth. To him who responds, more light will be given:

The disciples came to him and asked, 'Why do you speak to the people in parables?' *He replied, 'The knowledge of the secrets of the kingdom of heaven has been given to you, but not to them. Whoever has will be given more, and he will have an abundance. Whoever does not have, even what he has will be taken from him. This is why I speak to them in parables: 'though seeing, they do not see; though hearing, they do not hear or understand."*

In them is fulfilled the prophecy of Isaiah:

You will be ever hearing but never understanding; you will be ever seeing but never perceiving. For this people's heart has become calloused; they hardly hear with their ears, and they have closed their eyes. Otherwise they might see with their eyes, hear with their ears, understand with their hearts and turn, and I would heal them.

But blessed are your eyes because they see, and your ears because they hear (Matt 13:10-16).

He said to them, 'Do you bring in a lamp to put it under a bowl or a bed? Instead, don't you put it on its stand? For whatever is hidden is meant to be disclosed, and whatever is concealed is meant to be brought out into the open.

If anyone has ears to hear, let him hear.'

'Consider carefully what you hear,' he continued. 'With the measure you use, it will be measured to you — and even more. Whoever has will be given more; whoever does not have, even what he has will be taken from him' (Mark 4:21-25).

This repeated promise of additional light to those who obey the light they have is a basic and very important biblical truth concerning God's justice and judgment. Cornelius, the Roman officer, responded to the light he had with prayer and good deeds. God did not leave him in ignorance and simply accept him on the basis of his response to the initial light he had received. God sent Peter to him with additional truth (Acts 10). To him who had, more was given. Since this is revealed as God's way of dealing with

Of course, His method for sending this light is a human messenger. Paul makes clear in his letter to the church at Rome (10:14, 15) that the solution to the terrible lost condition of men is the preacher who is sent, the "beautiful feet" of him who goes. Ultimately, then, the problem is not with God's righteousness, but with ours.

But suppose no one goes? Will God send some angel or some other special revelation? Scripture is silent on this, and, I believe, for good reason. Even if God did have such an alternative plan, were he to reveal that to us, we who have proved so irresponsible and disobedient would no doubt cease altogether obedience to the Great Commission.

But the question will not go away. How does one respond in a Japanese village when a new convert inquires, "What about my ancestors?" My response is simple: I am not the judge. "Will not the judge of all the earth do right?" (Gen 18:25). Abraham pleaded with God for the salvation of innocent people who did not deserve to be condemned and destroyed along with the guilty. We can be very sure that every person has received adequate light to which he may respond. God's existence and His power are made clearly evident to all people through creation (Rom 1:18-21) and through each person's innate moral judgment or conscience (Rom 2:14, 15). To the one who responds obediently, God will send additional light. He was appealing to God's justice, and God responded with grace more than

Abraham dared ask. This crucial question recorded in the first book of the Bible is answered in the last: "Yes, Lord God Almighty, true and just are your judgments" (Rev 16:7). We are not called as judge — either of God, whose ways we do not fully know or of man, whose destiny we are not called upon to settle. Rather, we are commissioned as His representatives to find the lost, declare amnesty to the captive, and release the prisoner.

We may not be able to prove from Scripture with absolute certainty that no soul since Pentecost has ever been saved by extraordinary means without the knowledge of Christ. But neither can we prove from Scripture that a single soul has been so saved. If there is an alternative, God has not told us of it. If God in His revelation felt it mandatory not to proffer such a hope, how much more should we refrain from such theorizing. It may or may not be morally right for me to think there may be another way and to hope there is some other escape. But for me to propose it to other believers, to discuss it as a possibility, is certainly dangerous, if not immoral. It is almost as wrong as writing out such a hope so that those who are under the judgment of God may read it, take hope, and die. As long as the truth revealed to us identifies only one way of escape, this is what we must live by and proclaim.

Consider the analogy of a security guard charged with the safety of residents on the 10th floor of a nursing home. He knows the floor plan posted in a prominent place, and it is his responsibility in case of fire to get the residents to the fire escape which has been clearly marked. Should a fire break out and lives be put in jeopardy, it would be his responsibility to get those people to the fire escape. If he discusses with the patients or with a colleague the possibility of some other unmarked fire escape or recalls to them the news report he read of someone who had jumped from the 10th floor of a building and survived, he could surely be charged with criminal negligence. He must live and labor in obedience to the facts that are certain and not delay to act. He must not lead people astray on the basis of conjecture or logical deduction from limited information.

When all has been said that can be said on this issue, the greatest remaining mystery is not the character of God nor the destiny of lost people. The greatest mystery is why those who are charged with rescuing the lost have spent two thousand years doing other things, good things, perhaps, but have failed to send and be sent until all have heard the liberating word of life in Christ Jesus. The lost condition of human beings breaks the Father's heart. What does it do to ours?

In a dream I found myself on an island — Sheep Island. Across the island sheep were scattered and lost. Soon I learned that a forest fire was sweeping across from the opposite side. All were doomed to destruction unless there were some way of escape. Although there were many unofficial maps, I had a copy of the official map and there discovered that indeed there was a bridge to the mainland, a narrow bridge, built, it was said, at incredible cost.

My job, I was told, would be to get the sheep across that bridge. I discovered many shepherds herding the sheep which were found and seeking to corral those which were within easy access to the bridge. But most of the sheep were far off and the shepherds seeking them few. The sheep near the fire knew they were in trouble and were frightened; those at a distance were peacefully grazing, enjoying life.

I noticed two shepherds near the bridge whispering to one another and laughing. I moved near them to hear the cause of joy in such a dismal setting. "Perhaps the chasm is narrow somewhere, and at least the strong sheep have opportunity to save themselves," said one. "Maybe the current is gentle and the stream shallow. Then at least the courageous can make it across." The other responded, "That may well be. In fact, wouldn't it be great if this proves to be no island at all? Perhaps it is just a peninsula and great multitudes of sheep are already safe. Surely the owner would have provided some alternative route." And so they relaxed and went about other business.

In my mind I began to ponder their theories: Why would the owner have gone to such great expense to build a bridge, especially since it is a narrow bridge, and many of the sheep refuse to cross it even when they find it? In fact, if there is a better way by which many will be saved more easily, building the bridge is a terrible blunder. And if this isn't an island, after all, what is to keep the fire from sweeping across into the mainland

and destroying everything? As I pondered these things I heard a quiet voice behind me saying, "There is a better reason than the logic of it, my friend. Logic alone could lead you either way. Look at your map." There on the map, by the bridge, I saw a quotation from the first under-shepherd, Peter: "For neither is there salvation in any other, for there is no other way from the island to the mainland whereby a sheep may be saved." And then I discerned, carved on the old rugged bridge itself, "I am the bridge. No sheep escapes to safety but by me." In a world in which nine of every ten people are lost, three of four have never heard the way out, and one of every two cannot hear, the Church sleeps on. "Why?" Could it be we think there must be some other way? Or perhaps we don't really care that much.

ENDNOTES

Note: Biblical references without the ESV notation are passages where the text was not directly quoted.

INTRODUCTION

1   Don Barry. *Water Under the Bridge: A Journey Into Values-Shaped Leadership.* Castle Publishing, 2015. (11).

2   John 5:39-40, ESV.

3   2 Corinthians 5:17.

4   John 10:10.

5   John 3:16.

6   Jeremiah 2:13 and John 7:37-39, ESV.

7   These three terms were used by James "Buck" Hatch in his courses on psychology and family that shaped my biblical perspective of people. Mr. Hatch also inspired me, in his course design, to always start with the questions of, "What is God like?" or "How does God do this?" — in terms of communication, discipline, intimacy — every aspect of marriage, family and relating to people. His questions inspired me to rethink leadership from the starting point of God.

8   Revelation 3:20.

9   Hebrews 11:6.

10   Romans 12:7-8, ESV.

11   1 Corinthians 12:27-30, ESV.

12   2 Corinthians 4.

13   Matthew 9:36-38, ESV.

14   Barry, (60-63,66).

15   Pete Scazzero. *The Emotionally Healthy Church.* Grand Rapids: Zondervan, 2nd edition, 2010. (54). I have used his categories and then included my descriptions.

16   Matthew 28:18-20, ESV.

17   George Cladis. *Leading the Team-Based Church: How Pastors and Church Staffs Can Grow Together into a Powerful Fellowship of Leaders.* San Francisco: Jossey Bass, 1999. (4).

18   Ibid, pg. 6.

19   See the following references as examples: Romans 8:15-17, Romans 12:1-2, Titus 2:11-15, Ephesians 1:3-6, Ephesians 4:1-3.

20   Mark 10:35-45, ESV.

CHAPTER ONE

1   Romans 12:12, ESV.

2   Jeremiah 33:3, ESV.

3   Mark 1:35, ESV.

4   Henry T. Blackaby and Richard Blackaby. *Experiencing God Day-By-Day: The Devotional Journal*. Nashville: Broadman & Holman Publishers, 1997. (9).

5   1 Thessalonians 5:16-18.

6   David Hansen. *Long Wandering Prayer: An Invitation to Walk with God.* Downers Grove: IVP, 2001. (I have used several quotes from his introduction 'Orientation to Wandering' pages 11-25.)

7   Michael H. Crosby. *The Prayer That Jesus Taught Us* (quoted in Christianity Today, March 2009, (56.)

8   Mark Batterson. *Wild Goose Chase: Reclaim the Adventure of Pursuing God.* Colorado Springs: Multnomah Books, 2008. (86).

9   Mark 6:46, ESV.

10   I John 5:14,15.

11   Luke 17:11-19.

12   Hebrews 5:7, ESV.

13   Blackaby & Blackaby, (26).

14   Philippians 4:6-7, ESV.

CHAPTER TWO

1   Hebrews 4:12, ESV.

2   Octavius Winslow. *The Precious Things of God.* Published in 1859. Public domain.

3   http://www.brainyquote.com/quotes/quotes/a/aleksandrs132503.html

4   Luke 2:52, ESV.

5   Jeremiah 15:16, ESV.

6   Luke 24:32, ESV.

7   Psalm 1:1-3, ESV.

CHAPTER THREE

1   Acts 1:8, ESV.

2   John 13:34-35; John 15:12,17; John 17:22-23.

3   Luke 10:25-37.

4   1 Thessalonians 1:4-10, ESV.

5   Romans 14:17, ESV.

6   Wilbur M. Smith. *The Biblical Doctrine of Heaven.* Chicago: Moody Press, 1969, (132).

7   Ibid., 135.

8   John 10:10.

9   John Bright. *The Kingdom of God*. Nashville: Abingdon Press, 1952, (197).

10   Bright, (248).

11   Bright, (216).

12   Bright, (262-263).

13   Luke 17:20-21.

14   Bright, (218).

15   Bright, (219).

16   Bright, (210-211).

17   Bright, (221).

18   Bright, (223).

19   Bright, (250).

20   Larry Poland. *Rise To Conquer: A Call For Committed Living*. Chappaqua: Christian Herald Books, 1979 (Used as an outline for this section).

21   1 Thessalonians 1:9.

22   Matthew 19:13-14.

23   Matthew 22.

24   Matthew 7:24, Matthew 8.

25   Luke 14:25-27, Matthew 10:37-38, Hebrews 11:26, Matthew 20:20-28, Matthew 21:43.

26   Matthew 13.

27   Supporting passages: John 6:63, Matthew 6:33, Matthew 8:11-12, Acts 10:40-41, 1 Chronicles 29:11-16, Exodus 29:43-46, 2 Chronicles 7:14-16, 2 Chronicles 16:9, 2 Chronicles 20:6, 2 Chronicles 20:15, 2 Chronicles 20:17, 2 Chronicles 36:23, Ezra 1:2, Nehemiah 1:5, Psalm 11:4, Psalm 14:2, Psalm 20:6, Psalm 57:3, Psalm 73:25, Psalm 102:19, Psalm 136:26, Isaiah 63:15, Isaiah 65:1, Jonah 1:9, Daniel 2:18, Daniel 2:19, Daniel 2:28, Daniel 2:37, Daniel 2:44, Matthew 19:30, Matthew 20:16, Mark 9:35, Mark 10:31, Luke 13:30, Isaiah 63:12, Romans 14:17.

28   Matthew 13:10-12, 19, 24-26, 31-33, 36-52, ESV.

29   Luke 12:29-34, ESV.

30   White, James Emery. *Praying Kingdom Come*. Church & Culture Blog, Dec 05, 2013. Vol.9 No. 97. www.churchandculture.org .

CHAPTER FOUR

1   A.W. Tozer. *Tozer On the Holy Spirit (365 readings)*. Wingspread Reissue, 2015. See April 21.

2   1 Corinthians 12:4-11.

3 John 16:7-11; Acts 4:8; 2 Corinthian 3:14-4:6.

4 Matthew 28:20; John 14:17-21.

5 Ephesians 6:18, Jude 20.

6 John 16:12-15.

7 Acts 1:8.

8 Luke 4:1,2. ESV.

9 Luke 10:17-24, ESV.

10 John 14:8-14, ESV.

11 Roger Von Oech. *Creative Whack Pack (cards).* 1992 (Roger has several books, cards and team resources to stimulate creativity.)

12 2 Peter 1:21

13 John 1 and Hebrews 4:12

14 See: Luke24:32, 1 Corinthians 2:12-16, Hebrews 4:12.

15 1 Corinthians 2:12, ESV.

16 James Long. "The Care & Feeding of the Creative Mind: Random Thoughts on this Indispensable Gift." Outreach Magazine, Jan/Feb 2009 (70- 74)

17 James 1: 5-8.

18 1 Corinthians 12:7, ESV.

19 Barry, (173.)

20 Dallas Willard. From my notes taken in a two week course as part of a D.Min. at Fuller Theological Seminary, 2004.

21 2 Corinthians 4:7, ESV.

22 See: Matthew 8:5-13; Matthew 14:13-21; Matthew 15:29-39; Matthew 16:5-10.

23 Romans 8:32, ESV.

24 Ezekiel 34:15-16, ESV.

25 Romans 15:23, 2 Corinthians 5:2, 2 Corinthians 7:7, 2 Corinthians 7:11, 2 Corinthians 9:14, 1 Thessalonians 2:17, ESV.

CHAPTER FIVE

1 Matthew 5:8.

2 Luke 2:19, 51.

3 Mathew 5:28.

4 Matthew 13:15

5 Matthew 19:8

6 Mark 3:5; Mark 6:52; Mark 8:17.

7 Mark 16:14.

8   Matthew 6:21.

9   Matthew 11:29.

10   Matthew 12:34; Matthew 15:18 – 19; Luke 6:45.

11   Matthew 15:8.

12   Matthew 18:35;

13   Matthew 22:37.

14   Matthew 13:19; John 13:2.

15   Luke 18:1.

16   John 14:1; John 14:27; John 16:6, 22.

17   See Psalm 107 for a vision of his steadfast love.

18   Mark 10:35-45, ESV.

19   The following books assist you in going deeper in exploring the aspects of a biblical perspective on yourself and leadership

Hansen, David. *The Art of Pastoring: Ministry Without All The Answers.* Downers Grove: IVP, 1994.

Lencioni, Patrick. *The Five Dysfunctions of a Team.* San Francisco: Jossey-Bass Publishing, 2002.

McQuilkin, Robertson. *The Five Smooth Stones: Essential Principles for Biblical Ministry.* Nashville: Broadman & Holman, 2007.

Swenson, Richard. *A Minute of Margin: Restoring Balance to Busy Lives.* Colorado Springs: NavPress, 2003.

Hart, Archibald. *The Hidden Link Between Adrenaline and Stress: The Exciting New Breakthrough That Helps You Overcome Stress Damage.* Dallas: Word Publishing, 1995.

Scazzero, Peter. *The Emotionally Healthy Church: A Strategy for Discipleship that Actually Changes Lives.* Grand Rapids: Zondervan 2003.

Scazzero, Peter. *Emotionally Healthy Spirituality: Unleash a Revolution in Your Life in Christ.* Nashville: Integrity Publishers, 2006.

20   1 Corinthians 6:19-20.

CHAPTER SIX

1   Matthew 13:12-17, ESV.

2   Romans 3:11-20, ESV.

3   John 5:19-20, ESV.

4   Exodus 3:2-4, ESV.

5   Blackaby & Blackaby, (66).

6   Varney, Tom. *Sacred Discontent: Adjusting Our Vision of the Church.* Mars Hill Review, Issue one. http://www.marshillreview.com/issues/toc1.shtm

7 Robert Coleman. *Evangelism in Perspective.* Harrisburg, PA: Christian Publications, 1975. (94-95). Coleman footnotes Malcolm Muggeridge, "Living Through An Apocalypse," Let the Earth Hear His Voice, op.cit. (449).

8 John 12:24-32, ESV.

9 C.S. Lewis. *Mere Christianity.* New York: Macmillan Press, 1943. (104)

10 Ron Dunn. *When Heaven is Silent: Live by Faith and Note by Sight.* Nashville: Thomas Nelson, 1994. Also go to rondunn.com for sermons and resources.

11 Deuteronomy 8:2-3, ESV.

12 Tozer, see July 11.

13 See: http://www.azquotes.com/quote/773294

14 2 Kings 6:15-17, ESV.

15 Isaiah 66:2, ESV.

16 Zechariah 7.11, ESV.

17 Blackaby & Blackaby, (4).

18 Mark 1:22, ESV.

19 Bill Hybels. *The Power of a Whisper: Hearing God. Having the Guts to Respond.* Grand Rapids: Zondervan, 2010.

20 Matthew 10:16-23, ESV.

21 Luke 12:10-12, ESV.

22 Acts 9:10-18, ESV.

23 Amos 8:11, ESV.

24 Exodus 6:7-9, ESV.

25 Matthew 17:5, ESV.

CHAPTER SEVEN

1 Numbers 12:3, ESV.

2 Isaiah 6:5, ESV.

3 See Quotes of C.S. Lewis, http://www.goodreads.com/quotes/311692-telling-us-to-obey-instinct-is-like-telling-us-to. First appears in Abolition of Man chapter 2.

4 John 12:24,25, ESV.

5 Matthew 16:24, ESV.

6 Geri Scazzero. *I Quit! Stop Pretending Everything is Fine and Change Your Life.* Grand Rapids: Zondervan, 2010. See pages 70-74. This is an excellent book and is written for the woman who serves in a pastoral role alongside her husband.

7 2 Corinthians 1:8-11, ESV.

8 Dan Allender. *Leading With a Limp: Take Full Advantage of Your Most Powerful Weakness.* Colorado Springs: Waterbrook Press, 2006. (138).

9   E. Stanley Jones. *In Christ.* Abingdon Press, 1961. (95).

10   See: Ephesians 5: 21; Philippians 2:1-3; Romans 12:10.

11   Jim Mellado. "Editorial: Ministry on Steroids", WCA News, Volume 8, Issue 1 (Jan/Feb 2001), (2).

12   J. David Lundy. *Servant Leadership For Slow Learners.* Waynesboro, GA: Authentic Lifestyle, 2002. (47).

13   Barry, (175,178).

14   Hebrews 11:6.

15   Richard C. Halverson. *Perspective: A bi-weekly devotional letter for business and professional men.* Volume 29, No. 2, January 19, 1977. Published by Concern, Inc. Washington, D.C. (During the time Dr. Halverson was the chaplain of the U.S. Senate).

16   Thomas a'Kempis_*The Imitation of Christ._*

17   Luke 18:9-14, ESV.

18   2 Corinthians 3:18 ESV.

19   Robertson McQuilkin. *The Five Smooth Stones: Essential Principles for Biblical Ministry.* Nashville: Broadman & Holman, 2007. (Robertson devotes chapter 18 to examining this passage as an outline for leaders living under the Lordship of Christ.)

20   The chart is adapted from one in Nancy DeMoss's book *Brokenness: The Heart God Revives* (Chicago: Moody Press, 2002).

21   Coleman, *Evangelism in Perspective,* (102).

CHAPTER EIGHT

1   Many of the ideas for this section on Abraham came from sermon notes I had taken while listening to Ron Dunn. See www.rondunn.com . I have added some of my thoughts after my own reflection and study.

2   Galatians 2:20, ESV.

3   Jeremiah 17:5, ESV.

4   Blackaby & Blackaby, (152). *All For Jesus.*

5   Robert Morgan. See Day 7 in his daily devotional

6   Matthew 10:28.

7   James 1:2-4, ESV.

8   Gary Thomas, *Daily Readings: Simply Sacred.* Grand Rapids: Zondervan, 2011. Oct 9.

9   Colossians 1:27, ESV.

10   2 Peter 3:9-11, ESV.

11   Isaiah 40:5, ESV.

12   Luke 8:15, ESV.

13   2 Thessalonians 3:5, ESV.

14   Titus 2:11-14, ESV.

15   Romans 13:11-12, ESV.

16   See Romans 8:17-18.

17   Thanks to my African American students in the seminary for this proverb.

18   See John 21.

19   John 21:22, ESV.

20   John 14:21, ESV.

21   Luke 6:43-49, ESV.

22   Gary Thomas. *Simply Sacred: Daily Readings*. Grand Rapids: Zondervan, 2011. (See Nov 24.

23   Henri Nouwen. *Life of The Beloved: Spiritual Living in a Secular World*. Crossroad: New York, 1992, 85.

24   Ibid. 87.

25   Often referred to as the principle of proportionate giving.

26   David Croteau. *Tithing After the Cross: A Refutation of the Top Arguments for Tithing and a New Paradigm for Giving*. Gonzalez, FL: Energion Publications, 2013. (Summarized from pages 55-63).

CHAPTER NINE

1   Luke 5:4, ESV.

2   Blackaby & Blackaby, (73).

3   Psalm 86:11.

4   Philippians 4:8, ESV.

5   2 Corinthians 1:8-11, ESV.

6   Hebrews 11:6.

7   2 Timothy 1:7, ESV.

8   Matthew 8:25-26, ESV.

9   1 Thessalonians 4:13, ESV.

10   Romans 8:31-39, ESV.

11   http://mosaic.org/

PART THREE INTRODUCTION

1   Carl Honre. *In Praise Of Slowness: Challenging The Cult Of Speed*. New York: HarperCollins e-books, 2009. (4, 15).

2   C. Christopher Smith and John Pattison. *Slow Church: Cultivating Community In The Patient Way Of Jesus*. Downers Grove: IVP Books, 2014. (13).

CHAPTER TEN

1   Henri Nouwen. Henri Nouwen Society. http://wp.henrinouwen.org/daily_meditation_blog/?p=2027

2   Stephen Covey. *Seven Habits of Highly Effective People: Restoring the Character Ethic.* New York: Simon & Schuster, 1st Ed., 1989. (150-170).

3   Dallas Willard, D. Min. Course notes.

4   Henri Nouwen Society. (Found in one of the daily meditations).

5   Thabiti M. Anyabwile. *The Faithful Preacher: Recapturing the Vision of Three Pioneering African-American Pastors.* Wheaton: Crossway Books, 2007. (82).

6   Graves, Steve. *Work Hard, Rest Hard.* April 11, 2014. http://www.stephenrgraves.com/articles/read/work-hard-rest-hard

7   Gleanings, Christianity Today, March 2015.

8   Luke 5:15-16, ESV.

PART FOUR INTRODUCTION

1   Barry, (89-91).

2   For more on Mosaic go to http://mosaic.org/ .

CHAPTER ELEVEN

1   For additional practical wisdom see: Dennis Bakke. *Joy At Work: A Revolutionary Approach To Fun On The Job.* Seattle, Washington: PVG, 2005.

2   Marcus Buckingham & Curt Coffman. *First Break All Of The Rules.* Simon & Schuster, 1999.

3   Unknown source - shared with me by student Eugene Wade 29 Aug 13, 2014.

4   Paul David Tripp. *Wednesday's Word.* What is Love? 13 May 2015. Paultrippministries.org.

5   John 13:34-35; John 17:22-26.

6   Matthew 5:24, ESV.

7   Martin Luther King Jr., *A Knock at Midnight: Inspiration from the Great Sermons of Reverend Martin Luther King, Jr.* "Loving Your Enemies".

8   Ibid.

9   See the website for Gateway Church in Hamilton, New Zealand http://www.gatewaychurch.org.nz/ and read chapter five in *Water Under The Bridge* by Don Barry.

10   Ron Dunn is deceased but many messages and writings are available at rondunn.com.

11   See Isaiah 55:8-9.

12   These studies are condensed from work by Dale and Juanita Ryan and can be found in a small group study at www.christianrecovery.com . You can find a more complete version and other resources on their site.

CHAPTER TWELVE

1   I have written a book, *Helping the Church Live Well,* on how organizations experience stages in a life cycle and go through seasons in their work so I am only going to introduce the major idea here. If you are leading change in an organization you may find this resource a practical guide.

2   Ecclesiastes 3:1, ESV.

3   1 John 2:6

4   Matthew 6

5   James 4:13-17

6   Study Romans 15: 1-17 to see how Paul reminded himself and the church of God's heart for the entire world and how Paul saw worship and ministry as intentionally being priests bringing an offering of Gentiles to God.

7   See 2 Corinthians 1:1-21 for an example of how Paul viewed his ministry as radical dependence on God and the prayers of other believers.

8   Luke 9:23 is a good principle for God's activity. The encounter with the rich young man who Jesus loved but walked away is a good example.

9   Exodus 19:4, ESV.

10   See: John 12:24, Luke 9:10-17, Luke 8:15.

CHAPTER THIRTEEN

1   Bill Hybels. Note in my journal from a message at the Willow Creek Leadership Summit.

2   Gene Getz. *Sharpening the Image of the Church.*

3   Charles Swindoll. *The Bride.*

4   Rick Warren. *The Purpose Driven Church.*

5   For a full study on the purposes of the Church see Robertson McQuilkin's *Five Smooth Stones: Essential Principles for Biblical Ministry.* Nashville: Broadman & Holman, 2007.

6   Michael Card. *A Sacred Sorrow: Reaching out to God in the Lost Language of Lament.* Colorado Springs: NavPress, 2005. (32, 86).

7   Jean L. McKechnie (editing supervisor). *Webster's New Universal Unabridged Dictionary, Deluxe 2nd edition.* New York: Simon and Shuster, 1983.

8   Revelation 21:1-7, ESV.

9   Revelation 22:1-5, ESV.

10   Charles G. Finney. *God's Love for a Sinning World.* Grand Rapids: Kregel, 1966. (26-27).

11   1 Thessalonians 4:13-14, 5; 8-11.

12   Pete Scazzero. *Emotionally Healthy Church,* (171).

13   Ecclesiastes 7:4.

14 Psalm 30:5.

15 Michael Card. *A Sacred Sorrow: Reaching Out to God in the Lost Language of Lament.* Colorado: NavPress, 2005. (12 – Foreword by Eugene Peterson).

16 Jerry Sittser. *A Grace Disguised: How the Soul Grows Through Loss.* Grand Rapids: Zondervan, 1995. (9).

17 Sittser, (23).

18 Card, (20-21).

19 Card, (31).

20 Card, (17).

21 Card, (158).

22 Sittser, (33).

23 Pete Scazzero. *Emotionally Healthy Church,* (157).

24 Sittser, (19).

25 Leith Anderson. "Good Friday Surprises", Christian Reader Magazine (March/April 1997). Can be found on line at http://www.empoweringchristianwomen.com/2008/03/good-friday-surprises.html (January 4, 2015)

CHAPTER FOURTEEN

1 1 Peter 2:9, ESV.

2 Matthew 24:14, ESV.

3 Isaiah 61:1-2, ESV.

4 Coleman, *Evangelism Perspective,* (31-32).

5 See Luke 2:10.

6 John 16:20-24, ESV.

7 Alex McManus as recorded while giving a lecture at the Lake Hickory, NC learning communities of the Hollifield Leadership Center (www.hollifield.org) in 2007.

8 1 Thessalonians 1:8-10, ESV.

9 Richard Triplady ed., *One World or Many? The Impact of Globalisation on Mission.* Pasadena: Willliam Carey, 2003 (212).

10 Mark 4:18-19, ESV.

11 Reggie McNeal. *Kingdom Come: Why We Must Give Up Our Obsession With Fixing The Church—And What We Should Do Instead.* Carol Stream, IL: Tyndale Publishers, 2015. ISBN: 978-1-14143-9187-8. (xiv,xv, xxi, 8,9)

12 Coleman, (72).

13 Coleman, (113-114)

14 My summary outline of *The Master Plan Of Evangelism,* Robert E. Coleman reprinted over 63 times since its publication in 1963.

15   Craig Groeschel. *IT: How Churches and Leaders can Get IT and Keep It.* Grand Rapids: Zondervan, 2008. (114).

16   Dwight McGuire "Mass Media & Church Planting" in Bottom Line Connection. A Pioneers-USA publication, Spring 2009.

17   2 Peter 1:3-4, ESV.

18   Mark 14:9, ESV.

CHAPTER FIFTEEN

1   Robert Morgan. *All To Jesus: A Year Of Devotions.* Nashville: Broadman & Holman, 2008. ISBN: 978-1-1433657786-1.

2   Coleman, *Evangelism in Perspective,* (56-57).

3   Ibid., (58).

4   2 Corinthians 1:8-11, ESV.

5   Stan Nussbaum. *The American Cultural Baggage: How to Recognize and Deal with It.* Maryknoll, NY: Orbis Books, 2005. Stan lists American proverbs and unpacks how they reveal the values and 'treasures' of the American heart. He writes to an International student coming into the States. Seeing his work on American culture is a vivid example of how the study of proverbs in any culture can help us understand the hearts we are seeking to touch with the love and truth of Christ.

6   Ephesians 4:11-12, ESV.

7   Alan Hirsch and Michel Frost. *The Shaping of Things to Come: Innovation and Mission for the 21ᵗ Century Church.* Peabody, MASS: Hendrickson Press, 2003. Also see new learnings by Hirsch in *The Forgotten Ways: Reactivating the Missional Church.* Grand Rapids: Brazos Press, 2006. (Alan has served as church planters and denominational catalyst in Australia).

CONCLUSION

1   Luke 14:26-33, ESV.

2   John 15:15, ESV.

OTHER BOOKS BY ROY KING

Helping the Church Live Well: A Consultant's Approach to Assisting the Church
Published 2015, ISBN: 978-1517479398

If you could have a consultant visit your congregation or ministry organization, what questions might he or she ask? Where would you start to unravel challenges and problems you are encountering? What different perspectives might help you understand the group's history and present moment? In this book, church consultant Roy King offers advice for finding answers to some of those questions. An examination of life cycle theory and a developmental change model form the framework for diagnosing the health of churches and organizations. Informed by more than twenty years of consultations with groups of various sizes, from a variety of denominations, and from all stages of an organizational life span, this practical guidance will help you appraise your leadership setting and chart a course for your church or organization to not just survive, but to live well.

Available on Amazon.com in paperback and Kindle formats

Time Management is Really Life Management
Published 2009, ISBN: 978-1448656240

How we see our time says a lot about how we view God. In this study, Roy King examines the way that God views our time and provides helpful suggestions on how to bring the use of our time into alignment with God's perspective.

Includes study guide questions for each chapter.

Available on Amazon.com in paperback and Kindle formats